BabyTalk

Sally Ward qualified as a speech and language
rapist in London before marrying and moving to
nchester, where she had three children. From 1980 she
rked at the Mancunian Community National Health
rvice Trust, and was appointed Chief Speech and
Language Therapist with responsibility for children with
nguage, hearing and learning difficulties. She was also
pointed Advisor in Developmental Language Disability
the Royal College of Speech and Language Therapists.
llowing the completion of her PhD, she became the
ust's Principal Speech and Language Therapist. From
ere she went on to develop the BabyTalk Programme.
dly, Sally died in 2002.

Praise for *BabyTalk*:

'Just half an hour of chat can have amazing results'
Express

'A common-sense approach to spending
fun time with your baby'
Sunday Herald

n all Dr Sally Ward's many years as a leading language
erapist, only a handful of parents haven't responded
with immediate enthusiasm to her pioneering
BabyTalk Programme'
Daily Telegraph

BabyTalk

DR SALLY WARD

arrow books

Published in the United Kingdom in 2004 by Arrow Books

1 3 5 7 9 10 8 6 4 2

Arrow Books
The Random House Group Limited
20 Vauxhall Bridge Road, London, SW1V 2SA

Random House Australia (Pty) Limited
20 Alfred Street, Milsons Point, Sydney,
New South Wales 2061, Australia

Random House New Zealand Limited
18 Poland Road, Glenfield,
Auckland 10, New Zealand

Random House (Pty) Limited
Endulini, 5a Jubilee Road, Parktown 2193, South Africa

The Random House Group Limited Reg. No. 954009

www.randomhouse.co.uk

A CIP catalogue record for this book
is available from the British Library

Papers used by Random House are natural, recyclable products
made from wood grown in sustainable forests. The manufacturing
processes conform to the environmental regulations of the
country of origin

ISBN 0 09 929720 5

Typeset by Roger Walker

Printed and bound in Great Britain by
Biddles Ltd, King's Lynn

Acknowledgements

I should like to thank my literary agent Luigi Bonomi for having the idea for this book, and my editor Kate Parkin for her wonderful editorial skills. I am most grateful to both of them for their support and encouragement.

I am also aware of the wealth of knowledge I have acquired from many colleagues, in person and in reading their work. I am indebted to them all.

To my children Caroline, Tim and Jonathan
who have taught me so much about
language development.

Contents

Introduction

MY STORY

I have always loved words, and this, together with a very strong interest in language and in working directly with people, led me towards a career in Speech and Language Therapy. Speech and Language Therapists treat the full range of communication difficulties, from those experienced by adults who have had a stroke to those in babies affected by cleft palate. I qualified in London, and then married and went to Manchester. There I also qualified in the related area of audiology, which is concerned with the diagnosis and management of hearing and listening problems.

Soon after this, I had three children of my own, a daughter and two sons, who taught me a very great deal about language and communication development in the succeeding few years!

From 1980 I worked part-time in Manchester, in what is now the Mancunian Community National Health Service Trust, setting up a pre-school parent guidance service for hearing-impaired children, and also working in clinics with children who had a wide range of speech and language problems. I was subsequently appointed Chief Speech and Language Therapist with responsibility for children with language, hearing and learning difficulties, and taught courses on these specialist areas to Speech and Language Therapists and other professional groups. I was also invited to be Advisor in Developmental Language Disability to the Royal College of Speech and Language Therapists, and am consequently able to advise any member of the profession in this country who asks for my help.

I was then awarded a major three-year grant by the North West Regional Health Authority, and the resulting study established an accurate means of detecting infants at risk of language delay in the first year of life. This, together with a related study of the ways in which hearing impaired, learning disabled, deaf and autistic children respond to sound, resulted in the award of my PhD. Following this, I was appointed Principal Speech and Language Therapist, with responsibility for all speech and language impaired children within the Trust.

In the course of all my work, I had become particularly interested in listening and attention in young children, and in discovering more about the ways in which these relate to language development. I then had the wonderful opportunity of carrying out regular clinics for pre-school children with my colleague Deirdre Birkett, whom I had long respected as an exceptionally skilful Speech and Language Therapist. Deirdre and I learned an enormous amount from each other as we worked together, helping our young patients to talk and communicate. We developed an extremely effective programme, based entirely upon empowering parents to help their children's development. We found to our delight that in every instance where the child had a language difficulty or delay, however severe, and it was not associated with deafness, autism, neuro-developmental difficulties or general developmental delay, if parents were able and willing to spend just half an hour a day following our programme, the children made excellent progress. They often attained the ability to understand and use language normally expected for their age in a very few weeks or months. The joy on parents' faces as their child begins to communicate remains one of the most rewarding aspects of my professional life. Not surprisingly, we both became and remained totally committed to using the programme as a method of intervention.

Many of the children we were treating in Manchester came from economically deprived backgrounds. Since then, I have had the opportunity of using the programme which we developed, now known as the BabyTalk Programme, with families from many different parts of Great Britain and across the whole social spectrum. The results have been consistently successful.

THE BABYTALK STUDY

Deirdre and I had developed our intervention programme to help children who were already experiencing language difficulties, but it occurred to us that it might be possible to prevent language disability from occurring in the first place, by adapting it for use with very young children. In the course of the screening study, in which Deirdre acted as research associate, we had visited the homes of 373 ten-month-old babies. Our first observation was that even at this very early stage, the infants were showing great differences, not only in pre-language skills, but also in their general developmental levels. The infants' environments differed considerably, as did the amount and ways in which they were spoken to, and these factors appeared to relate strongly to their language development. By the time the screening study was completed, we felt that we could pinpoint those babies likely to develop language delay.

I was awarded a second major three-year grant by the North West Regional Health Authority in order to test out this idea. Using the screening test that had been developed, we discovered a group of 140 ten-month-old infants who were showing varying degrees of delay in language development, ranging from very mild to profound. These infants were divided into two groups, matched for language development, general development and social background. One group received the programme, and the other did not, acting as a control group. Over the next four months, Deirdre and I visited the BabyTalk group four times, discussing with parents a number of aspects of their lives, such as background sound and television, the amount the infants were talked to and the exact ways in which they were talked to. We then asked them to follow the BabyTalk Programme for half an hour a day.

We were very pleased to find that, just as we had seen with toddlers at our clinics, the BabyTalk infants made very rapid progress in their language development, and all who had completed the programme had caught up with their normally developing peers in under four months. Moreover, their parents told us how much they and the infants had enjoyed the programme, which delighted us!

The BabyTalk children at three years old

It was extremely important to know whether the effects of the BabyTalk Programme would be permanent, so we followed up both groups until they were three years of age.

We chose this age because there have been a number of studies in which children with delay in language development at three have been followed up over a number of years, some into adulthood. All the studies showed that many of the children continued to have problems with speech and language, and a considerable number also had educational difficulties as a result.[1] [2] [3] [4] [5]

We were astonished by the results when we looked at our children at the age of three. Eighty-five per cent of the group who had not received the BabyTalk Programme were still showing language delay, in some cases very severe. By contrast, almost all of those who had received the programme were up to the normal standard, but many in this inner-city area were showing language development *above* their age level. (Only three, all of whom had experienced adverse circumstances in their lives, were below the normal standard.) Some were showing understanding of speech and ability to put sentences together normally seen in children of four and a half years! These children were able to understand very long and complex sentences, and could express themselves with amazing fluency. One little boy called John, just three, could follow with ease for example, enormously long sentences like 'Go and find the thick wax crayons, and give them to Billy to hand out to the girls' which normally could only be followed by a four and a half year old. He also had no trouble discussing his interest in dinosaurs in great detail, including words such as 'extinct'. At this stage, too, there appeared also to be considerable differences in the children's ability to play, and in their conversational skills.[6]

These results appeared to indicate that changing environmental factors and the way in which the infants were talked to had a profound effect on preventing language difficulties as well as helping children who were falling behind their peers to catch up. The results were so exciting that we decided to have both groups of children followed up again at the age of seven.

The BabyTalk children at seven years

We recruited two psychologists and, without revealing which children had received the BabyTalk Programme and which had not, asked them to assess our two groups. They used fully standardised tests, including the intelligence tests which are the most commonly used in this country with children at this age.[7] [8] [9]

Once again, the results of this study were astonishing! Only four children in the BabyTalk group were showing any delay in language development, compared with twenty in the control group. In fact, the ability of the BabyTalk children, both to understand complex sentences, and the kinds of sentence structures they were able to use was, on average, one year and three months ahead of the control group. Some of them showed language development typical of ten and a half year olds! The reading ability of the BabyTalk children was also on average a year and three months ahead.

The same results were found on a test of vocabulary which, interestingly, is the best predictor of intelligence.[10] The most advanced children understood, for instance, words such as 'catastrophe', 'exhibition', 'fragment' and 'lecturing' which are not usually understood by children under ten and a half years old!

The most exciting finding of all was that there was a very considerable difference in general intelligence between the two groups. The average IQ of the group who had received the BabyTalk Programme was in the top third of the population, and between a third and a quarter of these children were in the intellectually gifted range. In contrast, the average IQ of those who had not received the programme was in the bottom third of the population, and only one child was in the gifted range.

These differences were reflected in the government's Standard Attainment Tests (SATs) which all children sit at the ages of seven and eleven. All the BabyTalk children reached the target standards or higher, while a third of the other group had failed to reach the targets.

There were also noticeable differences between the two groups in emotional and behavioural development, social skills and ability to concentrate. The psychologists who did all the testing made many comments on the test forms of the BabyTalk children like 'excellent concentration', 'forthcoming and friendly manner', and 'he's so friendly, and expresses himself so easily and effectively'. Conversely, on the forms of over a third of the other group were comments about the fact that the children were extremely easily distracted and needed many breaks to enable them to finish the tasks. Saddest of all were the comments about some of the children in that group who clearly found the whole situation stressful and greatly feared failure, with which they appeared familiar. Most of the BabyTalk children, on the other hand, appeared to enjoy the activities very much. A comment, made by a number of parents of the BabyTalk children, also pleased us very much: the expression 'He's such a confident communicator now' was often heard. Similar comments were even made by a camera crew who interviewed some of the children while making a television programme about the results. The cameraman was very struck by the way one little boy, once his mother had told him that it was fine to talk to the crew, engaged them in conversation, asking questions about their equipment, and comparing it with his father's camera. So impressed were they that they let him make the concluding comments of the programme!

In conclusion, our findings, independently tested, led us to realise that the programme developed for the prevention of problems would work for all children to enhance their development. It was clear that parents could be enabled to use the BabyTalk Programme from the time of their children's birth to give every one the opportunity of developing to his or her maximum potential.

These studies resulted in a number of publications in scientific journals, presentations at national and international conferences, and a considerable demand for teaching about the screening test and the BabyTalk Programme, both to Speech and Language Therapists and to other professionals. I am now engaged in further research on the development of attention in infancy, but hope never to stop doing clinical work as well: contact with the children and their parents is still the most rewarding part of the work to me!

How Language Develops

Despite our knowledge that children whose language development is not up to the normal standard for their age are very highly at risk of educational, social and emotional problems, we do not yet have a definitive answer to how the helpless newborn essentially masters the language in only four years.

The earliest theory[11] of how this wonderful thing happens was that the baby makes random sounds, and the adults around him 'shape' them by rewarding those closest to words. For example, the baby would frequently babble 'mama' at an early age, and every time he did so his mother would appear. He would eventually link the word with her. The great linguist Chomsky, however, rejected this view in the 1950s and 60s.[12] [13] His view was that children are born with an innate capacity for language learning, and when hearing language, automatically begin to use what he called a 'Language Acquisition Device (LAD) to help them make sense out of what they hear, and later on to help them to put sentences together for themselves. He considered that the amount of language the child heard and the way in which adults spoke to him was of little importance. Chomsky himself has developed his ideas and his view is now that we are born with a knowledge of grammatical rules, for example that nouns and verbs agree: for example, 'the boy jumps' is correct, as is 'the girls jump'; but 'the boy jump' and 'the girls jumps' are not.[14] This theory still assumes that language development is only possible because of this inborn knowledge, and that the amount and kind of speech heard is of little importance.

Pinker, another great linguist writing more recently,[15] also holds the view that children have knowledge from the start of life about the different types of words and the parts they play in language, which are universal in all languages. The little child knows, for example, that whatever causes an event is the subject of the sentence. Seeing the cat knock over a vase of flowers, for example, and hearing his mother say 'That naughty cat', he rightly assumes that the cat is the cause of the problem and therefore the subject of the sentence.

There is still no total consensus of agreement about this innate knowledge, but there is general agreement that some kind of innate knowledge or mechanism is needed to explain the amazing speed with which human infants learn language.

The extent to which such mechanisms are sensitive to input from the environment is still a matter of considerable debate. Chomsky and Pinker, as we have heard, both claim that it is of little importance, but other much acclaimed researchers[16][17][18] stress the vital importance of social interaction and input to the process of language acquisition. Their view is that early language skills are acquired through children's meaningful and active involvement with the people in their lives. While accepting that we are pre-programmed for language in some way, its learning is seen as extremely dependent upon this interaction between the child and his environment, in which the kind of language he hears significantly influences the extent to which the child realises his potential.

This view is supported by evidence from studies that examine the relationship between adult input and the rate and nature of language development. Many of these were carried out because of the interest generated in the 1970s as a response to Chomsky's claim that there must be a 'language acquisition device' because the speech used by adults to children is too complex, disorganised and deviant to allow language acquisition to take place otherwise. (It appeared that Chomsky may not have had much contact with babies and small children, as most adults are instinctively aware that they do not speak to these as they do to their friends!)

Although it is evident that certain language milestones are relatively independent of environmental influences (deaf children begin to babble at the same time as do hearing, and the age of first word production is the same in children in highly stimulating and in deprived backgrounds), there can be little doubt that environmental influences are critical in shaping future language and social development. There is, for instance, a substantial amount of evidence that the quantity of speech addressed to the little child correlates positively with their development, in that the more they are talked to the more rapidly they learn language.[19][20] The content of this speech has also been shown to have extremely important implications for language learning.[21][22] There, is too, much evidence that babies and young children show a marked preference for certain kinds of speech, and listen to and therefore learn more from this.[23] Studies have also shown that the acquisition of specific vocabulary and grammatical structures relates to the input the children receive.[24]

In all Deirdre's and my clinical experience and research, parents modification of their speech to their children has been a crucial factor in their children's dramatic progress, and is consequently an extremely important part of the BabyTalk Programme.

To summarise, while it does seem very likely that we have an inborn language learning mechanism, there is a substantial body of evidence that the way children are spoken to has a very considerable bearing on their language development – as you will hear as you go through the programme. Lenneberg, a biologist writing in the 1960s, summed up this mid position when he stated that 'Infants are biologically programmed to develop language in the same way as much animal behaviour is programmed. To occur satisfactorily, however, the organism must be intact, and the environment provide an appropriate quantity of the right quality of input.'[25] This is in accordance with other species, interestingly. The basic song of the chaffinch, for example, appears to be innate as it occurs in birds reared in isolation, but for the full song to develop the young bird needs to be exposed to model songs from adults.[26]

The outcome of the BabyTalk studies very much supports this middle view. I can help you to help your baby to sing his or her fullest song!

WHY THINGS GO WRONG

Language is what distinguishes human beings from the rest of creation, and there can be little doubt as to its importance to our society and culture. Despite this wonderful ability to talk, however, we still often have great difficulties communicating with each other. I was interested to hear from a veterinarian friend the other day that almost all the second opinions she is asked for are not in fact due to a wrong diagnosis, but to a lack of communication. We went on to speculate about how many wars and other serious conflicts might be due to such misunderstandings.

It is clear, therefore, that there can be few things more important than ensuring that our children acquire the very best communication skills that we can give them. Delay in language development, however, is recognised as the most common childhood disability[27] having been estimated to affect up to 10 per cent or more of all seven year olds, and considerably higher numbers in inner-city localities.[28 29 30 31]

You may be wondering why this is so. Language delay is inevitably associated with learning difficulties, autism, and hearing impairment. It can also result from specific neuro-developmental problems as in specific language impairment, dyspraxia, and attention deficit hyperactivity disorder (ADHD) which are discussed in Appendix 1 (see page 319). Problems with producing speech sounds also result from conditions such as cleft palate and damage to the nerve supply to the lips, tongue and palate.

For the many otherwise perfectly normal children, however, who constitute the largest number of speech- and language-impaired children, Deirdre and I have long been convinced that the delay in language development results from a mismatch between the language addressed to the little child and the actual level either of his use, or more commonly of his understanding, of speech. Adults automatically tend to adjust their speech to the age and size of children, and if a little child gets behind his age group, particularly in understanding, which can occur for a variety of reasons, it is very easy for such a mismatch to arise. Periods of intermittent hearing loss associated with catarrhal conditions, for example, are extremely common in babyhood and early childhood, and can very easily result in the little child finding listening difficult and ceasing to do so, with consequent effects on his understanding. Prolonged illness in baby or mother also can cause the problem, as can many of the stresses and demands of life, such as the need to move house, maybe to somewhere far away from the support of the wider family.

It is of the greatest importance to recognise, however, that only in the most rare and tragic situations of abuse or severe neglect can this ever be said to be parents' fault.

I feel very strongly about this, as I have seen so many parents blame themselves for something I know full well is not their fault in any way!

ISN'T INTELLIGENCE FIXED AT BIRTH?

There has been a general debate since the eighteenth century, just as there has been about language acquisition, as to whether human intelligence is the product of genetic attributes only, or is affected by experience. Scientists now agree, however, that the baby does not arrive as a genetically pre-programmed automaton, and are looking at the many ways in which genetic predisposition and environmental circumstances interact. It is now known that at twelve weeks after conception, neurones already show co-ordinated waves of activity, and that these waves actually change the shape of the brain. The same processes that wire the brain before birth drive the astonishingly rapid learning that takes place afterwards. The infant's brain at birth has virtually all the nerve cells it will ever have, but the pattern of wiring has not at that point been established. The information the infant receives through his senses results in neural activity, and innumerable connections are made, starting soon after birth. (A recent report summarises recent work on this.) [32]

The earliest years, therefore, particularly the first three, are a time of huge developmental plasticity, when the completion of neural circuits in the brain needs appropriate stimulation. This stimulation is, therefore, critical in shaping future development. By the age of two years, the little child's brain has twice the number of synapses, and consumes twice the amount of energy as that of an adult. Those connections which are made at that time and not used are gradually eliminated after the age of ten years.

It is not surprising, therefore, that there is much evidence that lack of stimulation can have the same devastating effect on development as does sensory deprivation. The tragic outcomes for many of the Romanian orphans show that deprivation of stimulation has an irreversible effect on intelligence. It was found earlier in this century, when childcare was less well informed, that institutionalised infants, who were well cared for physically but received relatively little interaction from adults, showed a developmental lag from the age of three months which was irreversible.

Other studies, which showed so clearly the immensely powerful effect of early stimulation on intellectual development, led to the establishment of the Headstart programmes in the United States and similar programmes here, which were designed to compensate culturally deprived children. These are nursery programmes starting at three years, which give the children rich play opportunities and language input, and many of the children show definite intellectual gains. Interestingly, though, it is now the view of many involved in the programmes, that starting at three years offers too little too late.

There can be no doubt that there are real differences in inborn intellectual capacity from the beginning. After all, we can't all be Einstein! The evidence is also clear, however, that there is nothing fixed or permanent about IQ, and that in the early stages of life, enormous changes can be made by environmental stimulation. It is possible that the most important of these is in boosting language development. Language is our main vehicle for thought and, therefore, language and thought are extremely closely related. Once again, there is no absolute agreement amongst psychologists as to the degree and nature of this relationship, but there is certainly a consensus that it is a very strong one.

There is much research interest in the way in which these two areas overlap. Most theorists consider that both intellectual and language development come about from the child exploring the objects, events and people in his environment, and it is evident that there is mutual dependence between the two areas. The little child, for example, needs to achieve certain stages of intellectual development for the acquisition of words to be possible. He needs to have a concept that objects continue to exist even when they are out of sight before he can label them. Conversely, intellectual development is clearly very greatly facilitated by language. Imagine the very young child trying to figure out where the pieces go in a jigsaw puzzle. An adult giving him words like 'turn it', or 'it's too small' will enable him to transfer his learning to another situation. Concept formation is also greatly facilitated by the addition of a verbal label. For example, the baby initially only relates the word 'cat' to the family cat, but the use of the word cat in other situations soon enables him to generalise the idea to any cat in any situation. Still later, children can use language to plan and discuss their activities before actually embarking upon them. Four year olds, for example, can be heard saying things like 'You can have the first turn with this and I will then have my turn' or 'After we've been to the park I think I will play with my guinea pig'.

Language helps us all to remember, and to give and receive information. By the age of four and a half, language is fully internalised, and can be used as a substitute for action, as it is in adulthood, acting as a short cut to arriving at solutions to problems. For example, the child is able to think through how to solve a puzzle before actually trying to do so, mentally working out how he will arrange and move the pieces. Language becomes, in fact, the key to understanding the world, and remains so for life.

THE BABYTALK APPROACH

The BabyTalk Programme aims to establish the foundations for all later learning. These foundations include not only the understanding and use of language, but also listening, attention and play. Many people do not realise that these skills actually develop in stages, still less that it is possible to do much to help infants and young children to move easily and effectively through them.

The approach is at all times developmentally appropriate and totally stress free for both parent and child. Although it is soundly based in extensive clinical experience, linguistic theory and cutting-edge research, it is also firmly rooted in natural interaction. No artificial teaching situations are ever set up: BabyTalk fits into the normal relaxed pattern of your child's day.

There is currently very great concern about the increasing numbers of children with literacy and numeracy problems. I was recently talking to a teacher in a large comprehensive school who told me that she had been shocked to hear that more than half the children arriving at the school at the age of eleven have reading attainments below their actual age level. There is a move to address this very worrying problem by instigating the very early teaching of numbers, colours, shapes and the alphabet. This move is highly controversial, and some educators consider that it is mistaken. There are growing indications that this 'hot housing' not only stresses the child, but also creates in many children the very problem it seeks to prevent, by engendering anxiety and aversion in children who are not ready for such teaching.

In a parallel situation, I have seen many children in my clinics recently who have been 'taught' to say their sounds correctly at an inappropriately early age when they do not understand what is required, and just get the message that the way in which they try to communicate is not acceptable. They become, as a result, anxious, sad and virtually silent children.

Jasper, just three and a half, was brought to me by his extremely worried mother in order to continue the intensive work on his speech sounds which had been done for the past year in another part of the country. This little chap peered at me from under his fringe, and clearly had decided that talking was definitely not on the agenda. His mother reported that he now only spoke at home, and was even becoming very quiet there. She was aware that he hated his Speech and Language sessions, and that he had obviously become very aware that he had a speech problem, but she had been assured that the therapy was necessary. I gave her the BabyTalk Programme, and told her to take him home and forget about Speech and Language Therapy. She telephoned me a few weeks later to tell me that to her delight, not only had Jasper's speech sounds sorted themselves out, but she had her delightfully outgoing and chatty little son back again!

Parents following the BabyTalk Programme do not need to feel anxious or guilty about going to work, or that they need to spend huge amounts of time with their children to ensure their optimal development. In the highly sensitive early stages of development, a little of the 'absolutely right' stimulus has huge effects. Thirty minutes a day is fine, although you are very likely to find that some of the suggestions will carry over naturally and effortlessly into other daily living situations.

DON'T FEEL GUILTY ABOUT BEING A WORKING PARENT!

You will also see that the emphasis changes considerably as your child grows up, and that for example, your role and that of books and play will change in accordance with the child's stage of development. I hope that you will be aware that your baby's development is fuller and richer for what you are doing, and that you always know exactly how best to help him or her. At whatever point you are starting, I hope that you and your baby or little child will have fun together as you go through the programme.

A VERY IMPORTANT NOTE FOR PARENTS

The stages of normal development have been included so that you can marvel at and celebrate your little child's development, and see how the programme matches the levels he or she has reached, but *not* so that you can 'test'! There are very big variations in normal development, resulting not only from the environment, but also from the baby's genetic inheritance, and from the interplay of different aspects of development. A baby who achieves very early mobility, for example, is very likely to be slower to acquire words, and may also be slower to play in particular ways. Your child, like all others, will have his or her own unique pattern of development.

DO NOT BE TEMPTED TO 'TEST' YOUR CHILD!

There is a great difference between observing and noticing, and setting out to test. The latter might lead you to try and teach your little child, as opposed gently to create the conditions in which he or she can develop towards his or her maximum potential.

As a general guideline, in any of the aspects of development we are discussing, it is very unlikely indeed that there is any need to worry unless you notice that your baby is behind:

★ more than two months in the first year
★ three in the second year
★ four in the third year, or
★ six in the fourth year.

More details are given in each chapter. If you do become concerned at all, however, about any aspect of your baby or little child's development, do seek reassurance from a Speech and Language Therapist, Health Visitor, or doctor, as it is difficult to enjoy your baby or little child fully if you are anxious about him or her in any way.

About the Contents of the Book

The book is divided into age bands, four in the first year, three in the second, two in the third and one in the fourth. Your baby is referred to as 'he' or 'she' in alternating chapters.

Within each section, the following are covered:

★ A detailed account of communication, speech and language development at that stage.
★ Stages of general development.
★ The development of listening and attention.
★ Play at each stage, with suggestions for the most appropriate toys and books.

The BabyTalk Programme is detailed at each age band. It covers:

★ How to create an environment which is most helpful for your baby's development.

★ How much to talk to your child and what to talk about.
★ What to do outside your daily half hour.

The programme is illustrated by case studies, and answers to questions parents commonly ask are contained in Appendix 2 (see page 322).

You will find that some themes run throughout the entire programme, and that some of the suggested activities go over several time periods, sometimes with small differences, or for different reasons.

You may come upon this book when your little child is leaving or has left babyhood. If he has experienced any cause for delay in his language development, such as trouble with his ears or prolonged illness, you may notice that his language levels are at a lower level than his age. If this is the case, go to the section of the programme that is at the level of his understanding, and start there. I hope that you will see a rapid improvement, but please do not hesitate to ask for a referral to Speech and Language Therapy if you are at all concerned.

If your baby or little child is affected by any of the problems with which language delay is associated, such as learning difficulties or autistic spectrum disorder, you will almost certainly have been referred for speech and language therapy. The BabyTalk Programme, I believe, will help considerably in addition to whatever other help you are receiving, so talk to your speech and language therapist about it. It will certainly be very helpful while you are waiting for treatment, and cannot possibly cause any harm.

A friend of mine who has a little boy with Down's syndrome, called Bennie, asked me when he was four if I thought the programme would be helpful to him. I replied that I was quite sure that it would be. I explained that it was vital that rather than going to the programme section for his actual age, she observed him for a few days to see how much he was understanding, and to start the programme there. She found that the right place to start was at the two-year level, as he was understanding quite a few names of people and objects, and some little phrases. She and Bennie loved their times together, and in six months Bennie made six months' progress in his understanding and use of language. His genetic endowment will prevent him from continuing to progress at that rate, but his mother is now confident that he will reach his maximum potential.

Listening and attention

You may wonder why listening is covered by the programme. We live in an increasingly noisy society and, as adults, take for granted the ability to 'tune out' background sound; focus on what we wish to listen to; and maintain that focus for as long as we desire. (Just take a moment to stop and listen to all the sounds you have been ignoring.) This ability, like that of controlling and maintaining attention, develops in stages, and ever more children are failing to acquire it. Large numbers of children with perfectly normal hearing are showing enormous problems with listening, and clinicians and teachers are increasingly voicing the opinion that the basis of many children's learning and language problems is an inability to listen. I was interested to hear from a friend whose eleven year old has just started at secondary school that the head-teacher in his welcome address to parents said that he was certain that there was one problem shared by all the children, and that problem was listening.

Children need adults around them to make possible the development of the ability to select, from the many sounds around them, what to listen to, and to keep listening for as long as they wish. The programme will explain how to do this.

Attention development is covered for equally important reasons. Many people consider that children (and indeed adults!) either do or do not pay attention. In fact, the ability to focus attention and maintain that focus, shifting it as required, particularly in the presence of a distracting environment, develops in well-defined stages in early childhood.[33]

In very many children of school age, however, this development has not occurred. Teachers increasingly complain that the children are not able to sustain attention to classroom activities, particularly in a noisy, busy classroom.

Not only is it obvious that learning is severely impeded when this is the case, but in the early stages of language learning, particularly the stage of starting to link words with their meanings, it is absolutely vital that the infant and adult are able to share the same focus of attention. Further, attention control is traditionally regarded as central to adult intellectual functioning. There is some evidence that the ability to inhibit attention to irrelevant or distracting stimuli relates strongly to adult intelligence. Trying to 'make' children pay attention only makes matters worse. Instead, they need help which enables them to progress through the normal stages.

The BabyTalk Programme will tell you how to identify the stage your child has reached and how to enable him or her to progress to the next.

Play

Play too, has a very important place in the programme. It has often been termed the 'work of childhood', as it is the child's way of learning about the world, developing his or her social relationships and expressing him or herself. Play and language development are inextricably linked, as play is the most wonderful vehicle for the adult to add language around. The child can explore objects and materials, and discover new ideas while the adults around him or her provide the words to go with his activities. Dropping things from a high chair once the baby has learned to release objects is much more fun, for example, when an adult says 'gone' with a smile each time!

Early adult-child play is also of very great importance, because it gives adult and baby shared experiences and ideas, and provides the basis for future shared memories, which will become important topics of conversation. At later stages, pretend play is powerfully affected by language, increasing complexity and richness in one leading to similar expansion in the other. As this play develops, language enables the child to play-act many daily routines, thereby increasing his under-standing of 'how his or her world works'. At still later stages, language can be used to problem-solve and develop creative imagination.

Creative activities are also a wonderful vehicle for lan-guage learning, language again serving to enhance the play. Wonderful words can be applied to water play, for example, such as 'drip', 'drop' and 'swish'!

Play is another area of development which occurs in well-defined (although overlapping) stages. The programme will help you to identify your child's stage and show how both to use the play for language input and to facilitate richer and more enjoyable play at each stage.

CONCLUSION

In this book, I will show you how to maximise your child's developmental potential in ways that are often basically simple. You do not need to spend huge amounts of time: as little as thirty minutes a day can make an enormous difference. And, above all, you will find that following the programme is totally stress free and fun for both you and your child. You will have the satisfaction of knowing that you have given him or her life-long advantages by making full use of this critical time for development.

The many years I have spent working in the field of child language have led me to believe that there is no greater gift that you can give your child at the beginning of life than the ability to communicate. This book will teach you how to maximise this area of development, giving your child the best possible communication skills.

This book is written not only for parents, but also for grandparents and other members of the extended family. It is also for intended nannies, nursery nurses and child-minders, and indeed anyone who has the care of young children.

As you go along the way, I hope that you will come to

share my interest in this fascinating subject, and above all I hope that you and your baby will have fun together as you help him or her to achieve his or her maximum potential.

Sally Ward
September 1999

Birth to **3** months

An overview

Having a baby must rank as one of life's most intense experiences, and in the early weeks you will be completely absorbed in the fascination of getting to know your baby and how to take care of him. If this is your first baby, you may be, as I was, astonished at what a very full-time job this is! A tiring job it can be too, particularly until that magic moment at around six weeks when if you are very lucky he sometimes sleeps through the night.

He can do almost nothing for himself at first. He has very little control over his body apart from the ability to turn his head automatically towards the breast or bottle to feed. He cries loudly and frequently, but it can be hard in the early weeks to

Please note that the developmental stages described here are averages only.

All babies develop at slightly different rates, and often progress in one area can result in a temporary delay in another. Do not get worried or depressed if your child does not appear to be doing everything at exactly the time periods mentioned here. For further information, see Cause for Concern, page 35.

figure out what he wants. He has, however, means of learning about the world from the very beginning. He can see and hear (although not for a few weeks as well as he will later) and he can taste and smell. Another important sensory area is his skin, through which he receives many messages from the outside world, particularly of warmth and human touch and comfort.

You will find that he has some astonishing abilities in terms of communication and interaction, and although he has no means of communicating specific messages to you at first, he certainly will have by the end of this trimester!

The first month

THE DEVELOPMENT OF COMMUNICATION

In this section, and in all those to come, we describe the stages of communication and language, and link them to stages of development in other areas. The objective is to enhance your joy and fascination in your baby by increasing your awareness and knowledge of his development. (Remember, though, that babies do develop at different rates, and that in the early stages, even whether he was born a week early or late makes a difference.)

The new-born baby arrives totally helpless and dependent, but none the less amazingly well equipped in a number of ways to interact with the adults around him. He shows an emotional inclination towards people from the very start of life, and soon engages them in the communication process.

Soon after birth, the baby shows his responsiveness to the adults around him by the fact that he is quieted by being spoken to, by being picked up and by eye contact. Nature has arranged things so that he focuses best at the distance he is from his mother's face when he is in her arms.[1] He already shows interest in listening, ceasing his activity as a sound comes nearer, and by the end of the first month he fixates on a nearby sound.

He cries frequently, but soon starts to produce some vowel sounds other than crying. His **sound-making** is not in any way communicative at this stage, but he clearly signals his state of alertness and comfort by means of eye gaze and the presence or absence of crying or fussing, and will actively seek eye contact with adults.

In the early weeks, the baby cries and produces other vocalisations such as hiccups and burps, which are related to his bodily functions. Although these are not used to communicate intentionally at this stage, the adults around him respond to them and to his eye gaze as if they are, paving the way for true interaction a little later, as the baby learns that different behaviours receive different responses. For example, he cries and fusses, and his mother says 'Oh, you want your nappy changed'; or he looks towards a toy, and she says 'You want to see teddy' as she brings it towards him.

Faces engage his attention, having many of the qualities that he finds most attractive to watch: namely three dimensions rather than two, contrast between dark and light, and curved lines rather than straight.[2] [3] [4] By the age of only thirty-six hours, he already shows a preference for watching a video of his mother's face over one of a stranger, showing amazingly rapid learning.[5] He also prefers to watch the movements made by people rather than those made by animals or inanimate objects.[6] The new-born baby has an extraordinary ability, lost a few weeks later, of imitating tongue protrusion and mouth opening, if he has seen these actions modelled in motion.[7] He can also imitate facial expressions of sadness, happiness and surprise.[8] [9] [10] Nobody quite knows why these abilities exist at this time.

GENERAL DEVELOPMENT

In terms of general development, he is beginning to make rudimentary attempts to explore his world. He will turn his head towards a light, and although he has no binocular vision as yet, he already perceives that size and shape are constant even though objects are seen from different angles and distances.[11] He can, at this very early stage, discriminate between a cross, a circle and a triangle.[12]

He has very little control over his body, showing large jerky and uncontrolled movements. As is the case in all vertebrates, the general direction of the organisation of his body is from head to foot in that he gains control of his head first, then his trunk, and lastly his legs. At this stage he can already hold his head steady for a few seconds if he is supported at the shoulders. He shows some reflex actions which will later become purposeful: for example, clenching his hand on contact with a rattle. When he is held upright, he shows a complete and co-ordinated walking reflex, but this only lasts for a few weeks.

ATTENTION

There are two striking features of the young baby's attention. The first is that its span is extremely short in the main, and the second that he has no mechanism at all for coping with distractions.

In the first month, watch the way he will look at a toy only for a very short time. Similarly, he will look only momentarily at your face, and when you are feeding him, you will be able to catch his eye only very briefly.

LISTENING

The ability to listen – that is, to focus on what we wish, and maintain that focus, tuning out that which we do not – is an ability that begins at birth and develops in stages. It has a long road to maturity. It is possibly the most neglected and underrated developmental area, and yet it is vital to language and intellectual development. It is also an area of development which is very easily affected by the environment, as will be discussed in all the sections on listening.

A baby recognises his mother's and father's voices on his very first day,[13] and the fact that he is even more responsive to these sounds when they are recorded to simulate the way they would have sounded in the womb, shows that he has been listening to them for some time.[14] He will also respond to a television or radio show which has been frequently played in his vicinity during pregnancy.[15] (He has, in fact, been hearing for the past two months, as the auditory system is functional from the seventh month of pregnancy.)

The new-born's hearing is not yet as sensitive as an adult's,[16] but within days, he can distinguish recordings of his own cries from those of other babies, and can discriminate between the sound of a real baby crying and a computer simulation – crying harder in response to the former. At this stage, too, he shows a preference for speech that is high pitched and very tuneful, with lots of rise and fall.[17] [18]

Evidence that he is listening is also given by a reflex that makes him turn towards low quiet sounds,[19] and his cessation of activity at times when a new sound occurs near him. Initially, he does not respond any differently to the many sounds in his environment, as very few as yet have any meaning for him. (Can you imagine not knowing the meaning of sounds such as the rattle of a cup on a saucer, or the scrape of a key in a lock?)

Within a few weeks, however, he begins to understand the meanings of frequently occurring sounds that are important to him, such as the sounds connected with feeding. He can only do this at first when the sounds are very close to him, but as the links between the sounds and their sources become more secure, he begins to be able to recognise them at greater distances.

The second month

THE DEVELOPMENT OF COMMUNICATION

The magical first true smile is seen at about six weeks, and this acts as an extremely powerful and totally heart-melting stimulus to the adults around him, who are prepared to do almost anything up to and including standing on their heads to evoke it. At this stage, the amount he vocalises, and the frequency with which his facial expressions change do not differ according to whether or not he is looking at an adult, and he will smile to a range of stimuli, and not only at people.[20] He now, however, sometimes starts an interaction sequence with an adult by catching their eye, and concludes it by looking away.

In this period, the baby is showing more and more interest both in his environment in general and in people in particular. He often turns his head and looks in the direction of voices, and appears to listen intently to anyone speaking. He seems to respond to the speaker's tone of voice, and by the middle of this month will sometimes smile when he is spoken to.

His **sound-making** is also developing. Cooing emerges in this month, usually signalling that he is contented. Cooing is quieter and more musical than crying, and consists of a consonant type sound followed by a vowel type sound, with occasional repetition of the same sound. The baby often develops special sounds signalling hunger at this stage, which is the first time a sound has a particular meaning. He will now demand attention by vocal fussing.

GENERAL DEVELOPMENT

He has longer and more defined waking periods. His motor development is dominated by asymmetrical tonic neck reflex, in which his head is averted to the preferred side, with the arm on that side extended and the opposite one flexed. This position limits his visual field, but his control over his eye muscles is developing. He can now turn his head towards a rattle or moving light, and visually follow a moving object, first horizontally and then vertically. He is able to watch a play activity, and will sometimes fixate on an object for a long time. His head control is also increasing and he can lift it when he is lying on his tummy. His strengthening muscles are demonstrated by his vigorous kicking in the bath.

ATTENTION

There are changes in the second month. He develops the ability to sustain attention for a short time, first to an attractive object moving horizontally, and then a week or so later, to one moving vertically. Notice how he becomes immobile, gazing with great intensity at something that has caught his interest. He may also look at you intently, although still quite briefly. He will now be giving attention to all the voices around him, and not only to those most familiar to him.

LISTENING

By the age of one month, he is showing interest in listening to a wide range of sounds, and will fixate on an interesting sound for some time. An extraordinary feature at this stage is that by the age of four weeks, he can distinguish between phonemes, which are the smallest units in the language to signal meaning. This means, for example, that he can tell the difference between 'pat' and 'bat', which is a very tiny one.[21] It is tempting to conclude that the infant arrives closely attuned to speech, but it is also possible that speech is suited to the innate characteristics of human beings.

By two months, babies can tell the difference between male and female voices.

The third month

THE DEVELOPMENT OF COMMUNICATION

From the age of eight weeks, the baby's gaze and the little sounds he makes are more frequently directed at adults, and by twelve weeks, he shows a very well-established preference for people rather than any other stimulus in his environment. He vocalises much more to them than to anything else, and most of all to his mother.[22] He is, for the first time, responsive to his mother's facial expressions and tone of voice, and can himself now show facial expressions. He is more inclined to smile at familiar adults than at strangers.

The baby is now showing rapidly increasing interest in speech, and regularly looks around for and successfully locates speakers. He can differentiate between angry and friendly voices. He tends to watch lips and mouth rather than the whole face, as if he is realising that that is where these very interesting sounds come from. He shows increasing interest in sounds of all kinds, searching for them persistently with his eyes. He will look for example, for an opening door, the clatter of cutlery, and the sounds associated with housework. He shows by stilling that he is interested in music. He loves it all – pop and classical – but at this stage prefers it to be quiet rather than loud. Best of all is his mother singing to him.

His **sound-making** is also developing, both in terms of quantity and quality. He increasingly makes sounds to himself, occasionally now with two or more different syllables containing a consonant and a vowel, and can be heard to string ten or more little sounds together. He will sometimes produce a long vowel-like sound during or after feeding. By three months, he produces that delight, laughter, and will respond to a smile by smiling back.

At the same stage, cooing is his main vocal activity, and involves wholly intentional playing with sounds when he is contented. He also makes groping movement with his tongue and lips, making it look as if he is attempting to say words. This happens mostly when he is face to face with adults. There is a shift from sounds made at the front of the mouth to those made at the back, and a big increase in the range of sounds he uses. There are now also lots of expressive sounds like chuckles, laughs and squeals of pleasure.

Interactive vocalisation is also developing. He sometimes vocalises when he is being talked to, and will return an adult's glance with cooing accompanied with a smile – a totally irresistible combination. The very exciting beginning of adult and baby vocal interchange is therefore now occurring, which is truly the beginning of a lifetime's conversation. The baby vocalises more when he is being talked to, and most of all when this is by a familiar adult who is using a lively facial expression.

GENERAL DEVELOPMENT

Many of these developments have been made possible by the baby's newly acquired head control, and the fact that by the age of three months, he has control of all the twelve muscles controlling eye movements. He can now lift his head when he is lying on his back, and hold it steady when sitting on an adult's knee. He can glance from one object to another, follow a moving object in a circle and watch an object being pulled along.

The asymmetrical tonic neck reflex is losing sway, and many of the early reflexes are being lost. He enjoys a sitting position, from where he shows ever increasing interest in the world around him. He is beginning to become aware of familiar situations. He promptly looks at and shows excitement about toys placed in front of him, and shows crude reaching movements towards them. He also waves his arms around, bringing them into the midline and playing with his fingers, which he seems just to have noticed. He looks intently at them and can now grasp a rattle if it is placed in his hand. His kicking in the bath is still more vigorous.

Recent exciting research has shown that, contrary to what was previously believed, young babies possess surprisingly advanced awareness of the principles governing the physical world. They appear to know that solid objects should not pass through each other, and should not hang in mid-air without visible support.[23] There is also evidence that the infant, by three months of age, can remember that hidden objects continue to exist, and this memory includes information about hidden objects, and even that this representation includes information about position, size and properties such as rigidity and flexibility.[24] The mystery remains as to why babies don't use this knowledge, not searching for hidden objects until they are eight to nine months, the age at which it was previously thought that they understood that such objects do not cease to exist.

We now know too that infants begin to form concepts from birth. By three months, for example, if shown a series of pictures of horses, they are able to form a concept which excludes other animals, including zebras.[25] The new-born has become a surprisingly competent little scientist in three short months.

ATTENTION

The third month sees the very beginnings of the baby's ability to control his attention. He can, for the first time, intentionally shift his visual attention from one object to another, although at this stage only in brief glances. He can watch for a short time an interesting object moving in a circle, and also one pulled along by a string. He is showing more sustained attention to people, gazing at speakers' mouths and enjoying watching people moving about. By the end of this time, he is just beginning to be able to direct his gaze to where someone else is looking, and this is the first precursor to the later ability, vital to language learning, of sharing joint attention with an adult.

LISTENING

We have seen how the infant is primed for interaction, and his listening abilities and their development reflect this. We've heard how in the first months he looks for speakers and is quieted by voice, and how by four weeks he has the amazing ability to distinguish between phonemes. In the second and third months his interest in speakers in particular, but also in music and all the other sounds in his environment increase rapidly.

He has, however, at this stage, no ability at all to focus on foreground sound and tune out background. This has very important implications for the BabyTalk Programme.

Play

Play – at this period *and* at all later stages – combines beautifully with language input. At this time, it is based entirely upon adult-baby interaction, and does not yet involve external objects or events. Adults, therefore, are virtually the only play material needed at this time! Again, your baby will cleverly trigger you into the activities he finds most fun and rewarding.

In the new-born period, physical play with him is hugely enjoyed. You will be the initiator of the play activities at this stage. Pat his feet, gently tickle his face, allow his fingers to curl around yours, count his fingers and toes, and gently head butt his tummy. All these activities – as well as being fun for both of you – also help, alongside the verbal vocal input we discuss later (see page 38), to stimulate the baby, and maintain the best level of arousal to enable him to explore his environment with his senses. Play, too, even in these early weeks, is important in forming a trusting relationship, and is already building up a repertoire of shared intentions, activities and knowledge between you and your baby. This will become an essential basis for language at a later time.

By two months, the kind of vocal turn-taking described on page 41 becomes a lovely part of play but, at this stage, you will fit in with him rather than the other way around.

The Toy Box

★ Mobiles with sharp colour contrasts, particularly black and white, can be very interesting to look at.
★ Simple bells and other musical toys are good to listen to.
★ Brightly coloured objects that are easy to handle and safe to chew will be popular.
★ A variety of textures provide stimulation. A simple cloth is one of the very best toys at this stage.

By three months, there are a number of changes and developments. Your baby now needs things to look at and listen to, and towards the end of this period, to hold. Your baby will enjoy waving a rattle if you put it into his hand, and will start to reach towards objects and enjoy handling a number of them as you hand them to him. The baby's mouth is his main means of exploration, but he will also start to look at objects which are farther away, and needs changes of viewpoint so that he has different things to look at. He needs time to play alone with lots of different objects as well as lots of play with you and other adults.

He will love music and singing, and will also relish opportunities to kick and move relatively free from clothing.

TELEVISION AND VIDEOS

We are going to talk about television quite a lot in the course of the programme, as it has become a very prominent part of our society. While it can be of enormous value to children at certain stages, helping them to learn, opening up many facets of the world to them which would be otherwise closed, and being a wonderful source of entertainment, it can, however, also impede development at others, particularly in the very early stages.

Infants and young children, as we have seen, have a wonderful in-built propensity for communication and interaction and can make enormous strides in these with amazing rapidity in the early months and years. For this to happen, however, it is necessary for the baby to have a responsive, communicative partner, and the television cannot in any way fulfil this role.

Babies and little children also need many, many opportunities to explore and begin to understand the world around them – that enormous task which lies before them. There is no possibility of learning anything from the television until they have had many opportunities to explore and investigate their environment and the real objects and people within it.

At this very early stage, do not be tempted to use the

television to stop your baby fussing or crying. There is no doubt that it is a powerful stimulus in terms of its bright moving colours; that babies as young as a few weeks can be riveted by it, and will actively seek it out. Please resist the temptation to let this happen.

Summary

To summarise, by the age of three months, your baby is likely to:

★ Chuckle and laugh when you are playing with him, making it very evident how much he enjoys this.
★ Coo, making a number of different little sound syllables containing a vowel and a consonant.
★ Occasionally make sounds back to you when you talk to him: conversation is beginning.
★ Show you that he is very interested in speech by looking around for speakers and watching their lips and mouths.
★ Show his interest in other sounds, such as those associated with domestic activities.
★ Enjoy listening to music – and make this enjoyment evident.

Cause for concern

We have talked about the wide range of normal development but, as parents, we all want to know as soon as possible when there are indications that our children may have a problem. Below are circumstances in which it would be advisable to seek professional advice about your baby's development. (Please remember, though, that rapid progress in one area can result in a temporary delay in another.)

It is important to recognise, too, that no checklist can be a substitute for a professional opinion. If you are in any doubt, even if the reason for your concern is not mentioned here, do take your baby to see your Health Visitor or GP as soon as possible.

At three months there could be cause for concern if:

★ Your baby does not smile.
★ He is not quieted by voice or being picked up.
★ He does not coo with little vowel sounds.
★ He never turns towards a light or the sound of a rattle.
★ He does not cry when a feed is due.

The Baby Talk Programme

Here you are, home with your miraculous new baby, exalted, knowing your life is changed for ever, sharing every parent's desire to do the best for this utterly dependent little being.

You do not need to worry! As we have seen, it is clear that new babies are very far from passive partners in the interaction process, but instead bring an enormous amount to the party. Nature has arranged matters so that we as adults are biologically triggered to respond to them with the most appropriate communicative and interactive input at this stage. Many aspects of baby care need to be learned of course, but interestingly, in the very early stages, we seem to know all about communication, perhaps the most interesting aspect of human development. These biologically triggered responses are the same in almost all cultures although other child-rearing practices differ greatly.

Sadly, this is not the case at later stages, when we all need to learn what to do and how to do it. In the first few months, however, provided that some very important conditions are met, you are very likely effortlessly to get it right. We will discuss these conditions, and for later ages, I shall describe what you will almost certainly find to be happening. If any of it is not, any adjustments that you find you need to make will be easy and pleasurable.

HALF AN HOUR A DAY

The first essential, and one which runs through the whole programme, is to establish that you have half an hour a day on a one-to-one basis with your baby, when you can be totally focused on each other. This total availability is the greatest gift you can give him. It is of inestimable benefit to babies and young children, the particular benefits changing with the age and stage of the child. Unfortunately, it is so easy in our full lives to find that it actually never happens, or only rarely, particularly with children who are not first in the family. It really is worth going to almost any lengths to establish it.

At this stage, it can be done by extending feeding and nappy times rather than setting aside specific times. This time together will give you a wonderful opportunity of getting to know each other, for you to start to see the world from his viewpoint and to become fully aware of his amazing abilities.

> **Spend time alone with him**

THE SETTING FOR YOUR ONE-TO-ONE PLAYTIME

The next essential, which again will run throughout the whole programme, is that in these precious times, the environment is quiet, and as free from distraction as possible. This means no television, videos, radio or music (although these will all have their place at other times and in other situations). It is also important to have as little chance as possible of other people coming in and out. As we have seen, attention is beginning to develop in small, subtle but very important ways, but it can only do so in an environment relatively free from distractions.

Listening, too, is beginning the long developmental path towards the ability to structure the 'auditory field': that is, to be able to focus on a particular foreground sound and 'tune out' background noise. Babies need a much greater difference between background and foreground sound than do adults in order to be able to begin to do this.

At this stage, too, the magical ability to discriminate between phonemes – those small sounds that differentiate meaning, such as 'pin' and 'bin' – is developing. There is much research evidence that shows this can only occur if the environment is structured in such a way that these discriminative abilities have a chance to operate: that is, that the baby has plenty of opportunities to hear speech really clearly. This means that there must be times when the infant is listening to one adult speaking to him in an otherwise quiet environment. Interestingly, it has been found that a background of adults talking to each other is not helpful to this process. The implication of this is that although it would be lovely for different adults in your baby's life to enjoy the programme with him, it is very important that they do so at different times.

We live in an increasingly noisy and stimulating society, and very many children literally never experience a situation in which they are only listening and attending to one source of sound at a time. I found, in a research project involving several hundred babies, that this was the case for 86 per cent of them!

Keep the room quiet during your playtime

These two foundation skills of listening and attending are vital to all later learning. We will discuss many ways in which the development of these skills can be helped, but establishing these quiet times is by far the most essential.

TALKING TO YOUR BABY

Start talking to him on day one. There is a considerable body of research evidence which shows that the quantity of speech addressed to children relates strongly to their language development,[26][27] and you can't start too soon. Of course, he won't understand what you are saying yet, but your voice communicates your feelings clearly to him. It is one of the most powerful facilitators of the mutual bonding so essential to a lifetime's mental health. We have seen already how effective it is in soothing a baby, but it is also one of your main means of signalling your responsiveness to him, acknowledging him not only as a unique human being, but that you also see him as a social being with lots (as we have said before) to bring to the party.

What you talk about really does not matter at all at this stage, although it is very important indeed later on. Talk to him about whatever is happening, or what is in your

> **Talk to him frequently**

mind. You might say, for example: 'It's our playtime. You're looking at teddy.' I remember very clearly telling my three-day-old daughter all about the landmarks of the route on our way home from the hospital where she had been born. Alternatively, you might say something like: 'I do like this green paper with animals that we chose for your nursery. I hope you will too.'

★ In the quiet times when you are alone together, talk to him in a rather special way:
★ Use short simple sentences, which are very tuneful. You might say something like: 'Up you come', or 'You're on my knee'.
★ Notice how the pitch of your voice is a little higher than when you speak to adults.
★ Speak slowly, with pauses between each phrase or sentence.
★ Use lots of repetition, for example: 'Here are your fingers. One finger, another finger, another finger...' and so on, or 'Teddy's eyes, teddy's nose, teddy's mouth...'
★ Make sure that you are face to face with him, and close, and you will not be able to resist touching him a lot.
★ Use the kind of delicious nonsense that comes naturally at this time, such as: 'Who's gorgeous? You are. Yes, you are. You're just gorgeous.'

> **Use lots of repetition**

This is the in-built way of talking that the baby automatically triggers in us, and interestingly every aspect of it is not only what infants have been found to prefer from birth,[28][29] but is also the kind which is most helpful to them in a number of very important ways. They are particularly sensitive to rhythm, loudness and tunefulness, which we exaggerate at this time, and the high-pitched voice adults tend to use to them relates to the fact that the size and shape of the baby's outer ear canal resonates at higher frequencies than does that of adults. It is also

Speak to him in a higher-pitched voice

exactly the form of speech which best enables him to develop that amazing ability to distinguish between phonemes – those little sounds which change the meaning of words – by the time he is a month old.

This, too, is the speech most likely to gain the baby's attention. His attention is also attracted by the smiling, moving, changing face which accompanies this kind of speech. Linked closely with attention is the baby's level of arousal, and you will find yourself varying the frequency of your head movements and eye gaze to regulate this, ensuring that he is neither bored nor over-stimulated.

The repetition in this form of speech relates to the fact that, as we have seen, the child's brain is wired by repeated experience.

In the very early weeks, you may well find yourself and your baby vocalising at the same time. That's fine.

At around six to eight weeks, you will start to notice some little changes, in that you and he are beginning to build the beginnings of 'conversation'. Fit your vocal 'turns' into his activities. For example, coo back to him when he coos, move your head from side to side immediately after he does or return his smile with a beaming one of your own. This truly is the beginning of a lifetime of conversation. You will also notice that he coos more at this stage when you talk to him animatedly, with exaggerated facial expressions and lots of tune in your voice. You will find yourself responding more and more to what he is expressing by means of his sounds, his body language and his facial expression. You will respond as if he were intending to convey a specific meaning, saying for example 'Oh, you're hungry. Let's get you some milk,' as he fusses. This will help him to understand that our vocalisations can have particular effects, and so lead him toward being able truly to communicate specific messages.

As he approaches three months, you will find yourselves engaged more and more in interactive 'conversations' as you begin to copy the sounds he makes, and to  respond more and more often to his still unintentional communications. Copy his sounds a lot; it is the very best way of developing 'conversations' at this stage.

Do sing a lot to him too, during these months. He will love it, be soothed by it, and above all, receive reinforcement of the view that listening to voice is hugely enjoyable. This is going to be very important. From the listening point of view, there could be no better 'foreground' sound to listen to in a quiet background. Which songs, tunes or pop songs you choose to sing at this stage is not important; just sing any that you remember and enjoy. Frequent repetition of the same ones is helpful.

You may be wondering whether you will find yourself talking to your baby in this way outside the Babytalk Programme. It is likely that much of the time you will, but at other times – for example when you are busy with something other than with him directly – you will find yourself chatting away with a 'running commentary' about what you are doing or what is happening. An example would be 'I'm peeling the potatoes. Here goes one into the pan, and here goes another. I'd better hurry up. We need to have lunch early today.' This kind of talking serves two purposes. First, it keeps you in contact with each other when you are not directly involved with each other, and it also enables him to hear the whole 'shape' of the language, in terms of the rhythm, tune and stress of continuous speech. This is very important information for him.

QUESTIONS

A little word here about questions. I raise it here, as questioning is a large part of adult conversational input to children, and can be very helpful or very unhelpful, according to how, why and how much questions are used. In the first three months, you will find yourself asking lots of purely rhetorical questions, like 'Who's a clever boy?' Such questions expect no reply, are in fact emotive statements and are absolutely fine. The use of this and other kinds of questions will be discussed as we go through the programme.

TWO LANGUAGES

I have received many queries about which language to use to babies born into families where more than one language is spoken.

One father told me that he was French, his wife was Greek, and the family lived in London. He wanted to know which language they should speak to their month-old daughter. My first reaction, as always on hearing about situations like this, was to think what a lucky little girl to have the chance of becoming fluent in three languages, with all the access to the poetry and literature of the different cultures. My first comment was that the one language they did not need to worry about at all was English, as their little daughter would absorb that from the environment in due course. I then advised that he and his wife always used their respective mother tongues with their baby when they were alone with her, and assured him that she would learn both languages without any difficulty, particularly if they were able to follow the BabyTalk Programme. That grounding would enable her to acquire English as a third language extremely easily later on.

Many parents think that their children might be confused and held back by exposure to more than one language, but this

I recently saw an enchanting, Greek three-year-old girl called Elysia, as there was great concern about her delayed language development. Elysia was using mainly single words, with only the occasional two-word phrase, appearing to have great difficulty putting sentences together. Both her parents were Greek, and had English as a second language, but thought that as they lived in England, they should speak to her in English. Fortunately, the family was about to go to Greece for the summer, to stay with Elysia's grandparents. I recommended total immersion in Greek and the BabyTalk Programme daily. I saw the family again two months later, and Elysia's parents were astonished at how quickly she had acquired Greek. They continued to speak to her in Greek at home, and were soon equally astonished to see how quickly she learned English at her playgroup.

only happens if parents mix up the two to a very high degree, for instance by using a number of words from each language within one sentence, or speak a language which is not their own mother tongue to their little children. The latter is particularly important. It is well known that it is very difficult indeed to modify the way we speak in a language other than our mother tongue, and a very central theme of the BabyTalk Programme, as you will see, is to modify the way you speak to your little child in very specific ways in your daily playtimes. It is also very helpful to use traditional rhymes and language games with your baby, which you are not likely to know in a language which is not your mother tongue.

I was interested in what I was told when I was talking to a Russian-English interpreter a while ago, who of course had both languages to an extremely high level. Despite this, she felt that she could not speak to her baby daughter in English, knowing instinctively that it was better to use Russian, which was her mother tongue. (See also Appendix 2, page 322.)

Another anxious call I had recently was from the mother of a colicky three-week-old baby, asking if I thought it would be very damaging to give him a dummy when he was distressed in the evening. My reply was unhesitatingly 'Of course not!' As new parents, we all need all the help we can get, and I have not yet come across a baby or young child whose speech and language development I considered to have been seriously affected by the use of a dummy. The only possible problem could arise in the case of a baby or little child who had too little to interest him or to do, and so little interaction with others, that he ended up sucking a dummy or his thumb for hours every day. This will not be the case with your baby.

OUTSIDE YOUR HALF HOUR

★ Keep talking, about what you are doing or what is happening. It enables him to hear the whole 'shape' of the language.
★ Keep background noise to a minimum so that he can focus on one set of sounds at a time.
★ Use short sentences and lots of repetition.
★ Sing to him: whatever and whenever it takes your fancy.

3 to 6 months

An overview

This is a delightful stage, and in many ways easier than the preceding one. With luck, your baby will have settled into a routine of feeding, sleeping and playing, and you may as a consequence feel that life is a little more predictable!

You will find that she shows a delightful interest in socialising with other people as well as with you, and both they and you will be rewarded by enchanting smiles and laughter. She has no fear of strangers until right at the end of this age period, and can comfortably be left with other people, and will sleep in unfamiliar settings. This all changes at the end of the trimester. She becomes aware that strangers are just that, and needs your reassuring presence if she is to interact with them. She becomes very insistent on sleeping in familiar surroundings.

Please note that the developmental stages described here are averages only.

All babies develop at slightly different rates, and often progress in one area can result in a temporary delay in another. Do not get worried or depressed if your child does not appear to be doing everything at exactly the time periods mentioned here. For further information, see Cause for Concern, page 59.

She may become mobile for the first time, by means of rolling, so this is the time to start removing precious objects from her trajectory.

You will notice that she is beginning to understand the world around her, getting very excited for example when her feeds are being prepared. She watches everything around her intently, and begins to show interest in reaching and grasping objects.

The fourth month

THE DEVELOPMENT OF LANGUAGE

We saw how in the first three months, the new-born baby developed into a full partner in the interaction process, giving and receiving important social messages. In this second three months, we see her making huge strides again.

In this period, the baby builds upon the skills developed in the first three months as her innate interest in people leads her towards the very beginnings of true verbal language. She is still pre-verbal, but a number of enormously important developments occur along the path towards her magical first word.

In terms of social interaction, you will see changes in two immensely important areas.

First, there is the start of conversational turn-taking. The baby begins to vocalise back when she is talked to, which is truly the start of conversation.

The second is linked with her increasing control over her eye movements. She can start to explore her visual environment, looking longer at one object after another, and more easily visually tracking moving objects. She is also able to follow an adult's line of regard a little more readily, thus sharing attention focus.

Her newly developed control over her head and eye muscles also enables her to turn her head to locate speakers, and she shows increasing interest in the speech she hears around her. The baby's developing interest in people and in socialising with them is shown by her frequent laughs and smiles, both spontaneous and in response to those of others. She even smiles at herself in the mirror. It is also shown in her frequent search for speakers – not just those she is most familiar with – whom she often manages to find when they are out of sight.

In terms of **understanding**, she now knows something about the communicative intent of speech, for example whether what she hears is a greeting or a warning. She is also very much aware of the emotional tone of what she hears, showing a marked reaction. She is frightened by angry voices, and comforted by soothing ones.

Sound-making continues to develop. She begins to babble, repeating little sounds, most often those made with her lips: p b and m.

GENERAL DEVELOPMENT

At this age, a baby's ability to locate speakers is made possible by her growing control over her body. She can now sit with back firm if she is held in a sitting position, and can hold up her head continuously. She is also able to lift up her head and chest when she is lying on her tummy.

Alongside the developments in language, she begins to become aware of her hands, and to play with her fingers. She makes reaching movements towards objects that interest her, and can grasp a ring if it is given to her. She also resists the removal of something she is holding.

Intellectually, her great achievement, as we have heard, is that she now knows that objects that have gone out of sight do not cease to exist.[1]

ATTENTION

As mentioned earlier, the baby occasionally begins to alter her direction of gaze to coincide with that of her mother, which is a very important precursor to the establishment of a shared focus of attention.[2] This will later become vital in the development of her ability to link words with their meanings, and to learn about 'how the world works' in very many ways.

It has been found that the sensitivity of mothers' awareness of their babies' attention development at four months predicts language development at thirteen months.[3] The results of an interesting study showed that four-month-old babies whose mothers were aware that their baby's attention was very fleeting had larger vocabularies at seventeen months than a group whose mothers were not. This finding is likely to result from the fact that the greater awareness of the baby's attention focus in the former group led the mothers to talk to their babies about that focus for more of the time.

At this stage, too, the baby starts to find ways of attracting your attention to her when it is directed elsewhere. She makes strenuous body movements, sometimes accompanied by little sounds, to get you to notice her!

LISTENING

Because of her greatly improved muscle control the baby is now able to look around from side to side for sounds. This is an important first step towards the ability to locate sounds directly in order to link them with their sources. In this way, she will be able to build up her knowledge of the auditory world. At this stage, she cannot turn her eyes only, but has to turn her whole head. She shows a particular interest in voice, making strenuous attempts to find speakers who are outside her field of vision. She is so interested in voice that she will often stop her activity in order to enable her to listen more closely.

She is also, as I have said, for the first time beginning to attribute meaning to the speech she hears, in that she responds differentially to different tones of voice. She is aware that her mother's voice can express pleasure, warning or even displeasure. She is frightened by angry voices.

The baby appears to be listening to her own sound-making, and to enjoy this, clearly receiving feedback about the sounds she produces by means of all the different tongue and lip movements she makes.

The fifth month

THE DEVELOPMENT OF LANGUAGE

The baby's awareness, **understanding** of, and interest in her environment is rapidly expanding. It can be demonstrated by her excitement when hearing her food being prepared, for instance, that she is showing anticipation of an event for the first time. It is also shown by the fact that she stops crying or fussing when she's talked to or when she hears music.

The baby is already beginning to associate 'chunks' of language with particular activities or situations. She is likely, for example, to raise her arms when hearing a tuneful 'up you come'. The magical moment when she first associates a word with meaning also occurs within this time: she appears to recognise her name, promptly starting to look around for the speaker when she hears it called. She seems to realise that a particular sequence of sounds actually means something: in this case, herself. It's interesting how early this happens, and how very far ahead of using the first words it is. Soon after, she seems to understand what 'no' means, [4] although she does not often comply!

Visual following is now mature, and by five months she can usually find anyone speaking in her vicinity. This leads to more frequently shared attention focus between baby and adult. Visual perception, understanding the meaning of what she sees, is increasing too. She can now recognise her siblings and enjoys watching them play. She watches her mother too, which will lead to understanding of the meaning and purpose of objects and events: in other words 'how the world works'.

She plays a lot with **sound-making**, both when she is alone and when with others, and the range of sounds she uses is ever increasing. Some sounds made at the back of the mouth are now heard: for example, g and k, and she often develops a special sound to signal her displeasure. This is specific to each individual baby and therefore only recognisable to those frequently with her.

The baby's communication is still not intentional, but the wider range of her actions, sounds and facial expressions make it easier for the adults around her to understand what she is feeling and what she wants. This recognition of her intentions leads towards shared intention between baby and adult, which will become important in the development of language.

GENERAL DEVELOPMENT

Her increasing control of her body again facilitates the developments in communication. The baby can now sit up with only very slight support, can turn her head, and can lift her head when she is lying on her back. A very important event happens at this time for some babies. She may now roll from side to side, giving her the first experience of mobility, and some control over her environment. She can then begin to explore more widely, and can see objects and activities from different perspectives.

The baby is also moving towards being able to access and handle objects. She can reach and grasp things, although she sometimes over-reaches. She invariably carries the objects to her mouth, which is very much her main means of discovering their properties at this stage. Her awareness of her hands is developing, as is that of her feet, and she enjoys play with both fingers and toes.

ATTENTION

There is relatively little change in this month from the last in terms of attention development. The baby's span of attention is still extremely short in the main, and it takes almost nothing to distract her. Her method of attracting your attention to herself when she perceives that it is elsewhere is now to 'call': to make loud vocalisations in order to be noticed.

LISTENING

The baby is becoming more adept at finding the source of sounds, although she still needs to turn her whole head towards them rather than just her eyes. She can now eventually find the sources of sounds which are below her and not just those that are in line with her ears. She is likely to turn towards any voice in her vicinity (not just those of familiar people) although she is still most likely to turn toward the voices of people in her family. She is also beginning to associate more familiar sounds with their meanings, becoming excited, for example, when she hears the sound of a key in the door. She is becoming very interested in music, much enjoying being sung to, and starting to listen to musical sounds.

There are some interesting research findings which show that the baby at this age is already sensitive to patterns of rate, stress and tune which mark some of the boundaries between major parts of a sentence.[5] The Language Acquisition Device is already coming into play!

The sixth month

THE DEVELOPMENT OF LANGUAGE

This month sees more important landmarks in the baby's increasing awareness and of all the people in her environment. She responds differently to different people, in particular becoming aware that strangers are just that, and showing shyness for the first time. She shows awareness of her peers, smiling and vocalising to them.[6]

She now **understands** general meanings of speech such as warning or anger, and begins to understand a broad range of emotions, which will later come into her pretend play. Very excitingly, she now shows that she understands some frequently heard and important words such as 'daddy' and 'bye bye', again very well ahead of the time she will come to use them, for reasons we will discuss later. She is beginning to remember and respond to the routines of her day. She understands 'no' a little more fully, and now obeys about half the time!

There are big changes in her **sound-making** at this time, both in terms of the sounds she makes and the ways in which she uses them. More consonants are appearing, including sounds made at the back of the mouth: for example, g and k. She begins to produce strings of repetitive babble in which she repeats the same syllable several times. These usually involve the sounds 'mama', 'dada' and 'baba', which are sounds made at the front of the mouth and very easy to produce. These are sometimes thought to be the first words, but this little miracle does not happen just yet. It's very obvious that the baby is having lots of fun playing with sounds. A very important stage in her communication development is that she begins to address her babble to people, as if she has become aware that we all make lots of sounds to each other, and wants to join in the game. She will sometimes interrupt someone else's vocalisation, starting to make sounds without waiting for the other person to pause, and will now start to sing along with music. She will sometimes accompany a gesture with a vocalisation, and finds it very funny to imitate a cough.

There is also the beginning of a 'drift' towards the speech sounds of the language she hears around her. The sounds within her repertoire begin to become those of the language around her, and those not in that language begin to fade out. (Interestingly, babies who are exposed to more than one language can do this for both languages, which is why only those who have heard a language in infancy or very early childhood can speak it with a perfect accent.)

GENERAL DEVELOPMENT

At this time, the baby can almost sit unsupported, and shows a crawling reaction when placed on her tummy. Her ability to roll is widening her horizons. She loves being lifted and swung, and will put up her arms in invitation to adults to do this. Her reach is much more accurate, making it easier for adults to know what she wants. She sometimes accompanies reaching with vocalising – an early precursor to naming.

Now that she can reach and grasp objects, she begins to explore them. At this stage, she treats all objects the same way, banging and shaking them, and still trying to put all of them in her mouth. The very beginnings of cause and effect are now emerging. For example, she may discover that banging a toy makes a particular sound.

This is helped by her growing manual dexterity and skills. Hands and eyes are now working together, enabling her to start manipulating objects more purposefully. She can pick up a small object with one hand, can pick up a toy from a table, and grasp one held in front of her. She cannot yet voluntarily release objects, or handle more than one at a time. If given a second toy, she will drop the first. She is beginning to become aware of the function of objects: for example, that a cup is for drinking.

The baby at this age is visually insatiable. She watches intently everything that goes on. She will watch an adult play with a toy and try to copy what he or she does, and will have fun imitating facial expressions. Another step forward is that she will now look for a toy that has rolled out of reach.

ATTENTION

In the course of this month, there are some small and gradual developments, and one very important stage is reached. The baby's attention span gradually becomes a little longer, but only to objects and activities which:

- ★ have become meaningful
- ★ are her choice of focus, and
- ★ are close to her.

This is the very beginning of that ability to attend selectively to sound, focusing on what is important and interesting, so vital to later learning.

She is, however, still extremely vulnerable to distractions, and she can only attend to information from one sensory channel at a time: that is, from hearing or seeing or touching. When she is totally absorbed in exploring with her hands or mouth, she will not be listening. She will even give very much reduced eye contact when in this situation. You may even wonder fleetingly if she is deaf or autistic when she does this in this situation. She's not: she's just busy!

The most important development at around this time is the continued increase in being able to follow an adult's line of regard – to look where he is looking – so that they both come to share joint attention to the same object or activity. As we shall see, this opens up the way to a huge amount of learning.

The baby is now able to watch an adult play with a toy. She attempts to copy what the adult does, and then they engage in the play together, sharing it as a focus of attention. This opens up another enormously important learning pathway.

LISTENING

Some very important developments in listening occur at this stage. The baby is beginning to turn more quickly to find sound sources, but at this stage, she can only do so directly if they are horizontal with her ears and close to her. She can eventually, after some searching, find those coming from above her head or those coming from a spot in line with her ears or those below her. She shows enormous interest in listening, beginning to scan all the sounds in the environment, and to build up more meaningful links between them and what causes them. Her ability to listen is still, however, very limited. She cannot yet listen in a sustained way, as her auditory attention span is extremely short, but she can maintain focus for a little longer on sounds which have become meaningful to her. Even in this situation, she is extremely easily distracted. However, she is also beginning to be able to discriminate between sounds which are near to her and those which are further away.

For the first time, she is able occasionally to look and listen at the same time, a huge landmark. This has been totally impossible up until now, and at this stage is still a very fragile ability, very much depending on the environment for its expression. She can only do this if the room is quiet, if what she is listening to and looking at is the same thing and is something that she is very interested in. She is totally unable to listen if she is busy investigating something with her hands or mouth, and you will see that when you give her a new toy, there is no point in talking about it until she has finished her first exploration of it. This will continue to be the case for some time to come.

It has been widely observed that there are considerable differences in babies' ability to listen, even at this very early age. This suggests that these differences are due to environmental circumstances.

Play is again, as always, the perfect vehicle for language input. This section is set out in one-month age bands, but with play there is much more overlap between the different ages.

Two themes now run through play:

★ play which is based on one-to-one interaction between adult and baby, as was all the play in the first three months
★ play with objects which now also emerges, due to the baby's growing control of her body, eye-hand co-ordination and increasing perception of her environment.

THE FOURTH MONTH

This is the time for the beginning of repetitive, interactive play, which will be enormous fun for both baby and adult. In this play, the actions of adult and baby are both synchronised and structured, and form a setting in which the baby can begin to anticipate and predict what is coming next. It gives the baby the very early beginnings of control of a situation, and an inkling of understanding of a sequence of events and how and when she can join in.

At this stage, physical games involving the baby's body parts continue to be great fun, especially as she is just beginning to become more aware of these. She enjoys tickling games, and the frolics in response, showing her huge enjoyment in every limb.

Rhymes and songs become an important part of play, as they will be throughout babyhood and childhood, and again babies are very expressive in signalling their enjoyment of these, particularly when they are accompanied by rhythmic movements. This interest coincides with the baby's emerging interest in the rhythms of speech.

External objects also begin to become the focus of play at times. The baby at this stage also begins to enjoy exploring objects by means of rather unco-ordinated handling and mouthing of them. All are treated in the same way at this stage. It is very evident that her mouth is her main means of investigation, and she is learning all the time from these investigations.

THE FIFTH MONTH

The baby's enjoyment of very simple interactive games is still enormous, and now the anticipation of each partner's actions becomes a very important part of the fun. 'Peekaboo', in which the adult hides her face with an object such as a cushion and then suddenly removes it, has to be the all-time favourite at this time. The baby's body language and the sounds she makes show clearly that she is understanding each partner's role, that is, that the person hiding her face will decide when to reveal it, while the other waits in suspense with bated breath! She also makes it very clear when she wants the game to continue. She loves the repetitive ritual which makes it increasingly possible for her to anticipate what is coming next, and is beginning to take an active part in turn-taking. The foundations of a lifetime's pleasure in social interaction are being firmly laid down and her understanding of the communication process is also being forged. She still very much enjoys the play involving her body parts, and she has started playing with her fingers and toes.

The baby's relatively well-controlled ability to reach and grasp objects increases her interest in them. She is still exploring them by means of mouthing and handling them, but now starts to shake and bang them as well. The beginning of her under-standing of cause and effect starts to emerge, as she realises for instance, that banging or shaking an object will cause a noise. She appreciates having objects with a wide range of different properties of colour, texture and shape to investigate.

She is also now beginning to watch others play, both adults and children, and is learning by doing so. She will begin to copy play with toys, and also to join with another in the play with them. She will also now perpetuate the play, making it clear to the adult that she wants to continue the activity.

THE SIXTH MONTH

The baby is now a fully participating member of the ritualised turn-taking games she has been enjoying for the past two

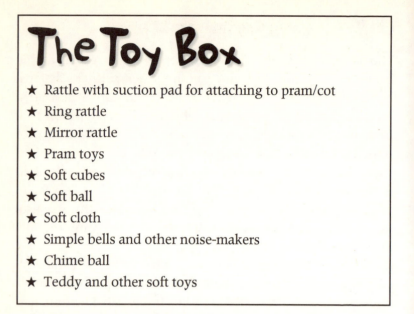

The Toy Box

- ★ Rattle with suction pad for attaching to pram/cot
- ★ Ring rattle
- ★ Mirror rattle
- ★ Pram toys
- ★ Soft cubes
- ★ Soft ball
- ★ Soft cloth
- ★ Simple bells and other noise-makers
- ★ Chime ball
- ★ Teddy and other soft toys

months. She loves games in which movement is linked with vocalisation, such as 'Patacake'. She also loves being jiggled on an adult's knee as she makes funny noises, and being lifted and swung as part of the play.

Her hands and eyes are working together now so that looking is part of her exploration as well as mouthing and handling, and her interest in toys and other objects is intense. She will now explore each for a little longer, and will become totally absorbed in this exploration, so much so that she will be unable to look at an adult as well.

She now watches her mother and others more and more, and is beginning, as a result, to learn about the function of objects and the sequences of events that she will later incorporate into her play.

She needs many objects to explore at this stage, as her attention span is very short, and she needs to be able to move rapidly from one thing to another.

The main need is still for a wide variety of textures, shapes and colours to explore and investigate.

The comments made in relation to the first three months (see page 34) still apply: there is still no place for these in her life. Her need is still, above all, for a responsive, interactive partner.

Summary

To summarise, by the age of three months, your baby is likely to:

★ Make it clear, by means of her body movements and her facial expressions, that she can now tell the difference between cross or friendly voices.
★ Begin to recognise some words which she hears a great deal, such as 'bye bye' or 'Daddy'.
★ Respond to little requests such as 'up you come'.
★ Appear to know what 'no' means, and will stop what she is doing some of the time.
★ Often play at sound-making, both when she is alone and when she is with other people.
★ Quite often start a 'conversation' in sounds, by clearly addressing someone with a sound.

Cause for concern

Below are circumstances in which it would be advisable to seek professional advice about your baby's development. (Please remember, though, that many children progress at slightly different rates.)

If you are in any doubt about your baby, even if the reason for your concern is not mentioned here, do take her to see your Health Visitor or GP as soon as possible.

At six months it would be advisable to seek a professional opinion if:

★ Your baby doesn't often look around for speakers.
★ She rarely follows a moving object with her eyes.
★ She seldom makes sounds back to you when you talk to her.
★ She doesn't make babbling sounds with a consonant and a vowel (for example 'pa' or 'goo').
★ She makes very few sounds apart from crying.

The Baby Talk Programme

In this second three months, as long as you follow some basic but extremely important guidelines, it is very likely that your baby will continue to trigger you into providing her with the kind of input most helpful to her development which, as we have seen, is extraordinarily rapid at this stage.

HALF AN HOUR A DAY

If you are lucky, she may be in a routine of feeding, sleeping and play, and you may be getting a better night's sleep as a consequence! If and when this is so, start your half an hour a day playtime when you and your baby can enjoy each other's company free from distractions, rather than finding the time around feeding and nappy changing times, as you have up to now. If this routine is not established yet, continue finding the time as you were before. Please do whatever is least stressful. Your full attention is the greatest gift that you can give your baby, and that which she will relish above all else. It is the most effective stress-remover for babies and little children that there is, and you will have seen how eagerly she seeks this at all times. Being there for her for part of each day, as a consistent partner in her gradual discovery of the world, is the most wonderful learning opportunity that you can give her. This is best built, in these early stages, around recurring repeated play times.

THE SETTING FOR YOUR ONE-TO-ONE PLAYTIME

As you know already, it is of the very greatest importance that the room is very, very quiet, with no radio, music, video or television. The small but extremely important developments in listening and attention that emerge at this stage can only do so in an environment free from distractions; in particular, background noise. The beginnings of her ability to focus on foreground sound and tune out background occur now and, as we have said, babies need a very much greater difference between background and foreground sound in order to begin to be able to do this. The baby also needs opportunities to hear her own sound-making clearly, so she can make the essential links between the tongue and lip movements she makes and the resulting sounds that ensue.

> **She needs to hear her sound-making clearly**

Your baby is very easily distracted still, and the span of her attention is, in the main, extremely fleeting. It is important, therefore, to have many interesting objects around for her to reach for or look at and that you can hand to her if she wants to bring objects into the play. Make a point of including some simple noise-makers as she is likely to enjoy these particularly.

Arrange the play space so that you and your baby are very close together, either with her in your arms or with you sitting on the floor with her in front of you in a little chair. In this way you will enable her to make all those very fine perceptions and discriminations of speech sounds which are possible for her at this stage. Make sure, too, that the toys are within your easy reach.

One extremely important principle of the BabyTalk Programme comes into effect already. It is essential that you *never* try to keep your baby's or little child's attention on an object or action for longer than she wants to. Nothing impedes the devel-

Never try to prolong your baby's attention span

opment of attention more than that. (Of course, there will be times later in her life when it will be appropriate to draw her attention to something and encourage her to keep it there, but not now, and never while you are following this programme.)

The reason for this is that in the early stages of attention development, any attempt to keep the baby's attention on a particular focus, after they have shifted it spontaneously to another, only serves to 'fragment' that attention, by splitting it between the child's and the adult's chosen focus. If this happens to any significant extent, it delays the child's progression through the stages of development, as well as causing much frustration for both child and adult. Sadly, this is a very common problem indeed, and it can be enormously rewarding to explain the situation to a parent and see the almost immediate change in a child.

Imran's parents were in despair, as Imran would not do anything they told him to, hardly played at all, and instead spent his time rushing around the house breaking things in his wake. His parents were trying harder and harder to get him to play with toys of their choice and to listen to them, and he was becoming more and more resistant – not only to their play suggestions, but to any directions at all, including those connected with eating and sleeping. His mother, in particular, was close to tears, saying: 'Of course I love Imran, but I'm finding it very hard to like him or enjoy his company'. Two weeks of daily playtimes, in which it was made clear to Imran that he was free to change the focus of his attention as often as he wanted to, brought about a change which astonished and delighted his parents. He played appropriately and for considerable spells with toys, and was very much more compliant. His mother was able to enjoy him once more!

HOW MUCH TO TALK

It's important that she has time to 'reply' now, so don't be tempted in your special playtimes to chat away to her on your own agenda. Instead, be very much aware of the 'conversations' in sounds between the two of you. Pause after you have said something to give her time to reply, and watch for her pauses, which will allow you to. You are likely to find, as a result, that there is now less overlap between your vocalisations and hers. By giving yourself this undivided time with her, you will progressively increase your sensitivity to her communications and interactions, and she will play an important part in leading you to respond to her in the most appropriate and helpful way.

Watch for her pauses

A study looked at the frequency with which mothers of five month olds responded to their infants' attempts to engage them in vocal turn-taking, by waiting for the baby to indicate that it was their turn, and giving the baby plenty of time to reply to them. The mothers' frequency correlated strongly with the level of the babies' attention span, symbolic play and understanding of words at thirteen months of age.[7]

HOW TO TALK

You will probably find that, at the beginning of this three-month period, your play and the language input that can so beautifully accompany it will focus on interactive play between the two of you. Later on, your baby's growing interest in toys and other objects she can explore will increasingly bring them into the play. As long as you and the toys are available, your baby can and will dictate the balance of this. The most appropriate ways of talking do not vary within each month age band at this time, so the programme is given for the whole three-month period.

Repeat her sounds back to her

Repeat the sounds she makes back to her very often. Copy either the last sound in the string or a single sound. For example, she says 'oo', and you say 'oooooo', or she says 'ayay', and you say 'ayayayayay'. (It can be fun sometimes to make your sounds longer than hers.) This is the earliest form of turn-taking, and a vital precursor to conversation. It is also one of the easiest things for a baby to focus her attention on, and is, therefore, very helpful for this area of development. You will see how she loves your evident enthusiasm for her sound-making, and will be encouraged to do more of this. You will find that the more you do it, the more sounds she will make. Later, she will start to make the sounds back to you again, and you will soon find that you are having a wonderful 'conversation'!

This also serves to enhance, too, her perceptions of her own sound-making, as it gives her the opportunity to hear one or two sounds at a time, rather than the extremely rapidly changing stream of sounds in normal speech. It enhances her perception of the effects of different lip and tongue movements on the resulting sounds. Yet another important effect is that it is one of the best ways of giving the baby the message that listening to voices is fun and rewarding. This is an extremely important message, and is another theme that runs throughout the programme.

> **Imitate the sounds she makes**

Do continue doing this, over and over, throughout this whole three-month period – she'll love it!

There is a common view that adults should only speak in 'real' words to babies. Not so. As I hope to show, BabyTalk has many important functions, apart from being a lot of fun.

A word of caution. Always regard making your baby's sounds back to her, as *you* responding to *her* in order to develop a conversation in sounds. Never think of it as an attempt to get her to copy you.

You can also make lots of 'play sounds' to go with what she is interested in at that moment.

These fun sounds can be made in many different ways. They can be single sounds like 'wheeeeeeee' as a ball rolls along. They can alternatively take the form of repeated

Susie and Charlotte both had very similar circumstances in many ways. Both were first babies, adored by the extended family, and received almost full-time devoted attention. They were extremely attractive, bright and alert. There was only one difference, and that was in relation to their mother's responses to their babies' sound-making.

Charlotte's mother responded joyfully to all her sounds, making them back to her and perceiving that this was an interactive conversation. Charlotte responded in turn by making more and more sounds, and by clearly taking great pleasure in both her own and her mother's sound-making.

Susie's mother, in contrast, saw her role in making sounds to Susie as doing so to get Susie to copy her. She made sounds, and then obviously and anxiously expected Susie to repeat them. Interestingly, as we have seen, babies know a great deal about communication, and Susie's response to this regime was gradually to cease making sounds altogether. Her distraught mother brought her to see me at the age of sixteen months and we put her on the BabyTalk Programme. Within a few weeks, her sound-making had caught up with that of her peers and she and her mother began having a lot of fun together!

sequences of words linked to interactive activities, such as 'up, up, up you come' as you lift her up, or delicious nonsense like 'oochi coochi coochi coo' as you walk your fingers up her tummy. Rhythmical ritualised vocalisations such as 'upsidaisy' also come into this category. The frequent repetition of these kinds of sounds greatly adds to the fun!

These play sounds also serve a number of important purposes, in the same way as does imitating the baby's own vocalisations. They too are extremely helpful in maintaining attention and arousal, and give the baby the message that voice really is great fun to listen to. You may also find that she begins to practise speech gestures, such as lip rounding, while she is watching your face

Play sounds make voices fun to listen to

at these times, showing clearly her enormous interest in speech sounds.

★ Use short simple sentences

Talk to your baby in short simple sentences, which are very tuneful, and speak slowly, with pauses between phrases. This way of speaking is important in that it attracts and maintains the baby's attention and level of arousal, as it is still the kind of speech that babies prefer at this age, and, therefore, focus on most easily.[8] [9] [10] [11] 'Here's Mummy. Here she is. Mummy's here!' is a great deal more interesting for a baby than 'I think I can hear Mummy's car coming down the road. She'll be here in a minute!'

Short tuneful sentences are also very important still in terms of the bonding between the two of you, as they carry emotional tone. Later in this period, they come to have another extremely important function in that they are enormously useful in helping the baby to link words with their meanings. It has been found that four-month-old babies pay much more attention to this kind of speech even when it is heard in the background than the kind of speech adults use to each other, and that they even pay much more attention to videos in which adults are using this kind of speech.[12]

> **Keep your sentences short and simple**

> **Speak slowly and tunefully**

★ Initiate language games

Ritualistic and repetitive language games, and turn-taking games, are of huge importance in laying the foundations of all conversation and social interaction, and also immensely enjoyable. They will help her to start anticipating events and so gain a measure of control, as well as very early experience of turn-taking. You will be the sole initiator of the turn-taking early in this period, but by the time she is approaching six months, you will find that she is becoming a full partner.

You will notice that she starts to pause between vocalisation, as if waiting for you to take your turn. She may say, for example, 'ah di baba' and then look expectantly at you for your reply. Early in the three-month period, initiate tickling games and those involving her body parts. Early on, these are likely to be simple activities such as counting her fingers and toes, later progressing to more complex action rhymes such as 'Round and round the garden', and 'This little piggy', which really come into their own at this stage. (If you can't remember how these go, try borrowing a book from your local library; there are some books that show hand actions as well as the rhymes and songs themselves.)

Later, other objects such as soft toys can be involved in the play: for example, playing 'Eyes, nose and cheeky cheeky chin' on teddy's face, or playing 'bang bang bang' with spoons. Make sure that your facial expression is always lively, as it has been found that babies vocalise a lot more when looking at such faces.

Play games in which she has the opportunity to anticipate your actions, which is turn-taking in its earliest form. At the beginning of these three months, for example, advance your face towards her slowly, giving her time to anticipate the 'boo' which will follow. By the time she's six months, she will love games like 'clap hands' in which you take turns in clapping your own hands and each other's.

Use lots of repetition

In the fifth and sixth months, sing and tell her lots of rhymes and action rhymes, which she will enjoy enormously. Use those with a strong beat, and repeat the same ones often, so that they become familiar and there can be an element of anticipation for the baby. Towards the end of this period, she will particularly enjoy those in which the words are accompanied by actions, such as 'Row, row, row your boat'. As we have seen, in the fifth month, she is becoming sensitive to the patterns of tune, rhythm and stress which will later help her to decode sentences, and this will help her with this process.

FOLLOW HER FOCUS OF ATTENTION

Start to become very much aware of and to follow your baby's focus of attention. Get into the habit of looking to see what she is looking at and making that the subject of what you talk about, following from moment to moment as she changes her focus of attention. If she looks at you, for example, start one of your interactive games, or if she looks at an object, give it to her, either telling her its name or making an appropriate 'play sound' to go with it. This is an enormously important theme throughout the programme.

> **See what she is looking at, and talk about it**

At this stage, you are the initiator of most play activities, but the principle can still be applied, in that you can be careful to stop an activity the moment she seems to be losing interest. As well, you can be alert to when, for example, she looks towards a toy, bringing it to her and including it in the game.

At a later stage, this principle becomes absolutely vital in helping her to make links between words and their meanings. At the moment, it is enormously helpful in facilitating the development of her attention. This is totally single channelled for most of this three-month period: remember that she cannot look and listen at the same time. As we have seen, however, she becomes able to look and listen in particular circumstances:

★ when there is nothing else to distract her
★ when the focus of her attention is one of her own choice
★ when what she is listening to and looking at is the same thing: for example a noise-making toy, or a person singing or talking to her about whatever her attention is focused on.

Following her focus of attention will help her to take this very important step.

QUESTIONS

You will find yourself asking a question and then pausing. If you listen to yourself, you will find that its purpose is to allow the baby response time, and not a true question. Examples would be 'Shall we do that again, then?' or 'Who's a very clever girl?' These are fine. You are also likely to find that you sometimes say 'What's this?' This again is not a true question at this stage, but rather an alerting device, used when you are aware that there is something in her environment that she is likely to find interesting. Again, that's fine.

OUTSIDE YOUR HALF HOUR

As mentioned in the previous chapter, continue to give a running commentary about what is happening, or what you are thinking about when you are busy and your baby is nearby. You might find yourself saying something like 'Shall we go to the shops now? No, I don't think so – it looks as if it's going to pour with rain. We'll go tomorrow instead.' Of course your baby won't understand what you are saying, but you will be giving her an opportunity to hear the rhythm and tune of the language.

6 to 9 months

An overview

By now your baby's routines are well established, and you and he have a comfortable and more predictable pattern in your lives. You will be in no doubt that you are the most important person in his life! He will make it clear by delicious smiles, laughs, shouts and joyful wriggles of his whole body how he relishes your company, and his increasing awareness of the difference between familiar and unfamiliar people and situations lead him to depend on you increasingly for a feeling of security.

You will find your baby very easy to amuse at this stage. He delights in his ability to reach and grasp, and all objects are fascinating to him. You will find that even a very simple object like a cardboard tube can keep him amused for a considerable

Please note that the developmental stages described here are averages only.

All babies develop at slightly different rates, and often progress in one area can result in a temporary delay in another. Do not get worried or depressed if your child does not appear to be doing everything at exactly the time periods mentioned here. For further information, see Cause for Concern, page 89.

time. He's also easy to distract if you want him to relinquish something or change activity. He may throw his body back in resistance momentarily, but everything is so interesting to him that he will soon engage with a new object or activity.

He may begin to make some progress forwards or backwards by means of crawling, but it's still possible to take your eyes off him for a few seconds – he won't get very far yet.

You'll find that he's very familiar with his daily routines now, and already starting to want to do little things for himself like holding a biscuit or putting his hands round his cup .

The seventh month

THE DEVELOPMENT OF COMMUNICATION

This third part of the first year again sees the baby making great strides towards becoming a verbal conversationalist. During this period, there are additional bursts of cell connections within the speech centres of his brain, and the network of nerves that allows for this to occur is believed to be very much affected by how much 'exercise' it receives.[1]

The influence of the environment, therefore, now becomes a crucial factor in the baby's development. This is reflected in the fact that from the age of six months, babies start to show a greater variation in the pattern and range of some achievements than they do at earlier ages, which is likely to be attributable to variations in their environments as well as to genetic factors. In a number of studies, for example, children living in families have been found to make much better developmental progress than those brought up in group nurseries.[2]

The enormous interest in speech that the baby has shown from the beginning of his life has resulted in the fact that he is already recognising the names of a number of familiar objects and people. At the beginning of this period, he even starts to look around for members of his family who are not present when he hears their names mentioned.[3]

At this time, too, he also shows by his actions that he **understands** something about the meaning of little phrases which he has heard a lot: for example, waving when he hears 'bye bye'. (It is rather like the way you feel when you visit a country whose language you do not know, and suddenly realise after a while that you do know the meaning of a few words.)

However, he can only do this when the phrases occur in a familiar context: for example, when one of his parents is routinely leaving for work. He cannot yet generalise to another situation, and may puzzle a parent who wonders why he doesn't wave bye bye when leaving the house of a friend he hasn't visited before.

His understanding of the emotional tone of speech is very much in advance of his understanding of words, and is well developed at this early stage. He is very clearly aware of his mother's or father's pleasure or displeasure. He very much enjoys listening to music and singing now, and shows his delight with his whole body.

His recognition that his own name means himself is also more secure, and he often vocalises back when he hears it, as if answering a call.

Your baby is developing a wide range of communicative behaviours at this time, which includes gesture, tugs, pulls, pushes and facial expression. He is also adept at communicating a wide range of messages, including drawing attention to himself, to other people and to objects, greeting, refusing, requesting, commenting and acknowledging. He is already a competent communicator, and is extremely effective by all these various means at controlling the people within his environment.

As early as six months, he realises that vocal **sound-making**, in particular, can be used to make things happen around him. He finds that making noises will bring his mother to him, and so begins to 'call' her purposefully. He also uses vocalisation intentionally to communicate with his peers, beginning to babble purposefully to them, and is very enthusiastic about joining in 'conversations' in sounds. By seven months, much of his play is accompanied by sound-making, and he is beginning to control the people in his environment by his shouts and other vocalisations.

During this three months, the baby is also progressively making many more links between the movements he makes with his lips and tongue, and the sounds that consequently ensue. He becomes aware, for example, that smacking his lips together makes a 'p-p-p' sound.

This monitoring is extremely important in the development of his speech-sound system, and its effect is seen in the continuation of the 'babble drift'. This is the process in which more and more of the sounds he makes are those of the language or languages he hears around him, with the simultaneous fading out of those that are not. At the same time, there is a marked decrease in the baby's ability to distinguish contrasts between sounds which are not present in the language around him whereas, as we know, he can make very fine discriminations between the sounds which are in that language.

He appears much more aware of the sounds he is making, and uses a smaller number with increasing frequency. He enjoys repeating them, producing more and longer strings of sounds, such as 'mamama' or 'bababa'. He also begins to use two syllables at times, rather than one, and may begin to repeat two or more different sounds, for example, 'bedebedebede'. His babble sounds more and more like speech in terms of rhythm and tune, and he is already making rudimentary attempts to 'name' objects, by referring to them with consistent sounds. Each baby will make its own particular sounds, which may have little or no resemblance to the real word. They mark, however, an extremely important stage, in that they signal the baby's recognition that specific sounds can refer to specific objects or events.

Strategies are being developed at this stage for exploring and interacting with his environment and the objects and people within it. As the baby's awareness grows, his social interactions start to involve a much wider range of topics, allowing him and his mother to begin to develop shared views of objects and events.[4][5][6] For example, he may have shared experiences of play with particular toys, and associate particular games with other people: he may know, for instance, that his brother loves to become involved in games of 'hidey peep'. The increase in the amount of shared focus of attention will lead to the crucial ability to attach meaning to words, for which it is vital.

This period also sees the development of vocal 'conversations' flourishing, which is such a vital precursor to true verbal conversation.

GENERAL DEVELOPMENT

These developments in the areas of social interaction and communication are occurring at the same time as big changes in the areas of motor and intellectual development.

The baby can now take his weight on his feet if he is held upright, and can sit with his head steady and his back straight. He can roll from his back to his tummy. He can adjust his position in order better to see a particular object, and his ability to grasp and manipulate objects is developing apace. He will attempt to grab an object which is just beyond his reach, and he can transfer one from hand to hand. His fingers close on an object with decision, and he can lift one hand towards a toy, imitate beating on a table with his hand, and bang two objects together. These are no small achievements. Reaching to grasp an object involves three joints in the arm and fourteen in the hand. Initiating a reaching movement involves more than thirteen muscles in the arm, and adjusting the hand to grasp an object uses more than twenty in the hand.[7]

Big steps in intellectual development are also occurring. By the age of seven months, babies can show that they understand some of the properties of partly obstructed objects, knowing for example that a soft object would be squashed by a rotating screen, but a hard one would not.[8]

Alice was six months old. Her mother was extremely concerned because she was neither showing any interest in voice or speech, nor was she doing more in terms of sound-making than making a few rather vague vowel-like sounds. Alice was clearly developing very well in many ways. In particular, she was very advanced physically, sitting firmly alone, rotating her trunk with ease and manipulating and investigating everything she could get hold of. She was also mobile, rolling at speed and navigating with considerable skill. These two areas, of mobility and manipulation, were clearly absorbing all her attention. We started the BabyTalk Programme, and within three months, her communication skills had completely caught up with her other areas of development. She is now considerably advanced in all areas.

Inevitably, the different areas of development impinge upon each other at this time, so that an early crawler, for example, may cease to be so interested in communication for a time, so enchanted is he by his new-found mobility. Similarly, nobody who has just learned to stand up unaided has an ounce of energy left to do anything else. It is very important to recognise this, so that you do not worry unnecessarily if development in one area seems to slow down for a little while. It is possible, however, to prevent language and communication falling behind other than very temporarily in these rather extreme and short-lived situations.

ATTENTION

As we have heard, the very beginnings of sensory integration, the ability to use more than one sense at a time – a very vital stage – continues to emerge in this month. In the main, however, attention is still single channelled, and you will still find that if you hand your baby an interesting object, he won't be able to listen to or look at you until he has completed his initial exploration. The baby can now attend to objects or activities of his own choice for still longer, but he remains extremely easily distracted. This increase in span of attention is very important – for both short- and long-term memory – and in fact, all later learning depends on the ability to maintain attention focus.

LISTENING

This is the beginning of a critical time in the development of two skills that are vital for successful speech and language:

★ discriminating and differentiating between all the different sounds in speech
★ understanding what words mean.

In terms of speech-sound discrimination, it has been found that there is a considerable difference in the ability of babies as young as seven months to do this, and it seems very likely that the different auditory environments of the babies would largely account for these startling differences. There are indications that both too little and too much sound stimulus can affect the process. Children who have been deprived of sound for much of their early lives by hearing problems often later show considerable difficulties, not only in discriminating between sounds, but also in making sense out of sound, and in listening in the presence of noise. Babies who have had to spend much time in incubators, in which the noise levels are very high, often show similar difficulties later. (It is important to recognise, however, that these problems can be overcome. We have had many children with very severe listening difficulties indeed in our clinics, and the parts of the BabyTalk Programme which relate to listening resolve the problems in a remarkably short time.)

In this month, the baby is continuing, gradually, to build up links between sounds and their meanings. He is still not able to localise sound directly – that is to turn immediately to a sound source – but has to look around until he finds it. However, he is now looking a little more directly for them, and can find those coming from above his head.

The ability to look and listen at the same time is still fragile. It continues to be essential that:

★ the focus of his attention is one of his own choice
★ he is not overly involved with either looking or listening
★ what he is looking at and listening to is the same object
★ his environment is free from distractions.

The eighth month

THE DEVELOPMENT OF COMMUNICATION

In this month, babies not only look for speakers who are out of sight, but begin to listen to whole conversations, turning to one speaker and then to the next, and then to the first again, looking for all the world like spectators at a tennis match.

They show that they **understand** the link between some common objects and the words that stand for them by turning to look at the objects when they hear them named. They usually recognise the names of all immediate family members at this time, and will usually listen intently when they hear their own name called.

By eight months, babies will usually respond to some familiar simple commands with an appropriate gesture: for example, putting their arms up on hearing 'up you come', or waving a hand when hearing 'wave bye bye'. They still need the support of a familiar situation for this understanding. They are extremely adept at this stage in understanding the speaker's feeling state and emotional tone from their gestures, facial expression and intonation patterns.

Babies' **sound-making** at eight months is continuing to come more and more into line with those of the language around them, and there is a marked decrease in their ability to detect small differences between sounds which are not in that language.

Babbling at this stage occasionally begins to sound more like little sentences in a foreign language, being full of rhythm, tune and stress patterns. There is much controversy about the relationship between babble and later speech. Research indicates that speech does not directly grow out of babble, but babbling does indicate that there is an underlying state of readiness of the nervous system in preparation for speech.[9] Babies at this stage will occasionally sing along with music, but without any true words as yet.

They are also still reliant upon non-vocal means of communication, which are now, however, becoming refined. They will make a request by opening and shutting their hand, and indicate refusal by pushing the adult away or shaking their head. They begin to combine a gesture with a sound: for example, waving their arms and gurgling at the sight of their mother.

GENERAL DEVELOPMENT

Babies of this age can usually maintain a sitting position for a few minutes. They can rotate both head and trunk while doing so, which allows them to look around more easily and so explore their surroundings. This is very important in enabling them to make the links between sounds and their sources. When helped upright, they will now take steps, placing one foot in front of the other.

Reaching is becoming more skilful. They will reach persistently for a toy, adjusting their position in order to enable them to do so. They can, for the first time, manipulate two objects at once: for example comparing two cubes by bringing them together. They can also pull a string to retrieve a toy, and will remove a cover from a hidden object or pull a cloth to retrieve an object resting on it.

ATTENTION

By the age of eight months, the baby can follow an adult's line of regard easily, but he still has to do this at this stage by turning his whole head; he cannot do it yet by moving only his eyes.[10] This continues to be extremely important, as it enables the establishment of an increased amount of shared focus of attention between baby and adult. This will be vital for a long time in helping him to understand his environment, and to come to share adults' view of the world, which is so essential for his intellectual development. The adult knows what is interesting him at that moment, and can give him information about it. It is of great importance in other ways too. It helps him to understand the reasons for the feeling states of other people, and so enhances his ability to relate and interact with them. It also, and perhaps most importantly of all, enables him to attach meaning to words.

His attention span is still very short and single channelled in the main: that is, he can only attend to the information from one sense at a time, despite his emerging ability, as we have described, to look and listen at the same time in very limited circumstances.

LISTENING

This month, if all has gone well up to this point, sees some extremely important listening developments. First, the baby is able to localise sound directly for the first time. This coincides with the ability to sit up alone, and is made possible by the completion of the covering of the nerve which connects the ear and the brain. The baby can now localise directly sounds which are horizontal with his ears, and within a few feet of him. The ability to localise depends upon being able to make judgements about the timing and loudness of the sounds reaching the two ears, and requires normal hearing in both ears.

With this new-found ability to localise comes the start of that crucial ability to scan his auditory surroundings, and focus upon a chosen sound. Scanning is very slow at this stage, and the baby is very easily distracted, but it is immensely helpful to him in making links between sounds and their sources. These links are now being built up more rapidly, and are vital not only to language, but also to understanding about the world.

The baby is now listening more closely to his own sound-making, and is comparing the sounds he makes with those he hears around him. This will eventually enable him to bring his sounds completely in line with those of his mother tongue.

He is immensely interested in sound now, and derives enormous pleasure from playing with noise-makers, and listening to vocalisations such as 'play sounds', rhymes and songs.

The ninth month

The baby's **understanding** increases considerably in this month. He may understand as many as twenty names of objects and people by the end of this time. He now responds appropriately to a wider repertoire of little phrases like 'Let's go', or 'Come to Daddy', although he still only understands them in a familiar context. He has a more substantial understanding of the meaning of 'no', and will now usually stop what he is doing on hearing it. He will also perform an action related to a routine on request, for example, rocking back and forth on hearing the rhyme 'Row, row, row your boat'. He still loves music and singing.

Now, for the first time, he can associate pictures of familiar objects with the objects themselves, and will enjoy being shown them for a short time, thus taking a first step on the road to reading.

He has a very wide range of communicative behaviours. He can use some conventional gestures as well as pointing: for example, shaking his head to indicate 'no', and waving as a greeting. He still also uses tugs, pulls and pushes, and facial expression to communicate, and is overall an extremely able communicator, giving information as well as greeting, protesting, acknowledging and drawing attention to himself and other objects and people. He is now well in control of the people in his environment and is beginning to understand the connection between his behaviour and adults' responses – and, as a consequence, to show off.

His own babbling contains an ever-increasing repertoire of **sound-making**, and is full of rhythm and tune. It can be hard at times to accept that it is not true language, as it sounds more and more like real sentences. The baby at this stage is very close, in two ways, to using true words.

★ He will now use a word invented by himself to denote an object, rather than a sound pattern as in the previous month, being delighted when the object appears.
★ He can now combine gestures with sounds and eye gaze: for example, looking intently at an object, pointing at it at the same time, and accompanying both with a loud 'uh uh' to make it extremely clear that he wants to be handed the object.

He loves to 'talk' back when he is spoken to, and enjoys speech games like 'Patacake' even more. He is also beginning to become a mimic, and will often imitate the sounds, tune and number of syllables used by others. He will also imitate facial expressions.

Intellectually, an essential precursor to the use of true language is developing, and this is the formation of concepts and categories. The baby's previous play activities will have enabled him to form concepts of what things are by now – for example, that cups are for drinking from – and also to begin to form categories: for example, that glasses and his bottle, as well as cups, are all for drinking from. These categories are very broad at first, and are subject later to finer and finer sub-groupings.[11] Concepts and categories such as these need to be in place before meaningful language becomes possible: we can't, for example, talk about cats and dogs unless we understand that they are two different kinds of animal.

By the age of about nine months, he has made a major realisation: that not only can vocal sounds magically bring about what we want to happen, but that specific sounds can bring about very specific effects. In fact, he is beginning to have a rudimentary appreciation of the amazing power of words. He does not yet have any true ones at his disposal, but he begins to develop some of his own: sequences of sounds which have a specific meaning and vary from infant to infant. The nine-month-old baby of a friend of mine, for example, firmly and consistently says 'oof' when she wants a drink. She is clearly enchanted when a drink consequently appears.

Towards the end of this period, the baby develops the beginnings of another very important skill: that of integrating the interactions of both objects and people. He can now use a person to acquire an object or do something with it: for example, by pointing at a toy car and vocalising as he looks at his mother, so that his mother winds it up and hands it to him. He can also use objects to gain attention: for instance, by banging loudly on his chair with a toy.

By nine months, he is using jargon – strings of sounds that have the rhythm and tune of speech – and which can sound, from a distance, very like a true language. This jargon contains no true words yet, but it is a wonderful vehicle for expressing feelings and emotions!

GENERAL DEVELOPMENT

The most marked feature in this month for many babies is the ability to get around the room other than by rolling, which considerably widens his horizons.

The baby's growing awareness of his environment is indicated by the fact that he will now look for a dropped toy, showing that out of sight is no longer out of mind. He will also imitate simple actions, such as ringing a bell, showing that he is watching closely and learning from the actions of others.[12]

ATTENTION

The baby is enabled, in this month, through the development of shared attention, to embark upon a stage of making very rapid links between words and their meanings. This establishment of shared attention is enhanced by a new ability which is emerging, that of following a point. By the age of nine months, he can follow an object which is close to him and straight in front of him. He cannot yet follow a point which would neccessitate turning his head.[13]

The range of his attention focus is also increasing. By the age of nine months, he watches people and moving objects at 3 metres (nearly 10 feet) distance with sustained interest.

Despite the fact that he is making links between words and meanings now, because his attention is still virtually always single channelled, he cannot yet relate words to what he is doing. He can either do or listen – but not yet both.

Being easily distracted is still a big problem, and will remain so for some considerable time to come.

One important development is that he can now pay attention, for up to a minute, to pictures when they are named for him by an adult. This is a first step towards sharing books, but at this stage usually lasts less than a minute.[14]

LISTENING

In this month, the baby's ability to scan the auditory environment, focus on what he wants to listen to, and inhibit responses to other sounds, gradually increases if environmental circumstances allow it. The time required for scanning becomes shorter and attention to the chosen sounds a little longer (if distractions allow). He systematically continues to increase his understanding of the meaning of sounds, such as those connected with meal times, by attending to and comparing the sounds he hears with those he has heard previously.

Play shows some important developments and, as always, is a wonderful vehicle for language input. The most marked feature of this stage is that more and more different objects and situations now become part of the play, as his understanding of the world and his interest in finding out all about the objects and people in his environment grows.[15] [16] (It's always important to remember that babies and small children readily move between stages of play. A tired two year old, for example, may want to be played with in just the same way he loved when he was six months old: sitting on his mother's knee while she recites 'Round and round the garden'.)

He continues to enjoy both interactive play and play with objects. The latter can be so absorbing that at times, he really doesn't want anyone else involved.

THE SEVENTH MONTH

At this time, he most of all loves interactive play which is highly predictable, both in terms of language and actions, so that he can begin to anticipate what will happen next. He can also understand the roles of the two partners, in terms of who does what and when it's his turn.[17] This means that he delights in having the same little rhymes and games repeated over and over again. This repetition makes the world safe and understandable, and he does not, at this stage, want any variation.

Very simple games such as 'Peekaboo', 'Incy-wincy spider' and 'Clap hands' fill the bill beautifully. The vocalisations are completely ritualised, and there is a delicious aspect of anticipation. The roles of each partner are very simple and clear, involving few words and actions, but they provide extremely enjoyable social interaction to both partners. The turn-taking element is a wonderful foundation for later social skills.

Chants, nursery rhymes and nonsense speech linked to body movements, such as the adult jiggling the baby on her knee as she makes funny noises, are still wonderful too. Babies at this age still love lots of physical contact in their play, and relish vocalisations that are linked to physical activity in this way. These activities are very helpful indeed in maintaining that all-important joint attention.

The baby also loves the adult to mirror his actions at this time, finding this immensely amusing. This helps him to become more aware of his own actions and the effects of them on other people, and also helps him to enhance the links between the information he receives through his senses and the movements he makes.

He wants to investigate a multitude of objects and materials now, and needs to have lots available, as his attention span is still very short, and he likes to move from one to another very rapidly on the whole. He continues to be very interested in shapes, colours, textures and the noises things make or that he can make with them. He will begin to remember these noises, and want to make them again.

There is research evidence that when parents make these kinds of play available, and enter into them, their babies show a greater variation and diversity in their play than do those who are left to their own devices for much of the time.[18]

THE EIGHTH MONTH

In this month, babies still relish interactive games such as 'Peekaboo', and still love them to be repeated many, many times. The turn-taking aspect of these games is hugely enjoyed, and his delight in anticipation, now that he is so familiar with them, can now be enhanced by little variations like a longer pause before the inevitable 'boo!' in 'Peekaboo'. His attention will be riveted and his amusement boundless. He is receiving, through these games, the message that listening to voice is rewarding and fun, and he is also building up a repertoire of shared experiences with his parent. He will begin to initiate some of these little games himself: for example, 'hiding' by putting a paper over his face. He loves surprises at this stage, such as those provided by pop-up toys.

Imitation, both by baby and adult, now becomes part of the play. Each begin to copy the facial expressions and movements of the other, and this leads on to co-operative games of give and take: for example, when the baby offers food to others.

Objects are coming more frequently into the play now, as the baby shows increasing interest in them. A common sequence at this stage is when he looks at an object, his parent follows his line of regard and hands it to him, and they then bring the object into their play: for example the adult rolling a ball to him or pushing a car towards him to catch between his legs.

He explores and investigates with great enthusiasm any objects he can get hold of: mouthing, shaking, hitting, looking at, throwing, feeling and nibbling them.

THE NINTH MONTH

Babies now show the most enormous enjoyment in being played with. Simple turn-taking games such 'Peekaboo' and 'Patacake' are still very popular but are developing in a number of ways. Not only does he initiate them now, but he also initiates 'conversations', vocalising to an adult and making it plain by his facial expression and body movements that he expects a reply. He also begins to create novel games: for example, teasing by holding out a toy and then withdrawing it, or making exaggerated protests. The biggest change is that he now wants variation in the games: for example, in a game of rolling a ball to each other, his parent rolling it to teddy instead. Very importantly, he is beginning to associate the games with the words they encompass, recognising for example which game is going to ensue when he hears 'clap hands'. His memory is beginning to operate, which has an impact on play. He remembers aspects of play, and will look for a toy he has seen hidden, and search for lost toys. His understanding about out-of-sight objects is still at a very early stage, though, and he still thinks that he is hidden from view if he covers his eyes.

Imitation is becoming an increasingly important part of play, and whereas earlier it was often automatic, it is now more often deliberate, as if the baby is trying to understand the meaning of different expressions and actions more fully by copying them. He can now play at the same time with a toy and with an adult fully for the first time, for example, in turn-taking games involving balls, cars or other objects.

The Toy Box

For exploratory play, he needs a very wide range of different objects to investigate, which do not need to be exclusively toys. Boxes, paper bags, and almost any objects which are safe to chew are good playthings at this stage. He is interested in different shapes and outlines, colours and textures, so make sure there is great variety in these. Examples of good toys are:

★ Push-over toy
★ Pop-up toy
★ Roller rattle
★ Activity playmat
★ Spinning toy
★ Baby mirror
★ Activity centre

★ Blocks and boxes
★ Vinyl ball
★ Paper: babies at this stage love playing with paper. It can be crumpled and waved around, and can be part of hiding games.

For enjoyment in listening to 'foreground' sound:

★ Noise-making toys are good – for example, rattles and simple musical instruments – but again household objects such as saucepan lids and spoons are just as good.

★ You can make effective noise-makers by filling containers such as plastic bottles with different substances such as rice or dried beans.

His passion for investigating objects continues unabated, and his increasing motor skills enable him to extend the range of his explorations to holding objects with a pincer grip; putting them in and out of containers; and now, at last, releasing them voluntarily. This leads to lovely games in which the adult is repeatedly 'asked' to return objects to him to drop again. He can now, for the first time, relate two objects, for example putting a cup on a saucer or a spoon in a cup. He still loves noise-making toys.

The baby can now play alone for up to twenty minutes if he has enough different objects to keep him entertained, but he usually insists that he is close to an adult. These times of solitary play are very important: he needs uninterrupted time in which he can give his full attention to his explorations. Remember, his attention is still single channelled.

He is now starting to move towards his infant peers, and will attempt to interact with them, waving toys enthusiastically in their direction.

The Book Shelf

Cardboard or fabric books can be included in the toy box now, but must be suitable for chewing and banging, which is what will happen to them at this stage. It's not too early, if he enjoys it, to sit him on your knee occasionally while you look at the pictures together.

TELEVISION AND VIDEOS

Do not be tempted to use these yet. Your baby has so much to learn at this important stage, and these would only hinder him.

Summary

To summarise, by the age of nine months, your baby is likely to:

★ Shout to attract your attention.
★ Imitate sounds that you make and the 'tune' in your voice.
★ Understand 'no' and 'bye bye'.
★ Babble with long strings of repeated sounds.
★ Often stop what he is doing when you say 'no'.
★ Understand the names of some familiar objects and people.

Cause for concern

Below are circumstances in which it would be advisable to seek professional advice about your baby's development. (Please remember, though, that many children progress at slightly different rates.)

If you are in any doubt about your baby, even if the reason for your concern is not mentioned here, do take him to see your Health Visitor or GP as soon as possible.

At nine months it would be advisable to seek a professional opinion if:

★ Your baby doesn't seem to recognise his name or those of close family members.
★ He seldom makes sounds to people as if he wants to talk to them.
★ He doesn't produce strings of babble sounds like 'mamamama' or 'babababa'.
★ He doesn't enjoy interactive games such as 'Peekaboo'.
★ He doesn't show any interest in noise-making toys.

The Baby Talk Programme

HALF AN HOUR A DAY

It is now of the greatest importance to get into a routine whereby you and your baby spend half an hour together every day, when you can focus entirely on each other, and in which he can take those small but essential steps in the development of social interaction. In this three-month period, your baby will begin to anticipate and look forward to this time, and will derive inestimable benefit from it. The assurance that he will have that immeasurable gift, your undivided attention, will engender calm, trust and reliance upon a safe and stable world. You will be able to develop routines and shared views about the world, which are vital to his later understanding and use of words.

You will find that the programme asks you to continue with some of the activities you have already been doing. You will be doing some of them now for different reasons, and your baby will respond in different ways now. There are also some small but subtle changes, which are very important.

If you have been on maternity leave you may be going back to work soon. If so, there is no need to worry. This half an hour a day will ensure that your baby continues to gain all the benefits of the programme, so do make sure that you keep it up. I hope that you are enjoying it so much that you will very much want to!

THE SETTING FOR YOUR ONE-TO-ONE PLAYTIME

We have seen that there are enormously important developments in terms of listening and attention during this period. The baby is beginning to structure the auditory field: that is to be able to scan what he can hear around him, focus on what he wants to listen to and maintain that focus for a little longer, thus building up his repertoire of the myriad links between sounds and their sources. He can only do this, however, in an environment free from background noise. Please remember: babies need a much bigger difference between background and foreground sound than we do to be able to listen to what is in the foreground.

> **Babies need a big difference between background and foreground sound**

You are likely to be invited to take him for a hearing test at some point in this period. It is very important to have this test, as even a very small hearing loss resulting from a catarrhal condition can affect this area of development. We localise sounds by comparing the way they sound to our two ears, and clearly this will be affected if hearing is different in the two ears. Even more importantly, slight hearing losses resulting from catarrhal conditions often vary from day to day. This has relatively little effect on an older child who has made firm links between sounds and their sources, and has learned to listen in the presence of background sound. For a baby at this stage, however, it can have a very serious effect by making the sense of hearing confusing and unreliable. Most babies so affected simply decide to focus on looking and handling, with disastrous effects on the development of their listening skills.

The development of his ability to look and listen at the same time can only happen in an environment free from distractions. The links between the baby's tongue and lip movements and the sounds he makes, and also between his sounds and the sounds of the speech he hears around him are also developing apace, and are essential to the establishment of his speech-sound system. Again, a quiet environment is essential if this is to happen satisfactorily.

Babies at this stage are becoming extremely interested in exploring many different objects and materials, and in bringing them into their play. As their attention span is still very short, they still need lots of different ones so that they can move from one to another as frequently as they want to. As we now know, an essential principle of the BabyTalk Programme is that we never ever try to keep a baby or small child's attention on something for a moment longer than he wishes to.

Make sure that you and he can be close together, with your faces on the same level, and that there are many toys and interesting objects within his easy reach. Making links between sounds and their sources is helped if the baby can move around freely, so make sure that the room is, as far as possible, baby proof. (I know that some people think that babies should learn from the **Make sure the room is still quiet for your playtime** beginning that there are things they are not allowed to touch. I believe that there are many more important things to learn at this time, and that they very readily understand that certain things are not for playing with at an age when you can explain why. It makes life so much easier at this stage for both you and your baby if you simply remove as many as possible of the things you don't want him to play with.)

HOW TO TALK

'Conversation' in sounds is really flourishing. It is important that you now see this play as one in which the two of you have conversations, rather than one in which you are principally talking to him. Always give him plenty of time to take his turn, and he will clearly indicate to you by the way in which he looks at you, and his movements, when it is yours.

His interest in exploring and investigating objects is now very great, and if you see that he is engrossed in this, give him a few minutes before you speak. Again, he will make it clear to you when the moment has arrived, by looking up at you, inviting you to do so. You will also notice that there are times when he is extremely interested in listening to his own sound-making, which is another time when it's important for you to remain quiet for a few moments.

★ **Play repetitive language games and rhymes**
He will continue to enjoy and benefit hugely from very repetitive simple interactive language games. In the sixth month, play 'Clap hands' and 'Peekaboo', using the same words and actions each time, and always with a lively facial expression. You will see from his facial expression how much he relishes this, how both of you are now sharing attention to an activity and how much these activities keep his attention.

Do lots of little repetitive rhymes and chants, such as 'Incy-wincy spider' and 'Ride a cock horse'. Make up your own if you can. Brief rhymes are best at this stage, as his attention span is so short.

As you have been doing before, jiggle him on your knee as you make funny noises, for example, 'dupedy dupedy dup' as you bounce him, or 'oo oo oo' as you move him back and forth. Again you will see his evident joy in listening to your voice by how closely he listens to you.

Copy his movements and actions as part of the game; for example, imitate his smiles and waves, and give him a chance to copy yours. You will see him busily working out the meaning of these actions, and making comparisons between his and yours.

As he moves into the seventh month, bring some little variations into some of your turn-taking games, such as making a little pause before the inevitable 'boo' in 'Peekaboo', or before a clap in 'Clap hands'. You will see by his body language that he is beginning to anticipate what is going to happen next. Pop-up toys will give him the same delicious sense of anticipation.

Continue with your rhymes, action rhymes and songs, and you will see his attention span gradually increasing and his enjoyment becoming even greater. It is also known that understanding of rhyme is a very important predictor of the ability to read. Always link the same words with the actions, and you will notice that he is beginning to link the words with the game, showing excited anticipation when you name a game. For example, as you say 'Let's play row, row, row your boat', he starts to rock backwards and forwards as soon as you say the first 'row'.

> **Use lots of rhymes, but keep them short**

As he moves into the ninth month, you are likely to find that he is beginning these games. Of course, you will respond enthusiastically. You can now build in variations, such as clapping teddy's hands as well as his and yours, or hiding behind a blanket for 'Peekaboo'.

★ **Make his sounds back to him**
It is extremely helpful to continue to make his sounds back to him. When you do this now, you will notice how intently he looks at you, and with what evident pleasure. You will also find that he now makes the sound or another back to you, so

engaging you in one of those delightful conversations which follow many of the rules of adult conversation, taking turns to

> **Make his sounds back to him**

vocalise, listening to the other speaker, timing the vocalisations and clearly enjoying the interactions. You will find that the more you do this, the more he vocalises, and how increasingly responsive he becomes. He's certainly getting the important message that listening to each other is fun.

Another reason why making the baby's sounds back to him is so helpful, and will continue to be for some time, is that it enables him to hear separate sounds, rather than the whole speech stream, which contains many hundreds of sounds. By

> **When having a 'conversation' give him plenty of time to reply**

doing so, you will be helping him very much to make those very important links between the movements he makes with his lips and tongue and the sounds that he makes, and also between the sounds he makes and the sounds he hears in the speech around him. You may well notice him 'trying out' different sounds, moving his lips and tongue purposefully and apparently listening with interest to the result.

At the beginning of this period, when he produces strings of repeated sounds like 'bababa' or 'mamama', repeat them back to him, and when later on he produces mixed sounds, like for example 'badigoo', copy those as closely as you can. Your imitation of squeals and exclamations will also be much enjoyed.

★ **Say for him what he means**

It is now very important that not only do you repeat his sounds back to him, but that now, as he is rapidly approaching the development of understanding words, that you also now give him the words to go with what he is trying to express by means of facial expression and body language. For example, when he cries, and you are not sure why, you could say 'Oh dear, you're sad. Johnny's sad', or you could respond to his gesture with

'Want up? Want to come up? Up you come', or 'It's gone' as at around nine months he discovers the new skill of releasing objects and does so repeatedly.

This kind of input will greatly help him towards understanding words, and you will notice by the end of this period that he is indeed making these links.

> **Give him the words to go with his actions**

★ **Continue to make lots of play sounds to go with what is happening**

These sounds, like 'shshshshsh' as water comes out of a tap, or 'gugugugug' as it runs away, continue to serve a number of important purposes. As they did in the previous age period, they add to the important message that listening to voice is fun, and they help him to notice all the different speech sounds because he can hear them separately. They also help him to link sounds with their sources, and are also extremely helpful in attracting and maintaining his attention.

I was talking about this the other day to the mother of an eight-month-old baby who, she said, had been showing very little interest in voice and speech. Every time I demonstrated a play sound to her mother, the baby whisked round with great excitement!

Examples of fun play sounds at this stage are 'brm brm' as you push a car along, 'eeeow' as a plane goes by, and 'oh-oh' as you drop something. You may even notice him trying to imitate you by the end of this period.

This brings us to another extremely important principle of the BabyTalk Programme. *Never, ever, under any circumstances, try in any way whatsoever to get your baby to say or copy sounds or words.* If you do, you will inhibit him, as sure as eggs. This is because that innate drive towards interaction and language includes a great deal of knowledge about communication. It is not part of normal communication to ask each other to say or copy words or sounds, and babies know it. I can think of many

> **Never make your baby copy sounds or words**

children I have seen over the years who have been virtually silenced by parents who were trying in the nicest and gentlest way possible to encourage them to speak.

> Harry was a delightful and very bright three year old whose understanding of speech was excellent, but who communicated constantly and highly effectively by every possible means other than speech. He pointed, mimed, and used complex series of gestures, but would not say a word. It transpired that his grandmother had come to live in the household when he was a year old, and had decided that it was time to teach him to talk. She bombarded him with 'Say…! Say…! Say…!', which had the inevitable effect. Removing this pressure, and seeing the almost immediate and incredibly rapid development of speech in children such as this has been one of the most rewarding parts of our practice.

★ Use short simple sentences

This is going to be very important indeed for the next few months. As we have seen, the baby at this stage is rapidly moving towards the magical time when, if the circumstances are right, he will be increasingly attaching meaning to words. If we were to use sentences such as 'We're going to the park, so we need to get our boots and coats on', how in the world would the baby know which of those many words refer to the things we put on our feet?. On the other hand, if we say something like 'Here's your shoe. Johnny's shoe. Shoe on. On it goes', he has a much better chance of understanding what 'shoe' means.

Don't use single words. This is not natural use of language, and is much more difficult to listen to than are little phrases and sentences.

Keep your sentences short, with pauses in between

Your sentences need to be tuneful, and slow, with pauses between each one. As earlier, this still attracts and maintains the baby's attention, and gives him time to take in each word.

As before, at times other than your special playtime, give a 'running commentary' about what you are doing, in order to keep the two of you in contact, and to give him experience of the 'shape' of the language.

★ Use lots of names
It is now very helpful to bring in names a lot, rather than pronouns (such as him/her/he/she/it/them/they), as the baby is rapidly moving towards linking names with the people and objects they refer to. Say, for example, 'Let's put *teddy* on the chair', rather than 'Let's put *him* on there'. The names of the most frequently heard objects and people are those earliest and most easily understood, so make a point of using often the names of family members and his favourite toys.

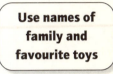

Use names of family and favourite toys

★ Follow his focus of attention
This is of the very greatest importance at this stage in helping the baby to make those vital early links between words and their meanings. As we have seen, he can only look and listen at the same time if what he is looking at and listening to is the same thing. If, therefore, we watch what he is looking at that moment and name it, he can listen to us, and can continue to listen if we follow that attention focus from moment to moment. If we do not, he cannot. When he looks at a toy in your playtime, name it for him in a little phrase 'It's a ball' and if his interest continues, bring it into the game: for example, rolling it gently towards him for him to catch. If it does not, and he looks at something else instead, name that for him too: for example, 'There's teddy'. Following his focus of attention is also the most powerful facilitator of the development of attention. At every stage, trying to make a baby or little child focus on something for longer than he wishes to only serves to 'fragment' that attention, and impedes his progress through the different stages.

You will notice in this time the great increase in the amount of shared attention between you, and how much of the time you are both focusing on the same thing.

Focus on the same thing as your baby

QUESTIONS

The same applies as in the last trimester. You may find that you are asking questions as a way of describing your baby's activities, such as 'Oh, have you kicked off your blanket?' Others are really comments, like 'Want your bottle?' or are alerting devices like 'What's this?' All these are fine, as they do not expect a reply.

OUTSIDE YOUR HALF-HOUR

Continue to talk a lot about what he is interested in. The more you get into the habit of observing his attention focus and speaking about it the better. When you are out, you might for example say something like 'There's a doggy ... he's running ... I can hear him barking' if that's what your baby is looking at, or 'Here's the potato, and here's some carrot next to it' when he is watching you putting his lunch on his plate.

9 to 12 months

An overview

Your baby will show further moves towards independence now. She may, for example, feed herself with her fingers or hold out an arm or a foot when you're dressing or washing her. She can be unco-operative at times though, and may well resist your attempts to put her hat on – and she won't be quite so easy to distract.

Her interest in everything is a real delight, even though at times it may be hard to appreciate it. She's likely, for example, to be fascinated by the pattern her spilt drink makes. She's great fun now, and loves to make you laugh by making funny faces or sounds. When you do, she'll repeat the performance for you.

> Please note that the developmental stages described here are averages only.
>
> All babies develop at slightly different rates, and often progress in one area can result in a temporary delay in another. Do not get worried or depressed if your child does not appear to be doing everything at exactly the time periods mentioned here. For further information, see Cause for Concern, page 116.

You'll really feel that you need eyes in the back of your head now. Not only is she likely to be getting round rapidly by crawling or shuffling, but she quickly forgets bumps and bruises, and is quite likely to repeat dangerous activities.

The tenth month

THE DEVELOPMENT OF COMMUNICATION AND LANGUAGE

Babies at this age are becoming very sociable, becoming much more aware of other people, and showing considerable sensitivity to their feelings and moods. They are also very interested in words, and will listen intently to new ones. If all has gone well, they can now listen to speech without being nearly so easily distracted.

A step forward in intellectual ability enables babies at this age to **understand** more clearly that both gestures and words can stand for objects. They begin to follow a point, first to near objects and then to those far away, and this ability coincides with the ability to understand object names.[1] The baby now discovers which objects and events her parent finds interesting, such as a new book; and which are upsetting, such as something being broken. In this way, she is not only becoming more adept at relating to other people, but also beginning to become sensitive to their reactions to the world. This awareness – that another person has feelings just as she does – is of great importance in the development of all future social interaction.

She also now begins to understand the connection between her behaviour and the adult's response, beginning to predict, for example, that if she spills her food on the floor, her mother will not be best pleased.

She also progresses in this period from understanding the meaning of the speaker's tone of voice and recognising in context the names of some very familiar people and objects, to understanding the names of more common objects in her environment, such as 'ball', 'teddy', or 'cat'. Babies' increasing social awareness is exemplified by the facts that they will now consistently look towards speakers who call their names, will give an object to another person on request, and will perform other routine activities on request, for example, waving 'bye bye'.

By this time, too, she can make all the necessary discriminations between the speech sounds of her mother tongue, and in fact can now only discriminate between phonemes (speech sounds which signal changes in meaning like 'pat' and bat') in that language. This matured discrimination interestingly coincides with the production of the first true words.

In this time, there is a complete change from a situation in which the adult interpreted her unintentional communication to one in which the baby controls the dialogue. She initiates much of the interaction, and can now terminate it by moving away. She is an immensely competent communicator, able to convey virtually all the meanings that adults do, although not yet in quite the same ways. Not only can she draw an adult's attention to herself, to objects and to other people, request objects, actions and information, greet, acknowledge and inform, but she can now even recognise when she has not been understood, and rephrase what she has said in order to help her listener, and can generally make adults aware of whether her communication has had the desired outcome.

She communicates mainly by means of gesture linked with vocalisation (usually pointing to something, accompanied by 'uh uh', meaning that she wants a particular object). She loves to participate in routine speech games like 'Clap hands', and will now initiate them. She also loves to copy ritualised adult vocalisations like 'oh oh' when something drops.

Her **sound-making** babble is very tuneful now, with all the rhythm and stress patterns of language, and indeed sounds increasingly like speech in a foreign language.

The baby can now sit alone for several minutes, and finds it much easier to obtain objects to investigate. She can now lean forward to pick them up, and turn sideways to stretch out for them. She is becoming more skilful in handling toys, and can consequently play with them in a wider range of ways. She is able to drop objects relatively easily. She can put cubes in and out of a box when she has seen this done, and can ring a bell by holding the handle. She will watch a ball rolling, and anticipates the direction of its movement. She can also throw toys, unwrap them, and will uncover a toy she has seen covered by a cloth. This increased ability to manipulate objects and explore them continues to be immensely helpful in building up concepts – such as hard, soft, heavy and light – which paves the way for words to be linked to the concepts later.

Mobility is often greatly increasing at this time, and this can bring about a temporary reduction in language and communication development, as it takes all her attention and, as we know, her attention is still single channelled. She can now get around, not only by rolling, but also begins to crawl or to shuffle. She may pull herself up by the furniture into a standing position, and stand for a while holding on, or even walk along holding tightly. She cannot yet sit down without help from this position.

She will actively help with dressing now, putting arms and legs into her clothes, and is adept at pulling off her hat!

ATTENTION

The baby at this stage is able to attend to an object or activity of her own choice for a short time, but is very easily distracted by noise or movement. Her attention is still almost totally single channelled, but she can just begin to be able to look and listen to an object at the same time if the level of distraction is extremely low. She and her parent are becoming much more efficient at establishing a shared focus of attention, not only by pointing, but also by following the direction of each other's gaze.[2]

LISTENING

This three-month period is an immensely important one in the development of listening. If all goes well, by the end of it, the baby will have achieved the ability to listen selectively: the vital ability to scan all the sounds in the environment, choose what to listen to and maintain that focus, 'tuning out' unwanted sound. By the time she is twelve months old, she will be able to listen to speech without being easily distracted, and will have made many links between sounds and their sources. As a result, the information she receives about the world through her ears will have become increasingly meaningful. These developments will have been greatly helped by her ability to move around and explore, now that she can go to find out about the sources of sounds, rather than just looking around for them.

Increasing numbers of children are failing to make these developments, and unfortunately the ability to listen selectively is not one that just comes with maturation, even many years later. It is the view of many teachers that difficulties in this area are the basis of very many children's learning difficulties. The problem has been growing over the last fifteen years or so, as our society has become increasingly noisy. I am aware that about fifteen years ago, nursery teachers were complaining to me about the numbers of children who couldn't listen, then infant teachers did so, then junior, and now secondary and even university teachers are aware of the problem.

I made a study of listening skills in nine month olds fifteen years ago, and found that an alarming 20 per cent of them had significant listening difficulties. These infants had made very few links between sounds and their sources, and were in fact listening less and less, as sound was meaningless to them. Many responded so little to sound that they were suspected of being deaf. Others showed highly erratic and inconsistent responses to sound, with huge amounts of ignoring, even of really loud or unusual sounds. They were unable to scan the sounds in the environment and select what they wanted to listen to, and could not listen at all if they were more than minimally occupied with looking at or touching objects. Needless to say, they were not making that astonishing progress in linking words with their meanings which is possible at this stage, and in fact tended to ignore voice more than anything else, almost as if they realised that they were unable to crack the verbal code.[3]

From the age of nine to ten months, the baby is beginning to scan the sound environment a little more, and to focus on a particular sound. Scanning is relatively slow, and her attention to the chosen sound is relatively short. This ability, however, greatly helps her to build up her knowledge of the meaning of sounds, listening to and comparing incoming sounds with those she has previously recognised. She is beginning to be able to listen to a sound made by something she is looking at or touching a little more easily. It is very noticeable that this skill can only operate in a quiet environment, where there is a big difference between the level of background and foreground sound.

The eleventh month

THE DEVELOPMENT OF COMMUNICATION AND LANGUAGE

The baby's **understanding** of words is coming on apace now. She will look around for more familiar objects and people when they are named in conversation, and will occasionally show that she is able to follow more simple questions or commands in context, such as 'Where's Daddy?' or 'Come to Mummy'. The object of the request must be visible. Her use of gesture is becoming more sophisticated. She will extend her arm to point out an object, and will use gesture to indicate 'Where?' and 'Gone' by her hand movements.

With **sound-making**, she enjoys imitating both speech sounds like 'shshsh' or 'bababa', and non-speech sounds such as raspberries, and very occasionally, words. She responds with much enjoyment to rhythmic music, moving her arms or her whole body. She has a great appetite for speech games such as 'Peekaboo' and 'Clap hands' and often begins them.

She 'talks' lots now, both when she's alone and when she's with others, babbling away with lots of different sounds. She certainly knows what a conversation is, and how to participate in it, gleefully taking her turns and anticipating her conversational partners taking theirs.

GENERAL DEVELOPMENT

Her understanding of her environment and her control over her body are both developing, enabling her to undertake more detailed exploration of objects. She can now pivot, twisting around in a sitting position to retrieve objects, and stretching to retrieve those out of reach. She will find a toy she has seen hidden in a box. She can begin to isolate her fingers, and to pick up small objects with finger and thumb. She stands more confidently, holding on to the furniture, and may even do so briefly alone. She cruises around the furniture, and may be able to crawl rapidly.

There are significant intellectual developments at this time. As her experience grows, she comes to understand the ways in which objects relate to each other – for example putting a cup on a saucer – and can link objects with events: for example using a brush to brush her hair. This is a very important foundation for the later linking of verbal concepts: for example, 'Bobby's brush' or 'Drink's gone'. She also begins to be interested in looking at pictures and to associate them with the objects they represent.

She becomes altogether more purposeful, beginning to use her ability to get around to solve problems such as how to reach a particular object, rather than just taking off for the purpose of general exploration.

ATTENTION

There is little change at this time, but just a more frequent shared attention and slightly longer attention to a particular focus.

LISTENING

If all is progressing well, the baby is becoming increasingly interested in listening to sound, and in particular to speech. She is less easily distracted now. Scanning is faster, and attention to particular sounds longer. She is beginning to be able to inhibit response to other sounds, which is extremely important, and the number of links she has made between sounds and their sources is growing apace. She is better able to listen while she is looking at or handling an object.

The twelfth month

THE DEVELOPMENT OF COMMUNICATION AND LANGUAGE

Babies now show intense interest in speech over a prolonged period. Interestingly, there is huge variation in how much different babies understand at this time, dependent upon their environmental circumstances, but the time of use of words is much more consistent, appearing to be very much more biologically fixed. (This is not the case later on.)

Most babies at this stage **understand** an increased repertoire of names and little verbal requests in context, such as 'Want some more?' They demonstrate this understanding by means of a gesture, such as a head shake, but may also, on occasion, try to comply vocally: for example by saying 'bye bye' when asked to. Babies can now start to integrate interactions with both objects and people, using people to acquire objects – for example by pulling at an adult's sleeve and pointing at an object – and objects to acquire attention: for example by banging vigorously on a tray with a spoon.

There is much **sound-making** with intent now, calling to people to attract their attention, expressing her desire for a change of activity, and she also very often vocalises back when she is spoken to. Tone of voice becomes an important part of her vocalisation and she uses much variation in melody and rhythm. Her parents find it much easier to understand exactly what she is trying to communicate. She now loves clowning and showing off, and loves an element of teasing to come into familiar games.[4] She joins in songs by singing along, and will try to say 'boo' in games of 'Peekaboo'. She chats away in long speech-like patterns throughout the day, both to toys and to people. The 'babble drift' (see page 73) discussed in the last chapter, in which the little child's speech sounds come increasingly into line with those of the language around her is almost complete, and she uses almost only the sounds of the language around her. Her repertoire of sounds now includes those made at the front of her mouth (for example p and b,) the middle (t and d), and the back (k and g). She begins to use sounds as if they were words, such as 'brm brm' for car, and also evolves some words of her own, individual syllables with a fixed melody which have come to be used consistently for a particular event or object. These are still idiosyncratic, and likely only to be recognised by those very familiar with her. The sounds are clear, but the meaning as yet is not. She also starts trying to copy words, again usually the names of familiar objects.

The magic moment of the first real word often arrives at this time, and some infants have as many as three by the age of twelve months[5] (although many babies take a little longer). They are most usually the names of familiar people or objects, and tend to contain sounds that she has long used in her babble, often p, b, d, and m: for example 'mama' and 'dada'. This is almost certainly why those words for parents are similar in many languages.

Parents are often very puzzled as to why there is such an enormous gap between the amount their baby understands at this time, and the very few, if any, words that she uses. She may understand as many as sixty and yet use only two or three. Perhaps a useful way of looking at this question is to think of ourselves hearing a complex name of a foreign politician when it comes into the media first. We recognise it the second time we hear it if we have been interested and paying attention, but we cannot accurately recall the sequence of sounds in it well enough to say it until we have heard it many times more. We only need to do this with the occasional word; the baby has to do it for hundreds and thousands of them. Like us, they can often recognise a word at the second hearing, and link it with its meaning, but they need to hear each one dozens of times before it can be recalled.

GENERAL DEVELOPMENT

Progress is also rapid in other areas of the baby's development. She can pick up objects and give them to an adult, imitate tapping with a pencil and hold a pencil as if to make marks on paper. She can push a car, imitate actions such as stirring with a spoon, and play 'Peekaboo' by covering her face. She gets around with increasing ease, crawling rapidly and with great facility. She can stand alone momentarily, and some babies take their first steps at the end of this period. This upright posture now frees her hands for action.

ATTENTION

By the age of a year, there is greater ability to listen to and look at objects at the same time, and the baby is not quite so distractible. At the end of this month, she is beginning to move into the next stage of attention development. In this stage, she shows, at times, spells of intensely focused concentration on something she has chosen to be interested in. So intense is this concentration that adults will find themselves totally ignored.[6] This alternates for many months with the fleeting attention of the first year.

LISTENING

If all has gone well, the baby has now achieved that vital ability to attend selectively, which will stand her in good stead in all her future educational situations. The world of sound is meaningful. These abilities, however, are still totally dependent upon her being in an appropriate environment.

Play

Play develops apace in this three-month age period. Exploration of objects continues, now in a somewhat more sophisticated way due to the baby's increased hand-eye co-ordination and control of her body, and in particular of her hands. We have seen how she has acquired the skills which enable her to play in much more purposeful ways: for example taking objects in and out of containers, opening containers, unwrapping toys, stacking objects, pushing cars, rolling balls, matching objects to pictures and fitting toys together. She very much enjoys all of these.

A lifetime's enjoyment of books can begin in this trimester, another great milestone.

By grasping a pencil and making a mark on paper, she is taking the first step towards writing.

She still loves the interactive play begun in the earlier months, and now becomes much more proactive in initiating and maintaining the games.

Yet another important development is that of interaction with her peers.[7] She will offer or show a toy to another baby, and point out things of interest to her. She can also grab toys from her, and thus the beginning of both co-operation and conflict emerge.[8]

THE TENTH MONTH

The baby now uses her index finger to poke objects, rather than just grabbing them with her whole hand, giving her further scope for her investigations, and enabling her to gain more knowledge about their textures and shapes. She still often conveys things to her mouth, but her mouth is giving way to her eyes and hands now as her main means of exploration. She is becoming very interested in details, and will look intently at the pattern on a doll's dress, for example. She relishes being able to move around, explore and handle many different objects and materials, gradually building up her understanding of the world around her. This mobility is of great importance, not only building up that understanding, but also in the continued development of selective attention, by enabling her to find out about the sources of sounds by going to investigate them.

She will also now start to copy an adult's actions with toys: for example, making teddy jump up and down when her mother has shown her how to.

All this exploratory play is immensely important in helping her to form concepts and categories, without which meaningful language is not possible. She will begin to form concepts – for example of which things are thick and which thin – and categories, for example, of all the different things which will roll or can be thrown. Words will be added to these at a later time.

At this stage, she treats all objects in rather similar ways, and her ideas of cause and effect are still very rudimentary, limited, for example, to the fact that banging a brick on a table makes a noise. She loves sound-making toys.

Rhymes are extremely important throughout this three-month period. The great linguist Pinker describes research which shows that human ears gravitate to rhymes as eyes do to stripes.[9] The Language Acquisition Device is in operation once more. The baby loves to sit on an adult's knee to enjoy rhymes. She prefers those with simple familiar tunes which relate to the world she knows and the activities and people she is familiar with. Good examples of these are 'Rockabye baby' and other lullabies relating to going to sleep, and 'Humpty dumpty' relating to falling down – a frequent experience at this age! Rhymes about clothes and dressing are much enjoyed too: for example, 'One, two, buckle my shoe', and 'Three little kittens have lost their mittens'. Rhymes relating to body parts still appeal very strongly. Good examples of these are 'I'm a little teapot', 'This little piggy' and 'Round and round the garden'. She will also love those linked with actions, such as 'Row, row, row your boat'.

The baby's participation in play becomes more active now, and she and the adult come to take equal parts in establishing games from this time.[10] She still enjoys a great deal of repetition of familiar games over many weeks. She clearly expresses, by means of gestures and vocalisations, her joy in knowing that the language and activities of the game are predictable, and that she knows therefore what is coming next. These games develop their own unique patterns of rhythm, tune and stress as they are repeated.

Turn-taking games are the most popular at this stage, interestingly just at the time when she is taking the first steps on the ladder towards becoming a verbal conversationalist. She relishes reciprocal games with an adult, such as rolling a ball or pushing a car to each other. She also loves games such as 'Hidey peep' or 'Catch', in which she and the adult take turns in the different roles.

THE ELEVENTH MONTH

The baby now starts to treat objects in a more differentiated way. She becomes interested in putting them in and out of containers – for example bricks in and out of a box – and opening containers. She can now competently roll a ball and push a car, this often accompanied by those early sounds used almost like words, such as 'brm brm' for a car. She much enjoys imitating an adult's initiation of these activities. She is beginning to show understanding of how objects relate to each other, that a cup and saucer go together, for example. This understanding is another vital precursor to the use of linked concepts in language.

The baby now has the ability to relate pictures to objects, and so takes another step on the path to a lifetime's enjoyment of books. She loves bright pictures of familiar objects and really starts to look at them rather than being more interested in chewing or handling the book. She even starts to turn the pages now.

By eleven months, she has begun to anticipate the body movements that go with rhymes.

THE TWELFTH MONTH

She now very much enjoys play with soft toys, and very simple pretend play is developing: she may hug teddy, or push a dolly in a buggy. She also very much likes playing with real objects like a cup or hairbrush. She has seen her parents use them, and now wants to know for herself how they work and what place they have in her life. She also now likes toys that represent real objects, such as toy animals.

Her play with objects shows that she now understands their function: she will push a car along, and make teddy walk, but not vice-versa. She also shows in her play that she is beginning to understand the use of adult's objects; for example, that a telephone is for talking into.

Her increasing hand-eye co-ordination and skill in controlling her hands enable her to put pegs into simple pegboards and stack toys such as beakers. She very much enjoys playing with paper and cardboard boxes, and loves a box big enough for her to get into.

She also very much enjoys the adult now bringing variations into games which are well established.[11] She finds this great fun, and it also has the function of encouraging her to

The Toy Box

REPRESENTATIVE PLAY

These are the kind of toys that will help her to understand what objects are for and what we can do with them:

- ★ Soft animals
- ★ Doll's buggy
- ★ Tea-set
- ★ Simple wooden vehicles
- ★ Doll's brush and comb

INVESTIGATIVE AND MANIPULATIVE PLAY

These toys will give her plenty of opportunities to use her new-found manipulative skills:

- ★ Cloth bricks
- ★ Stacking rings
- ★ Stacking beakers
- ★ Large soft ball
- ★ Pencil and paper
- ★ Cardboard boxes of different sizes, including one big enough for her to climb into

REAL OBJECTS TO INVESTIGATE

- ★ Plastic cup
- ★ Spoon
- ★ Soft hairbrush

NOISE-MAKING TOYS

These will help to show her that making and listening to sound is a lot of fun:

- ★ Bells
- ★ Drum
- ★ Xylophone
- ★ Maracas
- ★ Castanets
- ★ Containers with different substances inside: for example, rice, beans, lentils
- ★ Pan lids and spoons
- ★ Crumply paper

The Book Shelf

Now that your baby has reached the stage when she can relate pictures to the objects they represent, she will start looking at books, and even trying to turn the pages, rather than chewing and manipulating them. She will enjoy bright colourful card or cloth books, with lifelike realistic pictures of objects familiar to her, such as a cup or a toy duck. There are some lovely ones about, for example:

★ *Lucy Cousins' cloth books* by Lucy Cousins
  (Walker Books)
★ *First Focus* baby books (Ladybird)
★ A book of photos of the actual people and objects
  in her life would also be extremely popular.

Looking at books together can be an enjoyable part of your playtime. The most important thing by far – and extremely important it is – is that you make this a delightful interactive time, thereby giving books an extremely pleasant association from the very beginning.

Sit her on your knee, and give her plenty of hugs as you look at the pictures together and show her how you turn the pages. Be close together, and share the same angle of view. It can be fun to sometimes show her the actual objects that the pictures relate to. You can also make sounds to go with the pictures, like quacking noises to go with a picture of a duck. Give her lots of time to explore the book as well as looking at the pictures: remember she is still at the manipulative and exploratory stage as well as moving into others.

become a full partner in the games. The adult may, for example, make little pauses before the expected next action in the game, like delaying the 'boo' in 'Peekaboo', or in a game of 'come and catch me' waiting for the baby to indicate that she's ready to be chased. In other games she relishes changes to the routine like the adult gesturing that he or she is about to roll the ball to teddy, when she is expecting it to come to her.

PLAY MATERIALS

It is becoming more important to provide your baby with toys that are appropriate for the various different kinds of play which are now developing. Many will stand her in good stead for several months to come. Her attention span is still very short in the main, so she still needs a number of toys available, so that she can move from one to another with ease.

When your baby is playing with these materials, she will appreciate you being nearby, and sometimes showing her what you can do with the toys. You can at times enhance her play a lot: for example, by returning an object to her repeatedly when she has discovered her new ability to release objects. It has been found that babies will play more innovatively if a supportive adult is nearby. Resist the temptation to take over, though. It is better at this stage to start off a new way of using a toy, and then to withdraw. She needs to have time in which she can explore and work things out for herself.

TELEVISION AND VIDEOS

The comments made about this in relation to the last trimester still hold. Language is learned by interaction.

Summary

To summarise, by the age of twelve months, your baby is likely to:

★ Try to 'sing along' with music.
★ Understand her own name.

* Understand the names of a number of people and objects, as long as she hears them in their usual setting.
* Shake her head for 'no'.
* Use one to three words.

Cause for concern

Below are circumstances in which it would be advisable to seek professional advice about your baby's development. (Please remember, though, that many children progress at slightly different rates.)

If you are in any doubt about your baby, even if the reason for your concern is not mentioned here, do take her to see your Health Visitor or GP as soon as possible.

At twelve months it would be advisable to seek a professional opinion if:

* She never looks around for familiar objects, such as her hat, when she hears you talk about them.
* She doesn't turn towards a speaker when her name is called.
* She doesn't produce lots of tuneful babble.
* She never tries to start little games like 'Patacake'.
* She doesn't follow a point, looking in the direction you are pointing.

The Baby Talk Programme

Your baby will now relish her time alone with you above all else. Little children are inevitably directed by adults for a great part of their day, and to have some time when she is the boss is wonderful, and tends to make her much more compliant at other times. It has an enormously great effect on emotional and behavioural development to be sure of a communicative partner for part of each day. Please do not let your daily playtimes lapse, however difficult it may be to fit it in at times.

If you have twins, it is really worth pulling out all the stops to do the programme with each of them separately, however

I remember Kevin and Nelly, a delightful pair of red-headed twins. It was clear, when I first saw them when they were ten months old, that they were extremely alert, crawling busily in different directions, and investigating everything in sight. Kevin and Nelly only had the language development of six month olds, however. They only understood 'no' and their own names, and were producing very little sound-making. Their mother was very keen to help them. She managed to find a neighbour who was happy to look after one twin for half an hour each day, and she waited until their father returned from work to spend time alone with the other. The biggest problem at first was that the twins themselves were extremely reluctant to be separated. They soon discovered, however, the delights of having an adult's exclusive attention and the fun of being able to dictate the play – and the problem was solved. Their mother, too, found it immensely enjoyable having the company of her babies one at a time. Both twins made excellent progress, and at the age of seven were reading and doing number work like ten year olds.

daunting an idea this may sound. Twins often lag behind single children in terms of speech and language development, and

> **Keep up your one-to-one playtimes**

although many catch up by school age, some do not. The reason for this is that, as we have seen, one of the most helpful and important ways of enhancing a child's language development is to talk about her immediate focus of attention. This is extremely difficult to do for more than one child at a time, and is exactly the same reason why second and later-born children tend to be slower to develop speech than first-borns. If you can possibly have even twenty minutes a day with each twin you can prevent the problem.

THE SETTING FOR YOUR ONE-TO-ONE PLAYTIME

The setting for your playtime must still be very quiet. This is absolutely essential. This is an extremely crucial stage for the development of selective listening, which can only occur if the environment is appropriate. In terms of speech, your baby now has to notice which speech sounds go in which words, and so it is vital that she is able to hear them really clearly. It helps for you to be close to her in your playtime for this reason.

In terms of the amount your baby is spoken to at this stage, all the research evidence is that quantity correlates very highly with future language development.[12] So keep talking to her a great deal.

This is the stage at which your baby is beginning to link words with their meanings, and can do so with amazing rapidity if conditions are favourable.[13] The importance of what you do to help at this time cannot be overestimated. Let's think for a moment about that process of linking words with their meanings, and what an amazing feat it actually is. Think of the kind of sentence we commonly use: for example, 'Oh, look, the weather's clearing up; let's go and get our coats and our boots and go for a walk.' How in the world do we come to know that out of all those words, the one which stands for the things we put on our feet is 'boots'? Babies clearly need a lot of help with this, and the main focus of the BabyTalk Programme at this stage is to give her that help.

Other crucial areas of development occur at this time, in the development of selective attention, the discrimination of all the speech sounds in the language, and the beginning of the use of words. Your baby is also making great strides in understanding the world around her. You will notice once again that some of the programme items are continuations of those you have done before, but they now come to serve different purposes.

CONTINUE YOUR INTERACTIVE GAMES

The play you have mutually enjoyed in the earlier part of the programme, in which you evolved rituals in terms of language input and actions in your play, will now stand you in good stead. Do continue them during these three months. Whereas at earlier stages she just noticed the general shape and tune of your speech,[14] those familiar, repeated and enjoyable experiences will now greatly help your baby to link words with their meanings. You and she have now developed a shared understanding of the world, which has enabled her to know the meaning of significant objects and events, and she is ready as a consequence to understand the words that attach to them. She will, at this stage for example, link the actual words in a little phrase like 'up you come' directly with the action of being picked up.

These interactive games are also a wonderful way of establishing shared attention. The familiar repetitive routines with your shared intentions and shared anticipation are perfect for this. As we have seen, your baby progressively becomes more of an equal partner in these in this period. At the beginning of it, you will mainly be in charge of the turn-taking, but this experience will soon enable her to join in as an equal partner. Notice how she pauses between vocalisations now, as if to give you the opportunity to take your turn. You will also see that she often stops vocalising when you speak, and starts again when you stop. You have helped her to learn the basic rules of conversation.

Keep plenty of sameness in your games, but start to bring in the kind of variations we have discussed in the section on play. Pretend, for example, to get things wrong, or change the rules, or bring in long pauses before an anticipated event. These kind of activities will at this stage greatly encourage her to participate as a full partner in the game. They also help her to learn all the sequence of steps involved in an activity.

Games together help your baby to link words with their meanings

Games in which there are repeated naming rituals, such as 'eyes, nose, cheeky cheeky chin' are wonderful in helping her to link words with meaning. Once again, she is enabled to experience joint attention, shared intention and mutual highly enjoyable participation in the game.

CONTINUE TO MAKE HER SOUNDS BACK TO HER

This is very important at this stage, when her speech-sound system is finally coming into line with the language around her, and she has the huge task of noticing and remembering which

Keep having sound 'conversations'

sounds go where in all the thousands of words she hears. Making her sounds back to her helps greatly to reinforce the links between the movements she makes with her lips and tongue and the resulting sounds,

and in comparing her own sounds with those she hears others make around her. You will still be having those delightful conversations in sounds, as making her sounds back is the most powerful facilitator of this.

CONTINUE TO MAKE PLAY SOUNDS

These fun sounds, such as 'brm brm' as a car is pushed along, or 'swishshshsh' as you sweep, are not only great fun at this

Sean was brought to see me when he was eight months old, as he was virtually silent. He appeared an exceptionally placid and contented baby, making very few demands on his mother or his environment. He was initiating very little vocal interaction, and not showing a great deal of interest in communicating. His sound-making was at a level usually attained at around five months: just vowel sounds with few recognisable syllables. We put him on the programme and suggested to his mother that she should make lots of sounds herself and respond to his sound-making. Within two months his development was age-appropriate in all dimensions.

stage, but also continue to be enormously useful in the same ways they were earlier.

They help to encourage listening, by giving the baby the important message that voices are fun to listen to.

They also help in that essential process of making all the necessary discriminations between the speech sounds of the language, which can also be completed by the end of this trimester. They do so by enabling the baby to hear and focus on one or two sounds rather than the whole rapidly changing speech stream.

Play sounds make listening fun

Be increasingly inventive. It's amazing, for example, how many play sounds you can attach to a dropped toy: for example, 'bang', 'boom', 'crash', 'uh uh' and so on. Do continue to use your funny phrases like 'upsidaisy', 'whoopsie', or 'uh uh', which also come into this category.

FOLLOW HER FOCUS OF ATTENTION

The importance of this at this stage cannot be overemphasised. By establishing joint attention to an object or event, you are creating the ideal conditions for language learning, as language is learned entirely in the context of shared information. Not surprisingly, there is much research evidence that the extent to which adults' speech relates to objects which are the focus of the infants' attention, and the longer the episodes of shared attention, the wider the child's vocabulary and more extensive her understanding of grammatical structures later on.[15] [16] [17] [18] Specific comparisons of the understanding of names made between this situation and one in which an adult had set out to teach some of her choosing, showed that far more were learned in the former situation.[19] One study specifically showed that children learned names more easily and quickly when adults just named objects they were interested in rather than setting out to teach them specific names.

To enable you to do this easily, have lots of interesting objects nearby, and be close to your baby and face to face with her. Watch to see what she looks at or grabs hold of. Name it for her – 'That's teddy' – or if the focus of interest seems to be what has happened, describe the action: 'Dropped it'. The closer you can get, not only to the object of your shared attention, but to what is actually in the baby's mind, the more you will be helping her understanding. With a book, for example, her interest may actually range from chewing it, when you might say 'You're chewing it'; to turning the pages, where you might say 'Turn over another page, turn it over'; or in the actual picture, when you could appropriately say 'It's a car'. Try to work it out: usually it is not too difficult.

In the same way, when she looks at you, wait to see what happens. If she seems to be waiting for you to do something, point to something and name it, or pick up a toy and start playing with it, saying what you are doing, and making your meaning very clear. The moment she shifts the focus of her attention, you do too. Never try to keep it on something for a moment longer than she wishes to.

> **Watch to see what she is interested in**

HELP HER TO ENJOY LISTENING

This is a very critical stage in the development of the ability to focus on something she wishes to listen to and to tune out what she doesn't want to hear. By the end of these three

Harry was brought to the clinic at nearly a year old. He looked vaguely around, ignoring anyone speaking to him, even his mother. He took no notice of noise-making toys offered to him, even very loud ones, and totally failed to respond when a child in the next room started screaming loudly. I really thought that we had a profoundly deaf baby here, which was his parents' great anxiety. I asked his mother about Harry's favourite snack food, and she reported that this was crisps. I also asked if any of the toys Harry had brought with him were particular favourites, and she told us that a little teddy was.

We sent out for a packet of crisps, and I set to work. I sat in front of Harry, and gave him one crisp at a time, crumpling the packet as I did so. I then started a game with his little teddy, approaching and saying 'Coming, coming, coming … boo!' as I did so. Harry enjoyed both of these activities hugely. I then had someone distract him in the front, while I went behind and made the sound of the crisp bag, and spoke very quietly behind and randomly to each side of him. He located each sound accurately every time, however quietly I made them.

After four weeks on the BabyTalk Programme, Harry was responding perfectly normally to sounds all the time.

months, if all has gone well, and the environment is appropriate, she will be able to do this. Conversely, if this is not the case, babies can be in serious difficulties in terms of listening by this time. I have seen many children in my pre-school clinics, where there were serious suspicions of profound deafness, who turned out to have perfectly normal hearing. They had not been able to build up those crucial links between sounds and their sources, and the whole world of sound had become so meaningless that they had simply ceased to listen. Without help, they would go on to experience very serious problems in school.

In your playtime at this stage, give your baby lots of opportunities to get the message that listening is easy and fun. You can do this by providing her with easy to listen to fun 'foreground' sounds which she can listen to with no competition

Alexandra was eleven months old when I first saw her. She was a pretty little girl, very engaged in play and in relating to me and her mother. At nearly twelve months old, however, she was only just beginning to repeat little syllables in her babble as a normal six month old does. What was very marked was that she was not listening at all, ignoring voice and most of the sounds around her, although a recent hearing test had confirmed that her hearing was normal. Her mother reported that she often appeared to be in a world of her own. Alexandra was the less dominant of a pair of twins, and had a very extrovert older brother. Not surprisingly, she had never experienced time alone with one adult, still less a quiet time. She had also had a number of ear infections, since the age of three months, which may have affected her hearing at times.

We set up the BabyTalk Programme for her with emphasis on the listening sections. Her mother wrote to me a month later, telling me that there had been a very marked improvement, which had started almost immediately. She had become very responsive, her babble had developed enormously, in both length and complexity, and she was listening beautifully in her quiet times. I saw her again a month later, and her listening, sound-making and understanding of speech were all well within normal limits for her age.

from other noises in the background. Have plenty of noise-making toys available, and sometimes show her how she can use them to make sounds. Be sure to give her time to listen to them, and do not talk at the same time. It can be fun to show her how you can use them differently to make, for example, loud and quiet sounds.

One note of caution. Some commercially produced noise-making toys, particularly those which are computer operated, make sounds at very high levels, which can be damaging to a baby's ears.

Bring into your playtime some rhymes and action rhymes, or jiggle her on your knee as you make funny noises. Your baby will love this, and get the very important message that voice is very good to listen to. The fun rituals like 'upsidaisy' as you swing teddy into the air are also very good for this purpose.

Keep playing games that make listening fun

It is helpful, too, at other times, to help her to make the links between sounds and their sources, showing her, for example, that when you switch on the vacuum cleaner, or ring a door-bell, a particular sound results.

HOW TO TALK

The ways in which you speak to your baby now, some of which you have already been using for helping her attention, arousal and communication of feelings, are now crucial for helping her to understand words. This is a critical stage in language development.

★ Keep your sentences short and simple

It is extremely important that you keep your sentences short at this stage for a number of reasons:

First, in terms of understanding, as we have said before, it is much easier to figure out what a word refers to if it comes in a short phrase or sentence. It's clear, for example, what the sentence is about if we hear 'There's doggy', but a lot less clear if we hear 'I think that a dog and a cat just crossed the road'.

Second, we have seen how by the end of this period babies can make all the necessary discriminations between the speech sounds in the language around them. They now have a huge job, however, in noticing which sounds go in which words so that they are eventually

Use simple sentences, not single words

able to recall and say them. It is clearly very much easier to notice sequences of sounds in a short phrase or sentence.

It is a very important principle of the BabyTalk Programme that at every stage the adult's input is matched to the baby's level of understanding. At this stage, she is understanding at the single word level, so the appropriate input for her is little phrases containing one important word, for example, 'There's the cat,' or 'It's the ball'. Never use single words, as this is not normal communication.

Short sentences are also appropriate to your baby's attention span, which is also short at this stage.

Keep your little sentences simple, but always well formed and grammatical. For example, it's fine to say 'There's doggy, on the table', but 'doggy table' would not be grammatically correct. This is very important in helping her Language Acquisition Device to come into operation. Studies have shown that there is a significant correlation between mothers using less complex speech at this stage and a more rapid increase in the child's length of sentence.[20]

Make pauses at the end of each little sentence to give her time to take in each one. We know that infants first attend to the whole 'chunk' of speech between pauses, and then to smaller and smaller units, that is, to individual

> **Pause between sentences**

words and sounds.[21] Make a slightly longer pause when you change the topic. Studies of infants at this age show that they prefer to listen to speech with such pauses. Once again, they seem to know exactly what is most helpful to them.

Continue to speak a little slower and louder, with lots of tune in your voice. Babies of this age still attend very much more easily to this kind of speech, and the tunefulness and stress patterns also help them to understand the grammar of sentences. 'Here's Mummy' with a rising intonation and slight stress on the first 'Mu', for example, will help her to identify that Mummy is the subject of the sentence. Similarly, a slight stress on the word 'Teddy' in the sentence 'Teddy is coming' will help her to identify that here is a new word, and to attach it to the object. (Be careful never to distort your speech; it should always sound natural.) Make sure too that you continue to bring in plenty of names, for example 'Let's put the cup on the table', rather than 'Put it on there'.

Speech of this kind is also by far the most effective for gaining and keeping her attention and maintaining her level of arousal.

Repetition is also very important. We all need to hear a word many, many times in a variety of different contexts both fully to understand it, and also to be able to recall it. Once again, think of yourself learning a foreign language, or even trying to recall the names of a foreign politician who newly comes into the news. You want to hear that name over and over again if you want to be able to say it. That huge gap between recognition and recall is just the same for your baby.

> **Babies need to hear the same word many times**

Repetitive games and rhymes are wonderful for this, and you can also make a point of bringing names into a sequence of little sentences relating to the same object or event: for example, 'There's doggy. Nice doggy. Here doggy. Doggy's here.' Of course, washing, dressing and feeding times are excellent for this too.

This will all be great fun for your baby: babies of this age just love hearing words they know already.

★ Use lots of gesture
We have talked about the amazing process by which babies at this stage can rapidly form links between words and what they refer to if they are given appropriate help at this stage.

> Molly, a curly-headed three year old called a car a door, and a shirt a shoe. She was a tenth child, and had had no opportunity to have an adult follow her attention focus and, as a result, had made many wrong connections, through looking at an object and hearing another named. We established half an hour a day in which Molly was alone with an aunt, and in these playtimes, asked her aunt only to name objects when she was quite sure of what Molly was focusing her attention on. We also asked that Molly's family and teachers did the same as far as was possible, and also made a point of naming correctly objects that Molly had misnamed, as part of the natural conversation. Slowly but surely, Molly began to attach more and more correct meanings to objects, until finally mis-namings were very rare.

The use of gesture is a very important way of helping, in particular by pointing at objects which you name, and more importantly at this stage, naming what she is pointing at. Notice how at nine months your baby can follow a point straight ahead, but not across her line of vision. By doing this, you are confirming the object of your joint attention, which is crucial in helping her to make the correct links between the word and what it refers to. I have seen a number of children who have made the wrong connections between words and meanings.

Use gesture also to show her what you mean: for example, saying 'pouring the milk' as you do so.

It's fun sometimes to copy her gesture. This will make her laugh, and will encourage her to communicate more.

QUESTIONS

Do not use questions to make your baby speak

You will probably find that you are still asking questions as an attention-getting device, and questions that are actually comments. This is fine, but make sure that you never ask any questions to try to get her to say words.

OUTSIDE YOUR HALF HOUR

Continue to talk a lot about whatever she is interested in. Comment on the fun she is having in the bath, for example 'Splish splash – you splashed the duck. He's gone under – oh, here he is' or when she's playing with her stacking beakers 'on it goes … and another one'.

12 to 16 months

An overview

One of the most fascinating features of this stage is that your baby will be moving towards verbal language with great rapidity. You'll notice that his understanding of speech will increase enormously during this period.

Your toddler now seems to veer between being a baby and a little child. He'll be very keen to walk when you are out, for example, but after a short distance will want to be carried. He'll want to try feeding himself with a spoon, despite the amount that gets spilled but when he's tired or unwell, he'll want you to feed him as you cuddle him, as you did at an earlier time.

He'll still get into dangerous situations very easily, so that feeling you need eyes in the back of your head persists, and will

Please note that the developmental stages described here are averages only.

All babies develop at slightly different rates, and often progress in one area can result in a temporary delay in another. Do not get worried or depressed if your child does not appear to be doing everything at exactly the time periods mentioned here. For further information, see Cause for Concern, page 149.

for some time. You'll find that he gets very excited when you're about to go out now, and that when you do he's fascinated by all the animals, people and objects he sees. It's lovely to be able to dawdle sometimes at this stage, and to enjoy his intense interest in the world.

Your baby still wants lots of your company, and has a huge need for your help, reassurance and protection. Personality really starts to emerge at this stage, and you may see amusing resemblances to other members of the family in traits like excitability or persistence.

He won't be a baby much longer, so make the most of it!

There is another burst of brain development at this time, when many more connections are made, and research shows that this is very greatly affected by the amount of stimulation the baby receives. Babies who are not talked to and played with at this time are unlikely to fulfil their potential in the future.[1]

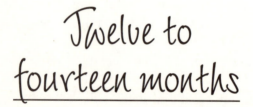

Twelve to fourteen months

THE DEVELOPMENT OF LANGUAGE

In terms of **understanding**, at the beginning of this period, your baby is just beginning to crack the language code. There are two very interesting elements to understanding at this stage.

There are huge differences between babies in how much they understand, indicating that unlike the use of words, this is highly dependent upon their experiences up to this time.

Second, there is an apparently huge gap between the rapidity with which understanding is increasing in comparison with the relatively slow increase in the number of spoken words. This once again reflects the enormous difference between the number of times we all need to hear a word to *recognise* it when we hear it again (which, for both adults and babies, can happen with just one exposure), and the number of times we need to hear it in order to be able to *say* it accurately. Babies demonstrate this very clearly. At the time at which they use words for a wide range of objects with similar characteristics, such as 'cat' for all four-legged animals, they can often point correctly to pictures of, for example, a cat, a horse and a sheep.

By the age of a year, babies for whom all has gone well can understand a number of words, and may already be saying two or three. Parents often notice that he understands several new ones every week by the fact that he looks around for people or objects who are mentioned. He is also now more adept at recognising the feeling behind what the speaker says, knowing, for example, whether his mother or father is pleased or cross about something he has done.

An important new departure is that he likes to look at books with pictures of familiar objects, and to have the pictures named for him. He soon learns to understand these – an important precursor of reading.

He will understand little commands now, particularly if they are part of a game: for example, 'Give it to Mummy' or 'All fall down'.

There are many important developments in social interaction at this time. At the beginning of this period, the baby is beginning to know that he is a separate person from others, and he has already become an equal partner in the interaction process. He often initiates 'conversations' in sounds, and speech gesture games like 'clap hands'. He is more aware of the likely effects of his different communications, for example anticipating being laughed at when he clowns, or expecting to be given an object he points to after looking at an adult.

By fourteen months, his **speech** has developed so that he is likely to use four or five words fairly consistently, and there is often a favourite one he uses very frequently. (One of my children said 'up', not only meaning that he wanted to be picked up, but in general that he wanted attention.) Interestingly, there is very little variability in the age and stage of use of these words between babies in very different environments, (although there are huge differences later). This indicates that this aspect of development is governed largely by a biologically determined milestone at this stage.

The first words are usually the names of familiar objects such as food, clothing, body parts or toys, followed by those associated with actions such as 'up'. At this stage, the baby only says them in the context in which he has heard them. For example, he is likely only to say 'spoon' in his own home at a mealtime.[2]

The ways in which these early words are used is also interesting: they are not used in quite the way that we use them. They are often used not only as labels, but can also stand for whole sentences, representing questions, requests for objects or attention, greetings, information giving, protests or commands. The word 'cup', for example, could mean 'I want a drink', 'That's my cup', or 'Where's my cup?' The baby becomes very skilful at making his meaning clear, expressing his different meanings by the use of intonation patterns supplemented by gesture. A rising tone, for example, can clearly mark a single word as a question. Even at this one-word stage, the baby tends to talk about aspects of his environment which are the most useful to him for giving information and communicating, largely about his toys and the people who are most important to him. As his world expands, so he gradually acquires new words.

When the baby doesn't know a word, he will use one that seems to refer to something similar. He may know, for example, that the nice furry purring animal who lives in his house is called 'cat', and apply this label to any furry creature that walks on four legs. Whole phrases may also be chunked together into one word, for example 'allfalldown'.

These first words are used sporadically over a period of time. They may be used for a few days or weeks and then not for some time. For this reason, parents can find it very difficult to answer the question 'How many words does he say?' Interestingly, the very first words often disappear for a considerable time. Nobody is quite sure why this is, but there is no need to worry: they always reappear eventually.

Despite all this, the baby still communicates most of his needs by pointing, accompanied by 'uh uh'. He uses long strings of very tuneful babble, and now puts his real words into it. He becomes quite a little mimic, and will try to copy both words he hears adults use as well as sounds like animal and vehicle sounds. He also imitates the sounds made by other babies.[3] He is very responsive to the vocalisations of children and other babies, and often initiates turn-taking speech games with them, such as 'Round and round the garden'.

GENERAL DEVELOPMENT

The developments in communication are paralleled by those in other areas. At the beginning of this period, he is busy exploring by crawling or shuffling around, and is now able to get up off the floor unaided to a standing position, and to climb onto a low step. He may take his first steps at this time.

His knowledge about himself and his environment is increasing. This is shown, for example, by the fact that he now looks in the correct place for a ball which has rolled out of sight, clearly keeping it in mind, and will repeat a performance which has made people laugh, remembering that it amused them previously. He is generally helpful and co-operative at this stage: for example, actively helping in dressing by putting out an arm or a leg. He is now capable of many emotions, including a sense of humour. He will laugh uproariously at surprise sounds, for example.

The baby's manual skills are developing apace, and he has many new abilities, which help him in his enormous task of exploring the world. He can put one cube on top of another, soon after twelve months, but can't let go of it for another month. He may begin to show a preference for one hand at this stage, although many babies do not do so until later. His ability to take hold of objects is approaching that of adults, and he can now grasp two cubes in one hand. He still loves to put toys and other objects in and out of containers, and to scribble. He very much enjoys looking out of the window and pointing out what he sees.

ATTENTION

Your baby will be starting to show spells of intense concentration on objects or activities of his own choice now, although his span of attention is still mainly very short.

The phrase 'of his own choice' is extremely important. He can at the beginning of this period reliably look where an adult is looking, but he is still very far from being able to give sustained attention to an adult's chosen focus. When he is concentrating in this way, he finds it virtually impossible to shift the focus of his attention in accordance with an adult's direction. He is not being unco-operative – he just cannot do it.[4]

As we have seen, the baby can now make more and more links between words and what the words refer to. Another important development is that he can now maintain attention to pictures for a short time, and to link name to picture. For both these to occur, it is essential that adult and infant share the same focus of attention so that the adult can make it clear to the infant exactly what the words refer to.

This co-ordination of attention is achieved at this stage principally by the adult following the direction of the baby's gaze and talking about the focus of his attention. The more that this is done now, the more effectively he will arrive at a situation in which an adult will be able to direct his attention, vital for all learning in school. It has been found that infants at this stage show more focused attention during interactive play with an adult than in solitary play.[5]

In this period, the baby begins to direct the adult's attention, and this direction shows considerable development during this time. At the beginning, he will point to an object and then look at the adult, indicating his interest to her. By the age of fourteen months, he will point to the object and look at the adult at the same time.

LISTENING

Your baby can now, if all has gone well, focus to some extent on foreground sound and tune out background. He is still only able to do this in conditions where there is very little background sound, and a low level of distraction. This important new ability can easily be lost if the environment is not helpful to it: it needs careful nurturing.

I saw Mary when she was fourteen months old. As the result of a genetic abnormality, she had normal hearing in one ear and none at all in the other, and her parents had been told that this would not cause any problems for her. This was not the case. We can only locate sound sources by comparing the differences in the sounds which arrive at our two ears. Mary, of course, had been unable to do this and so had not been able to attach meaning to the sounds she heard. Sound, therefore, was becoming more and more meaningless to her, and so she had totally focused on looking and handling, and had almost stopped listening. In particular, she was showing almost no interest in speech. She lived in a family where there were three older children and constant noise, which made things even more difficult for her.

We put her on the BabyTalk Programme, with emphasis on the listening sections, and those to enable her to attach meaning to words. The quiet environment they call for, with no competing background sound was absolutely essential for Mary, as having hearing in only one ear makes it extremely difficult to focus on a sound if there is any background noise. Giving her lots of fun noise-makers to play with, and making speech very easy and attractive to listen to by making it slower, louder and tuneful soon helped her to feel that listening was something that she wanted to do. Talking about her focus of attention soon enabled her to start attaching meaning to words. She started making progress both with listening and understanding words almost immediately, and in only four months had caught up with her age level in both areas of development.

This can be particularly essential if a child has any kind of hearing impairment, whether permanent or caused by catarrhal conditions, which are very common in babies and young children.

The baby's knowledge of the meaning of sounds is still building up steadily, and this helps him greatly in understanding his world. It helps him very much in getting to know the rhythm and sequence of his day, as he recognises, for example, all the sounds connected with mealtimes, bath times, visitors and going out.

You may notice that in noisy situations he becomes quiet, perhaps just when you are hoping he will be sociable. This is not because he is not sociable, but because he's too busy listening and trying to sort out all the different sounds around him to vocalise as well.

Fourteen to sixteen months

THE DEVELOPMENT OF LANGUAGE

The baby's **understanding** of words continues to increase rapidly. He now understands the names of many everyday objects like clothing and furniture, and can identify some body parts, such as ears or hair – not only his own, but also those of a doll. He is beginning to understand some words other than the names of objects or actions, for example words like 'in' and 'on'. He also begins to understand adults' gestural points, first only when they are close to him and later in this period when they are further away. He will show that he has understood a question by responding with a vocalisation accompanied by a gesture. For example when asked 'Where's your drink?' he will point to it, saying 'uh uh' as he does so.

Understanding is developing in quality as well as in quantity. Towards the end of this period, they learn to understand the names of smaller parts of a whole, for example 'door' and 'window' as parts of a house, or 'sleeve' and 'button' as part of a coat. They begin to understand a few very familiar phrases like 'Daddy's coming' now out of their usual context, and with no or limited visual cues.

A momentous step often taken at this time is that babies show the first signs of being able to decode sentences as opposed to only single words. They can now follow little instructions containing two important words, for example, 'Go to the *kitchen* and fetch your *shoes*'.[6]

The baby's early **speech** is often only understood by people very familiar with him, although by the age of sixteen months his babble contains virtually all the sounds of his mother tongue. The 'babble drift' – the process in which the sounds in his babble are only those present in the language around him – is nearing completion. These words are usually a simplified version of the adult form of the word. (My daughter, for example, referred to her comfort blanket as 'banna'.) Most families enjoy and retain a few of these early word approximations. In my family, rabbits were long known as 'bunnits', and guinea pigs as 'wiggy wigs'!

A wide range of speech sounds is coming into his words now, including those made at the front of the mouth, such as 'p' and 'b'; those made in the middle, such as 't' and 'd'; and those made at the back, such as 'g' and 'k'. He can round his lips with both a tight seal, as needed for the sound 'b' and a loose one, as needed for the sound 'p'.

By sixteen months, most babies use about six or seven words, and these now begin to appear within his babble. It's as if he knows full well that we don't speak in single words, but in long strings of them, and he is doing his best to do the same. His words work hard: even at this stage, much of his communication is accomplished by words, although he often needs to supplement this by gesture. His messages are becoming altogether much clearer.

Right at the end of this age period, some babies begin to show a more rapid acquisition of single words, although others may not do so until a later stage. Many at this time also enjoy trying out adult exclamations like 'oh-oh!' when something is dropped.

The baby loves to take turns vocalising with both adults and children, but most interactions are still quite short, being limited to one or two turns per partner. He is beginning to develop symbolic gestures, for example shaking his head for 'no', and now enjoys singing independently.

GENERAL DEVELOPMENT

Most babies usually attain an independent upright posture within this time period, which frees his hands for yet more investigation and exploration. He may take a few steps if he has not already done so, but cannot stop suddenly or go round corners. He walks with a 'wide base' – feet planted well apart for stability – and can climb stairs on his hands and knees. He tries to throw a ball, but cannot do so without falling over.

He begins to do more for himself, and now feeds himself with a spoon, although very messily, and can take off his hat, shoes and socks. He is also becoming able to control his own behaviour: for example, saying 'no' and withdrawing his hand when encountering an object he is not allowed to touch.

Manual dexterity continues to develop. He can build a tower of two blocks, releasing the second. Now that he can do this easily, throwing happens less often, but he still enjoys throwing and then picking up an object. He will offer a toy to an adult now and release it on request. He can roll a ball easily, and put several cubes into a container. He still enjoys playing alone at times as well as with an adult.

The baby's interest in books is increasing: he now helps to turn the pages, and looks at the pictures with interest, sometimes patting them.

There is a constant interplay between intellectual and language development, each enabling progress to be made in the other. A certain level of intellectual development is necessary for language to develop, and then language development can facilitate intellectual development.

At this stage, he is steadily acquiring concepts. He comes to understand, for example, that not only is there a cup and a coat which relate to himself in particular ways, but there is also a category of cups and coats containing many different ones. Such concepts begin as very broad global ones like 'things you eat with' and there are then progressively finer sub-groupings such as 'cutlery' and 'crockery' and finally 'knife', 'fork' and 'spoon'.[7] These concepts are essential for the acquisition of meaningful language. Concepts such as those relating to size and number, like 'one' and 'many', 'bigger' and 'smaller' are also being acquired. Without these, the words referring to them would be meaningless.

ATTENTION

The baby is now likely to show more frequent long spells of intense concentration on objects or activities of his own choice. It is of the very greatest importance that he has opportunities to engage in these periods of concentration when he chooses to do so. For much of the time, however, his span of attention is still very short, and he is still totally unable to give sustained attention to an adult's chosen focus. It's still enormously important that the adult observes the direction of the baby's gaze, and talks about that focus as often as possible.

His ability to direct an adult's attention is also continuing to develop. We saw how at twelve months he pointed to an object and then looked at the adult and at fourteen months progressed to pointing to the object and looking at the adult at the same time. By sixteen months, he is likely to look at the adult before pointing at the object, to ensure that he has her attention when he does so!

The baby's knowledge of the meaning of the sounds around him continues to develop apace. The scrape of his father's key in the lock or the voices of neighbouring children may produce great excitement now!

His interest in speech is also developing markedly at this time, and he will listen intently to people talking for quite prolonged periods. He makes it clear by his facial expression and body language that new words are very interesting to him, and he's not quite as easily distracted now when someone is talking to him.

He is very interested, too, in listening to the sounds he makes himself. This is important at this time as his speech-sounds system is rapidly coming into line with that of the language he hears around him, due to that very ability to compare his sounds with those he hears others use.

Babies at this stage are busily continuing their quest to find out 'how the world works'. They are doing this in a number of different ways, through investigative play, interactive play and now also with symbolic and pretend play, often involving interactions with other people. The development of the latter in this period is of great importance, as this is such an important precursor of creative imagination and all that stems from that.

Babies' new skills in manipulation and increasing control of their bodies helps in their investigations, and they now can literally learn from any situation and any materials. All their experiences help them to continue their understanding of their environment, and to form more and more concepts, for example of what is rough or smooth, big or small, which are all important if language is to be used meaningfully.

It continues to be important at this stage that babies have some time to play alone, and opportunities to work things out for themselves. Adult involvement, however, is enormously important, and babies are most helped by a sensitive partner, who knows when to join in and help and when to leave him to carry out his investigations alone. The development of pretend play can be greatly helped by an adult showing him the kind of things he could do, and all play can also, of course, be greatly enhanced by an adult adding appropriate language input.

INVESTIGATIVE PLAY

Babies' increased manual dexterity enables them to investigate toys with more sophistication at this stage. At an earlier time, their investigations took the form of shaking, banging and tasting in an attempt to find out the basic properties of objects, such as size, shape and texture. Now, while there is still much looking and touching, their increased intellectual ability, together with their greater control of hands and body, enables them to engage in more complex and wider investigations. They begin to become interested in fitting and matching, as well as stacking objects on top of each other, and will work hard, for example, at using a very simple shape sorter. They are beginning to find out how objects relate to each other, still enjoying putting objects in and out of containers, pulling toys apart and putting them back together. All these activities are enormously helpful in forming concepts of size and position, such as 'bigger' and 'smaller', 'in' and 'under'.

The very first use of tools appears now, with toys like wooden pegs and a hammer being used appropriately. This helps ideas of cause and effect, which are still rudimentary, to start to develop. In this case, for example, he learns that banging the pegs causes them to go down.

The baby starts to be able to handle pull along toys, and very much enjoys this. Water play begins to be a source of delight. This is wonderful for language input, as so many marvellous words like 'splash', 'splosh' 'drip drop' and 'pitter patter' go with it. Many concepts can also be acquired from it too, such as 'light' and 'heavy', 'float' and 'sink', 'full' and 'empty'.

The baby begins to look at books much more appropriately, opening them and really looking at the pictures instead of chewing and tearing them as he did earlier.

Investigation of sound is still very important. The baby still loves to play with noise-makers like musical boxes, cymbals, and squeaky toys. However, I cannot emphasise enough that some toys, particularly those with computers in them, produce sounds which are loud enough to damage babies' hearing. Do check before you give them to him.

Babies' desire to investigate now encompasses the mysterious ways of adults. At this stage, they begin very much to want to 'help' with chores like sweeping and dusting, in order to find out what these are all about. I remember feeling a little sad when I asked the mother of a little girl of this age whether she enjoyed helping with such activities. The mother replied: 'I don't ask her to help with the housework.'

Babies of this age love toys such as telephones that represent objects adults use, which enable them to find out what the objects are all about. They also enable the baby to demonstrate his skills at mimicry.

INTERACTIVE PLAY

Rhymes, finger rhymes and songs continue to be much enjoyed, particularly those with simple familiar tunes and words which relate to people, objects and actions the baby is very familiar with. Those involving body parts, such as 'I'm a little teapot' are still great fun, and he loves frequent repetition of these. Any songs are fine, but the traditional nursery rhymes in most languages tend to become part of the culture, because they have the qualities of strong beat, rhythm and repetition, which hugely appeal to this age group.

Interactive games involving turn-taking continue to be a very important part of play during this period, and are now more frequently initiated by the baby. He will also clearly, by body language, express that he wishes them to continue. These games now quite often involve toys and other objects. Activities like taking turns to put blocks in and out of a bucket, and throwing games, posting boxes, and putting rings on a stick all lend themselves very well to turn-taking. These basic turn-taking activities soon expand into games involving pretend, such as waving bye bye to each other. Such games often begin by the parent imitating the baby, and from there, they then develop into turn-taking games. The baby now clearly alternates turns with his partner, completing his before waiting for the adult to take his or hers. When the adult brings a variation into the game, such as patting the doll's back, he can now successfully imitate such new actions.

All such play, accompanied by language, is enormously helpful in enabling the infant to discover the ways in which language can be used to get things done, to understand the meaning of actions and events, and to enhance his interaction skills.

PRETEND PLAY

This is the period in which simple pretend play begins to flower. This play, in which pretend objects are used to represent other objects, thus using them as symbols, is critical to children's intellectual development. It is the precursor to the ability to think through problems in abstract and to find creative solutions to them. The ability to use the imagination freely and creatively helps in every aspect of life. Somebody recently told me that Einstein once said: 'Imagination is more important than knowledge.' Pretend play and language reflect the same underlying intellectual capacity: the ability to represent things symbolically.

The little child starts to act out simple familiar daily routines, and soon starts to involve toys in this play, like pretending to drink from a toy cup, followed by giving a doll or teddy a drink from the same one. At this very early stage of pretend play, the baby is active and teddy or dolly passive recipients of his actions – dolly receiving a brief hug, for example – but they gradually begin to 'act' on their own. Teddy, for example, will later hand back the cup. The baby loves to involve an adult partner in his pretend play, for example, offering his mother a soft toy to hug, or pretending to feed her in a simple tea-party game.

By the age of fifteen months, he will use objects which are less similar to the real ones, for example using a box as a doll's bed, or bricks for sandwiches. He will also start to relate more than one object together by this age, such as putting a dolly in a bed or a cover on the bed.

Infants benefit greatly from adult involvement in pretend play. They try out more different activities, and incorporate into their play extensions the adult has modelled for them.[8]

COMPUTERS

Please don't be tempted to introduce him to computer games yet. The under fives are being perceived by software manufacturers as a market potential, and programmes are being produced which target infants as young as nine months. The big worry about very little children using computers is that they have the same attractive qualities as do television and videos and there is a very real danger of little children spending hours on their own playing with them. Interaction and exploration is what children of this age are all about, and there is plenty of time for computers later. Starting later won't give him any disadvantage over those who started as babies, and the latter will have missed out on valuable play and interaction times for no good reason.

TELEVISION AND VIDEOS

There are many television programmes and videos being produced for young children, and these can be fun for your baby from this age, but it is extremely important that they are used in the right way.

The Toy Box

The following toys and play materials will enable the baby to meet his needs for investigative, interactive and pretend play in this period. Many will be used in different ways at this time period as he establishes his own games with them, and will also be used in different ways in the future.

When you are thinking about toys for pretend play, such as doll play and those which help him to copy your activities, do make sure that they represent reality. Talking trains and flying cars are enormous fun later on, but at this stage, when the baby is just learning about the world and how it works, can be very confusing. I remember hearing a snippet of a radio play about Martians when I was very small, and it was only years later that I discovered that there were no people living on Mars.

The toys suggested here are divided for convenience into those which encourage investigative and pretend play, but this is a very artificial divide and any of them could become the focus of interactive play. You will probably find that your little child will play with them in ways you would never have thought of.

Many excellent toys for this age group can be made at home for very little cost. Examples are boxes and tea-towels which can be used as doll's bed and bedding; boxes with holes in the lid or cardboard tubes which toys can be posted down; containers such as tins together with objects like cotton reels which can be put in and out of them. Paper and boxes still lend themselves to a great deal of fun. Continue to make wonderful noise-making toys by filling containers with different substances, such as rice or beans.

CONTINUED

INVESTIGATIVE PLAY

★ Toys he can push: eg, a baby walker or truck
★ Pulling toys: eg, a duck on a string
★ Thick wax crayons
★ Simple shape sorter
★ Chunky peg men in a boat
★ New noise-making toys: eg, drum, xylophone, maracas, or squeaky toys if he does not already have these in his toy box
★ Simple posting box
★ Pegs and hammer toy

PRETEND PLAY

★ Toy telephone
★ Simple large dolly and teddy, with bedding and doll's clothing
★ A simple train
★ Planes
★ Cooking utensils
★ Toy household objects like dustpan and brush or sweeper

Do limit video watching to half an hour a day at the most. Your baby needs to be spending lots of time interacting with people, and learning through play. This is a wonderful time in which this learning can be amazingly rapid. Opportunities lost now are lost for ever. The medium of television is so attractive because of its intense colours and rapid movements that babies and little children will watch for very long periods if they are allowed to. I have seen a number of children who watched for more than six hours a day. Not only were their language skills considerably delayed but, more importantly, so were their interactive skills, their play, and understanding of the world. They were very sad and confused little children.

The Book Shelf

The most important aspect of books for your baby at this time is that sharing books is a cosy interactive experience for him. You can now establish a foundation of pleasure in books that will stand him in good stead for a lifetime. Sit him on your knee so that you are close together while you look at the pictures. You won't have any difficulty in being more interested in him than in the book, but make sure he knows it.

The best kind of content should still be brightly coloured pictures of objects familiar to him, and photos of real people and objects in his life are wonderful now. (It can be fun too, to make books by cutting pictures out of magazines.) He will enjoy looking at small details now in pictures, so these can be more complicated or with more complicated backgrounds than those in his very first books. He will also very much enjoy some of the wonderful books now available for little children which have different textures he will enjoy stroking with his finger and those which you can press and make a noise to go with the picture. He will be enchanted to find, for example, that the duck actually quacks.

Follow his lead. He will help you turn the pages by the middle of this period, and will make it very clear which pictures he likes, patting and talking to them. Never try to keep his interest in a picture or book longer than he wishes to. Wonderful books for this age include:

★ *Touch and Feel Fluffy Chick*, Rod Campbell (Campbell Books)
★ *My Farm*, Rod Campbell (Campbell Books)
★ Touch and Feel (Dorling Kindersley)
★ *Clever Dog, Kip!*, Benedict Blathwayt (Julia Macrae)

CONTINUED

- ★ *Rosie's Walk,* Pat Hutchins (Bodley Head)
- ★ *Hide and Seek With Duck*, Jo Lodge (Bodley Head)
- ★ *Peepo*, Janet and Allan Ahlberg (Puffin)
- ★ *Where's Spot?,* Eric Hill (Puffin)
- ★ *The Very Hungry Caterpillar*, Eric Carle (Hamish Hamilton)
- ★ *Wibbly Pig* board books, Mick Inkpen (Hodder Children's)
- ★ *Dr Seuss* board books (HarperCollins)

Watch with him, so that the experience becomes an interactive one, and you can then make what he sees meaningful for him. A nursery rhyme video, for example, can be great fun if you both join in with the actions together.

The content should relate to the world as he understands it. Many programmes designed for older children, such as 'Thomas the Tank Engine', and 'Pingu', are fantasies, in which vehicles and animals do things that they do not in real life, such as talking and flying. These can be great fun for children who have enough experience of the world to know that they are fantasies, but they could be very confusing to babies at this stage. After all, he is only just finding out what people, animals and inanimate objects actually do.

Do not fall into the trap of thinking that the television can help him to understand words, now that he is beginning to be able to do this. It can't. Babies and young children are totally fascinated by the sight of the bright moving lights and colours of the television, and learn nothing from the sound. In an experiment, Dutch children who watched German television for extensive periods of time were found to have learned no German at all.[9] It is also the case that hearing children of deaf parents learn no language from television, instead picking up sign language from their parents.[10]

You may desperately need a short break, and the television can give you this, but do recognise that that is what is happening: the benefit is only to you.

Summary

To summarise, by the time he is sixteen months old, your baby is likely to:

★ Use from six to eight recognisable words.
★ Look with interest at picture books.
★ Use gestures to make his wants known.
★ Look at familiar objects or people when he hears them named.

Cause for concern

Below are circumstances in which it would be advisable to seek professional advice about your little child's development. (Please remember, though, that many children progress at slightly different rates.)

If you are in any doubt about your child, even if the reason for your concern is not mentioned here, do take him to see your Health Visitor or GP as soon as possible.

At sixteen months it would be advisable to seek a professional opinion if:

★ He never takes it in turns with you in making sounds to each other.
★ He doesn't respond by looking in the right direction to little questions like 'Where's your hat?'
★ He does not babble with lots of different sounds, sounding almost as if he is talking.
★ He is not interested in starting lots of games with you like 'Patacake'.
★ He never concentrates on anything for more than a few seconds.

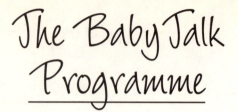

The BabyTalk Programme

This daily one-to-one playtime is still the very best possible situation for language learning. It also continues to be immensely important for your baby's emotional development. Nothing gives a little child more confidence than the certainty that he

---

Natasha was brought to me at the age of two and a half, because she was using only three words at that time. She was clearly bright, and immediately began to play with my toys in a very constructive way, busily setting out teddy's lunch for him. When I approached her, however, she completely ignored me, very much giving me the feeling that I was seen as an interference in her activity. Her mother reported that she had always shown a preference for solitary play.

We set up daily playtimes for Natasha and her mother, in which her mother began to operate the principles of the BabyTalk Programme, particularly following the focus of Natasha's attention and avoiding directing her play in any way. Natasha soon began to experience her mother's presence as enhancing her play and it was lovely to see the increased pleasure she and her mother took in interacting with each other. Natasha's language skills very quickly caught up with and exceeded her age level.

Just recently, Natasha and her mother brought Natasha's baby brother to see me, as they were in town. He was six months old, and as soon as we met, made it clear by his facial expression and body language that he was absolutely determined to relate and communicate with me. I found it impossible not to respond, and had to postpone conversation with Natasha and her mother for some time. Their mother was amazed, as we all were, at the difference in personality between these two siblings.

---

will receive undivided attention from a beloved adult on a daily basis. You will be particularly aware if you have more than one child of how powerful is their desire for such attention.

Babies and young children, like adults, vary a lot in personality, including in their eagerness for interaction. It can easily happen in a busy household that parents are only too happy that a particular child seems content to occupy himself for long spells, rarely seeking attention. Sadly, the effects of this are often noted when the little child reaches the age of around two years, and is not talking.

THE SETTING FOR YOUR ONE-TO-ONE PLAYTIME

We have heard how babies of this age have now acquired the vital skill of being able to focus on a foreground sound and tune out other sounds in the background. This skill, however, is still new and not yet well established, and needs very careful nurturing, or it can be lost. At this stage, it can only operate in quiet conditions, so a quiet background in your playtime continues to be of the very greatest importance.

> **A quiet setting is still extremely important**

Babies' play at this time ideally involves many more play materials than at an earlier age. The availability of these gives him the opportunity of developing exploratory, interactive and pretend play alongside each other. It's good to have quite a number of different objects available in the play space, as his attention span is still very short for most of the time. Make sure that they include those which will encourage all the different kinds of play.

As you did before, sit on the floor with him so that your faces are on a level, and the toys are within easy reach of both of you so that you can easily share joint attention.

He may move around the room a lot now. If so, do follow him. You need to stay close to him so that he hears everything you say and all the sounds you make really clearly.

We have seen how babies can hugely increase their understanding of words in this time period. There is a great deal we can do to help him with this process. In fact we can make all the difference now. Here's how to help.

★ **Follow his focus of attention**
The importance of doing this at this stage cannot be overestimated. There is a great deal of research evidence which shows that the degree to which adult and baby share the same focus of attention, the wider his vocabulary and the more complex his sentences are later.[11] Comparisons have also been made between two different situations:

★ one in which the adult tries to direct the child's attention at this stage to the objects and activities of her choice, and
★ one in which she follows the direction of the child's gaze and talks about that focus.

It has been found that words used in the latter situation are much more likely to be understood than those in the former. [12] Making links between words and their meanings can occur with amazing rapidity if this is done at this stage.[13] [14]

Another good reason for following the child's focus of attention is that even as young as this, little children just relish it. Don't we all as adults, enjoy people we love showing real interest in what interests us?

If you have been following this programme, you will already have begun to follow your child's attention focus, and it will be very easy for you now, as you and he will have a shared history of play together, and know what is important and interesting to you both.

As before, always comment on what is interesting him, and avoid questions and directions entirely. This is still of the very greatest importance, and is in fact one of the most important principles of the BabyTalk Programme. Questions give the baby the problem of trying to figure out the answer, and directions mean that he has to decide whether or not he wants to comply. Both interfere with his listening, whereas comments just add to the fun of what he is doing, and do not cause him any communicative stress.

It is still the case that the more closely you can work out what is in his mind at that moment, the more helpful you can be. It may be an object he's interested in, and would like named, in which case you might say, for example, 'It's a chick' as he looks at a picture, or a play sound to go with it might amuse him, when you might say 'cheep cheep'. His interest might be in what is happening, and you might say 'All fall down' as the bricks do so, or 'Crashshsh' as the cars collide. It usually isn't difficult to know what is appropriate. You are interacting with a pretty accomplished communicator now.

> **Questions and directions interfere with his listening**

I have seen many little children who had received a great deal of verbal direction literally turn their backs on me as I approached them to play, and continued skilfully to do this however cunningly I tried to manoeuvre myself to face them. Almost invariably, within half an hour, the moment they realised that I was following their focus of attention and adding to their interest by naming an object or making a play sound to go with it, like 'brm brm' when they picked up a car, round they came. That always amuses and pleases me very much.

★ Help him to enjoy listening

Do make a point of including noise-makers in his toys so that he can have fun listening to them in this quiet environment.

Take any opportunities to show him where sounds come from, for example in a 'noise' book. Opportunities can also be taken to show what sounds things make as he moves around the room. It could be fun, for example, to tap with your nail on the window, or run your finger across the slats of blinds if he shows interest in these items.

Rhymes, finger rhymes and action rhymes are still all wonderful for giving him huge enjoyment in listening to voice in this

> **Keep listening enjoyable**

quiet, interactive setting. These can be done when he looks at you expectantly, indicating that it's your turn to initiate an activity.

Do continue your turn-taking games, such as hiding, and clapping hands. He will still love them, and they are such an important precursor to later true conversational skills.

★ Help him to crack the language code

Some of the modifications which you have been making to your speech to help your baby to focus on your speech and maintain that attention focus, still serve to do these, but now continue to be enormously important in helping him to understand words. As we go through them, think of yourself trying to learn a foreign language, and see if you don't think they would help.

★ Use short simple sentences

You will already have been doing this to help your baby to increase his understanding of words, and it is essential that you continue to do so. It is only at the very end of this time period that he will be able to understand little phrases and sentences containing more than one important word. Following the principle, therefore, that it's important always to adjust our input to the level of the baby's understanding, it is still very important to use little phrases and sentences which contain just one important word, but to add a little to it. Examples are 'It's teddy', 'Your duck', 'Another car', or 'Here's dolly'. (Be sure to bring in the names of objects at this stage, rather than 'There it is' for example, as names are what he wants to learn right now.) If what is happening is the focus of interest, we can say 'It crashed', or 'They fell down'. Put a very slight stress on the important word, to help him to identify it, but as before, be very careful that you don't distort your speech; it must always sound natural.

Your little sentences must also always be grammatical. We wouldn't say, for example, 'It car' but rather 'It's a car'. Pause between each little sentence to give him time to take it in.

Isla's mother talked to her constantly, using sentences like: 'It's time we went to the shops. I wonder if we should buy the bread now, or wait until later.' Not surprisingly, at this stage Isla had only managed to pick out her own name, 'Daddy' and 'No' in terms of understanding words. As soon as her mother realised the importance of short sentences and began to use them, Isla learned the meaning of words incredibly fast.

Research studies have shown that the simpler mothers' speech is at this time, the more rapidly the little child's length of sentence increases later. I have seen lots of mothers and babies who were enjoying a very close and loving relationship, in which the mother talked a great deal to the baby, but in enormously long sentences.

> **Sentences must always be grammatical**

★ **Speak slightly slower and louder, with lots of tune in your voice**

These features are still very important in helping your baby to focus on your speech, and is still very much the kind of speech that babies of this age like to listen to best. You will notice that your baby listens to you intently when you talk to him in this way. Speaking like this also gives him the best chance of noticing which of those many speech sounds go where in which words.

★ **Use lots of repetition**

Think of yourself trying to learn a foreign language. Wouldn't you want to hear the same words over and over again to help you to recall them? So does your baby. We know that he has most of the speech sounds of the language within his repertoire now, and so the reason they do not yet appear in the right places in the right words is largely that he can't recall which goes where. The only way he will do this is by hearing the same words many, many times.

It is also very important for his concept formation to hear words in many different contexts, discovering, for example, that his hat is always called 'hat' whether it be on his head, on the floor, or squashed up in his mother's handbag.

The best way of bringing repetition in at this stage is by putting the name of an object into a sequence of little sentences for as long as his interest is focused on it. For

> **He needs to hear words many times in order to learn them**

example, as he picks up and plays with a ball, you could say: 'It's the ball. Your ball. Ball's rolling.' Little naming rituals, like 'Sock off, shoe off, gloves off' as you undress him are also fun, as are games like 'Johnny jump, Mummy jump, Daddy jump'. Put a slight stress on the key name as you say it the first time so that he identifies the name clearly.

★ Say his sounds back to him

This continues to be extremely helpful. We know that, at this stage, all the sounds of his mother tongue are now coming into the baby's sound-making, and this enables him to compare his own sounds with yours. As we know, there is still nothing like it for encouraging 'conversations' in sounds, with infants who are essentially non-verbal still. Saying his sounds back to him can be a little more complex at this stage, as his sound-making is so much more involved. If he produces a long string of sounds, try imitating the last couple of syllables. He will love it, and is likely to make more sounds back to you.

★ Continue to make play sounds to go with things that happen

Do continue with this. Sounds like 'brm brm', 'der der' and 'eeeeow' to go with cars, fire engines and planes, 'swishshshshsh' as you sweep the floor and so on, are still, at this stage, wonderful for gaining and keeping his attention. They give him that all-important message that voice is fun to listen to, and give him a chance to hear speech sounds separately. Little phrases like 'Upsidaisy' as you lift him up, 'dompedy dompedy domp' as you go upstairs, are still much appreciated at this stage, and you will see from his facial expression how much he enjoys them and how closely he listens when you do them, even if he is tired or a little upset.

> **Play sounds show that voices are fun**

★ Always respond to what he means

Now that he is able to use some words, don't try to encourage him to do so in any way. He will use them when he is ready, and he will be ready much sooner if he never feels under pressure to speak. The important thing is always to respond to what he means in whatever way he tries to tell you. He is adept by now at using body language, facial expression, gesture and even elaborate pantomime to express himself, so it is seldom difficult to know what he means. It has been found that the degree to which parents do this, paying attention to their baby's intention in whatever way this is expressed, does much to account for the differences in language development between different children.

★ Show him what you mean

A very important way in which you can help him to crack the language code at this stage continues to be by your use of

> Jerry's speech was in a state of great confusion, with many words attached to the wrong meanings. He called a button a coat, for example, and a fork a plate. He was one of a large family, and his mother suffered from long-term depression. As a result, he had not been talked to very much, and certainly had not had any one-to-one time. What had happened was that he had heard a word while he was looking at an object other than that which the word referred to, and so had made the wrong connection between them. Can you imagine what a confusing world he lived in? Just a few basic misconceptions are enough to cause confusion in all learning that follows. It took a very long time to help Jerry to sort out all his muddles. He did so eventually, after the adults around him had worked hard at following his attention focus when they talked to him, both in one-to-one playtimes and for as much of the remainder of the time as possible.

gesture. Again, think of trying to learn words in another language. He has to decipher exactly which word amongst several

> **Point to objects when you say their names**

stands for a particular object or event, and it is hugely helpful for him if we point as we name an object for him. For example, if he looks at the ducks and we say 'It's a duck', accompanying this with a point in its direction, there is very little chance of him being under any misapprehension about what that word 'duck' represents. Perhaps unsurprisingly, it is easy for children to attach the wrong meaning to words if they are not given this help. Speech and language therapists all see children who have attached the wrong names to objects.

Your facial expression and body language can also be used to help your baby's understanding of words, and give him much information about feelings and attitudes.

SOME 'DON'TS' FOR THIS AGE PERIOD

A couple of 'don'ts' are very important at this stage. This is the time period in which your baby is very likely to become mobile, and wants to explore and investigate anything and everything, including plug sockets, light fittings and your precious ornaments. It is all too easy to find yourself saying 'No', 'Don't touch', 'Stop it' and 'Put that down'. It is very much better not to. Continue as far as possible to avoid 'negative'

> **Keep language positive, not negative**

speech. You have been, and still are spending lots of time and effort giving him the message that voice is fun to listen to, and nobody likes to hear these kind of comments. Furthermore, it is always necessary at this stage to intercept and distract him physically, and it is much better to rely on that. (Please do not think that I am advocating letting him do anything he wants to: I'm not. My concern is how you stop him.)

Your baby is very likely to produce those magical first words at this time. Please resist the temptation to ask him to 'say it for Daddy', 'for Grandma', 'for Aunty', or for anybody else. As we have said before, babies know a great deal about communication, and they know all too well that this is not normal communication. It just serves to make them self conscious, and inhibit them. Share your jubilation on the phone when he can't hear you, but never comment to him about what he has said, or how he said it. Instead, always respond to the meaning of his communication. He will be enchanted by this, particularly when you respond to his very early words, which only you may understand.

> **Never comment about what he has said, or how he has said it**

I and many of my colleagues have seen many children who began to say words and then ceased to do so for six months or more because of overenthusiasm on the part of their family.

This is another very important theme which runs throughout the programme. We are never ever going to ask your baby to say or copy words or sounds. There is absolutely no need. Our job is to talk to him in the most appropriate way. If we do this, he will look after the talking.

QUESTIONS

Questions are very frequently asked by adults of children from this age. They are asked for two purposes: first to gain information – for example, 'Do you want an apple?' – and second to get the child to answer: for example 'What's this?'

The first is fine, and the second is not. The reason is that the former is true communication in that the adult doesn't know the answer, and even very young children are well aware of this. The second is nothing to do with communication, and is in fact a test. The little child also knows this. If he knows the answer already, the question adds nothing to his knowledge, and if he does not, it just makes him feel bad, and can seriously inhibit a child's communication. I saw a little boy in my clinic once who said virtually nothing but 'What's this?' It's not difficult to work out what he had been hearing over and over again.

> **Do not ask question 'tests'**

I'd go so far as to ban 'What's this?' at this age, and for some time to come, unless there were an odd occasion when you really did not know what something was and your child might.

(When he is much older, questioning skilfully done can help a child to think and work things out, and can be a way of passing the conversational turn to the child, but he is very far from that stage now.)

OUTSIDE YOUR HALF HOUR

You may be wondering how to talk to him outside your special playtimes, as up to now this has been different. It's fine to continue your 'running commentary', and pointing out interesting objects and events to him, at times when you are busy and want to keep in touch with your baby. But remember to keep your sentences short for much of the time now when you talk to him. The more that you can modify your speech now, the better for his language learning. It can be helpful to enlist the help of the whole extended family at this stage.

16 to 20 months

An overview

This is a very exciting period and you will notice many dramatic changes in your child's development as she moves from babyhood to the world of a confident toddler.

By sixteen months, she's really becoming a small person with whom you can share the routines of your life, particularly as her own routines are really settling down now. She will probably be sleeping right through the night most of the time – which makes things infinitely easier for you and the rest of your family – and she's probably down to only one or two naps in the daytime. Her mealtimes will be more regular, and although she will probably still want a bottle last thing at night and first thing in the morning, she will be becoming more

Please note that the developmental stages described here are averages only.

All babies develop at slightly different rates, and often progress in one area can result in a temporary delay in another. Do not get worried or depressed if your child does not appear to be doing everything at exactly the time periods mentioned here. For further information, see Cause for Concern, page 178.

skilful at drinking from a cup as well. She may well start to get very fidgety about sitting in her high chair – realising that she's the only one – and will prefer to be 'grown up' in a normal chair.

Other things are changing as well. She likes to have more control over her life now, and will take charge of games if she can. For instance, when you go for a walk, although you'll still take the pushchair (and she will inevitably get tired at times), she may well be keen to take turns with you pushing the buggy herself: she's definitely growing up! She'll really enjoy climbing onto things – sofas, beds and pretty much anything within reach – and now she can really start getting into trouble.

She'll generally be joining in and engaging with both you and other people around you more, and this desire to be part of things is reflected in how quickly her language skills are now developing.

This is a rich and crucially important stage in your child's development. Enjoy every minute of it!

The seventeenth and eighteenth months

THE DEVELOPMENT OF LANGUAGE

Your child's **understanding** of the world around her and the people in it, what objects are for and how people use them, is developing very rapidly indeed, and – particularly if she has lots of help from you – this will be accompanied by a dramatic increase in her understanding of words. At the beginning of this period, she is likely to recognise the names of many everyday objects such as furniture and clothing, and may have taken the momentous step of being able to begin to follow little sentences containing two important words, for example, 'Your *cup* is in the *kitchen*' or 'Let's find *teddy* and give him to *Daddy*'. You will find that you naturally put a slight stress on the important words, which is helpful in making it easy for her to notice them, but it is important never to exaggerate the stress as this would distort the rhythm of the sentence.

You will notice that she begins to respond appropriately to what is happening around her: going to fetch her shoes when you are preparing to go out, or sitting in her chair when you are cooking. She can also now associate words with their categories, recognising, for example, that a vest is an item of clothing, in the same category as shirt and socks.

She begins to be able to respond to simple questions such as 'Where's Teddy?' by looking in the right direction, but it's important to remember that some words can only be recognised in a familiar context: she may only look around for 'bowl', for instance, when *her* bowl is likely to be within sight.

At around seventeen months, you will notice a rapid increase in the number of words she recognises. Often she seems to understand something new every day, particularly the names of body parts, clothing or animals. She is also developing a strong feel for the way in which you use language, and will respond appropriately to a question such as 'Want an apple?', a comment like 'There's pussy' or a direction along the lines of 'Get your shoes'. She will also understand words other than names by now, and will know the meaning of some simple verbs like 'sit down' and 'come here'. It's interesting that her increasing awareness of herself as a separate person is demonstrated by her new-found understanding of pronouns like 'you', 'me' and 'mine'.

As her vocabulary increases, so does her ability to understand sentences and phrases containing two important words, rather than single words only. So she might now be able to follow little instructions, like 'Go to your *room* and fetch your *coat*' or 'Get your ball and give it to Johnny'. She may even bring you two things you ask for, responding to requests such as 'give me the brush and the spoon' – but only if she is in the mood to be helpful.

It's only natural that at this stage, with your child progressing so wonderfully, you'll be excited and keen to show off her new-found linguistic skills, but don't be disappointed if she doesn't perform as well with other people as she does with you. Many babies at this age will understand familiar adults much better than people they don't know well, and although this can be very frustrating, it's something that will change as she grows up a little.

Her **speech** is developing quickly as well, and although at sixteen months she is still using lots of babble containing a wide range of sounds, pitches and intonation patterns, and probably only around six or seven true words, spoken vocabulary will increase gradually but steadily. Most babies do not experience rapid vocabulary expansion until at least twenty months, and their use of words can seem bewilderingly behind their understanding. Don't panic! This is perfectly normal, and her speech will catch up in due course.

Unsurprisingly, children's early words tend to be the names of people and objects of great interest to them. They love to join in and be sociable, so will often learn words like 'hiya', and 'bye bye' very quickly. Other early favourites include words which accompany familiar actions, such as 'up', but her use of words at this stage will generally be restricted to specific contexts she knows well: for example, 'teddy' may only refer to her own teddy. Interestingly enough, as long as your child is interested in an object, the length of its name is not a key factor: my daughter had a toy hippo to which she was greatly attached as a child, and had 'hippopotamus' extremely clearly amongst her limited vocabulary at sixteen months.

Although your child's vocabulary will be growing fast at this age, the limited number of words she is able to use have to work extremely hard. Although some are used in too limited a way – for example 'ta' or 'bo' to refer to her own cat or bottle – others will be wildly over-used. When she doesn't know the correct word for something, your child will – very sensibly – use one which seems to her to be connected to it, so she might for example use 'ball' to refer to several round objects including the moon, a wheel, and even a teabag.

These early words also have to express a wide range of intentions. 'Car' could mean 'I want the car', or 'That's my car', or even 'I don't like the car!' so she will use facial expressions and body language to make it absolutely clear which she means.

Her conversational skills are improving steadily too, and she may now be able to follow a conversation in which each partner takes two turns. For example, she could say 'Car', and you might reply 'Here's your car'. She might then follow with 'Brm brm' as she pushes the car along, and wait for you to say 'Crash' as she crashes it.

By eighteen months, she will acquire many more abstract concepts about objects, events or people: for example, an understanding of the concept of 'dogginess', or 'shopping'. As a result, her use of words can move away from the specific, to the general: 'dog' can now mean all dogs rather than just the family pet. This may to some extent account for the rapid development of spoken vocabulary at this stage, as words are now beginning to be used as symbols.[1]

GENERAL DEVELOPMENT

A crucial factor in your child's language development is the fact that her intellectual ability, her ability to move around, and her manual dexterity are constantly helping her to increase her understanding of the world around her. Perhaps the most important intellectual development at this age is the rapid increase in the number of concepts she understands. Concepts which were initially very broad – for example four-legged animals – gradually becomes refined, so she begins to understand categories of birds, fish, dogs and cats, and finally individual animals.

You'll notice very quickly that your child is becoming much more adept at moving around the room, picking things up and handling objects that interest her, and all of this helps her to increase her understanding of concepts as she explores and investigates her world. For example, unless she has tried to pick up something that weighs too much it's difficult for her to understand the concept of 'heavy'.

Because her eye–hand co-ordination is increasing, she is now able to handle various materials in ways which are very helpful in forming concepts: for example, she can fill a container right to the top with bricks and then empty it. She now scribbles and dots purposefully with pencil or crayon, and examines the results with great interest. She likes to push and pull large toys and vehicles around, and so acquires better judgement about the size and position of objects. She is also more interested in completing what she starts: for example, parking all her vehicles in one place, or putting all her bricks into a truck.

Her increased ability to move around also helps her to explore the world. She can now kneel upright without support, and seat herself in a small chair. She walks confidently with a wide base, and enjoys pushing a trolley along. She can push a chair into position in order to climb on it to reach a toy, and she can walk upstairs two feet to a step if you hold her hand. She likes the idea of kicking a ball, but just walks into it at present.

Not all of her discoveries about the world involve purely physical developments: she's investigating things socially as well. Don't be surprised to see her engaging in a lot of imitation and mimicry, partly to find out how it feels to do the things she sees you doing, and also in order to find out how other people are different from and like herself. She loves to involve others in her games, and will invite you to join in by offering you a toy.

ATTENTION

It's still difficult for your child to control her concentration so you'll continue to see the rapid shifts of attention focus that she's been demonstrating for the last sixteen months, but they will now become interspersed with spells of intense concentration on something she becomes passionately interested in, and she absolutely doesn't want to be interrupted.[2]

Although when she is not so deeply engrossed she will show an increased interest in following your focus of attention, when she is concentrating hard on something she cannot even listen to anything you say to her – unless it is directly related to her chosen focus, and makes it even more fun. For example, she would be able to listen to the words of a game such as 'Where's your hand?' when she is trying to figure out how to put her arm in her sleeve, but would not at that time be able to listen to you pointing out a cat in the garden.

LISTENING

Your child should now be able to pinpoint sounds coming from most directions, which is an enormous help in making links between sounds and their sources. If all has gone well, she will now be able to scan the sounds in her environment, choose what she wants to listen to, and focus on that for a little longer, tuning out background sounds. This ability is still not well established, however, and needs favourable circumstances if it is to be maintained.

Sensory integration – the ability to look and listen at the same time – is also developing, but it is still only present in particular circumstances: when her surroundings are free from distractions, and when what she is looking at and listening to are not only the same thing, but also her chosen focus of attention.

She is increasingly interested in listening to speech now, and shows this by sometimes repeating the last word of a sentence she's heard. Her fascination is also shown by the fact that she's much less easily distracted when she's listening to someone talking.

The nineteenth and twentieth months

THE DEVELOPMENT OF LANGUAGE

The last two months have seen some dramatic progress in your child's **understanding** of words, but things develop even more rapidly in the nineteenth and twentieth months. If her circumstances encourage it, she will be able to recognise as many as nine new words every day!

However, it's not just in terms of sheer number of words understood that your child will be making progress. By around twenty months, she will begin to understand words and phrases outside the context in which she usually hears them: for example, she will respond to 'Tea's ready' in a neighbour's house, and not only in her own. Similarly, she will begin to understand that many words and phrases can stand for an object or person not actually present, so she can respond to familiar phrases like 'Where's Granny?' even when Granny isn't visiting. In other words, she is now truly beginning to understand spoken language, recognising the meaning of a word without the support of a familiar context.[3]

Her increased understanding of words as symbols is also reflected in the fact that she begins to recognise the names of model objects such as toy cars or doll's house furniture, as well as of real objects. She will also recognise the names of objects in illustrations. She might well look at pictures for up to two minutes now, and will point to parts of the body and clothing in them when they are named. Her knowledge of sequences of events such as going to the shops or bath-time, acquired through repeated experience, are a huge help to her. It is easy, for example, to deduce the meaning of the word 'towel' in the sentence 'Here comes the towel to dry you with' if she hears it as she is about to come out of the bath and knows that what happens next is being dried!

She will also become adept at using non-verbal cues such as gesture, context and the signals you make with your eyes to help her to understand what a word refers to, and can make quite sophisticated deductions about the object of your interest.

As earlier, **speech** develops alongside – although behind – understanding. Most babies at this age continue to vocalise for much of the time, using a wide range of sounds, pitch and intonation patterns, but there can be an enormous difference in the number of words used. Some use only nine or ten, while others may use up to fifty words meaningfully by the end of this period.

At around twenty months, some children will experience a huge and sudden increase in vocabulary. The majority of these words are still names of family members, pets and favourite toys as well as some action words like 'bye bye' and environmental sounds like emergency sirens. However, she will also now respond to speech with speech, for example saying 'bye bye' when asked to, whereas at the start of this period she would respond with a simple sound or gesture. You will find that gesture starts to become less important as words take over as her main means of communication. Those babies who experience this rapid increase in vocabulary at twenty months will now be using a wide range of types of words including verbs like 'drink', and adjectives like 'big' and 'little', and responding to speech with speech, answering simple questions like 'Do you want an apple?'

However, words are still used to express a wide variety of meanings and purposes, so 'Dadda' may mean 'Pick me up, Daddy', 'Come here, Daddy', 'Daddy's car', or 'Daddy's turn'. That said, as your child acquires a larger vocabulary, the over-extensions you've become familiar with will gradually decrease. A word used for all four-legged animals, for example, will be replaced by the names of different kinds of animals.

Children who reach a spoken vocabulary of about fifty words at around twenty months now begin to combine two words, although, of course, they will also use single words for some time. You will now hear your daughter's first sentences, and this is a really exciting and momentous stage. The first words which are truly linked to another are often 'gone' and 'more', as in 'Mummy gone', and 'More drink', but the earliest two-word combinations are usually two entirely separate words put together: like 'me car' meaning 'I want the car'. The word order may not, of course, be correct, and at this stage my daughter would firmly announce 'Mummy see' when she wanted to see me. These early two-word sentences often have several meanings. 'Mary hat' could mean 'I want my hat', 'Give me my hat', or even 'I don't like my hat'; so although she's speaking in sentences they might still need a bit of deciphering.

I've mentioned that babies at around this age are very interested in mimicry, and this extends to speech. Most will imitate two-word sentences, and they will continue to imitate environmental sounds: 'der der' when a fire engine goes by, or calling 'woof' when they see a dog.

Pronunciation, however, is far from mature and proud parents quite often find that they are the only ones to understand many of their child's words. This is largely because the child still has a very long way to go in terms of being able to remember which sounds go where in which words, but also because some speech sounds such as 'ch' and some clusters of sounds like 'scr' require extremely fine adjustments of tongue and lips. (Try them, and see how much more complex the movements are compared with those needed to say 'b' or 'p'!) Only by having lots of opportunities to compare the sounds that she makes herself with those she hears around her is your child eventually able to bring her speech-sounds system into line.

These are some of the most common mispronunciations of early childhood:

★ Difficult sounds are replaced by those which sound similar but are much easier to say: for example, 'wabbit' for 'rabbit', or 'tat' for 'cat'.
★ The same consonant may be used twice in a word where there are two quite similar ones: for example, 'goggie' for 'doggie'.

★ The fact that the child has not yet noticed all the sounds in words is revealed by some of her mispronunciations. The sounds at the end of words, for example, are often quiet and quite hard to hear and are therefore left out, as in 'bo' for 'boat'. Whole syllables which are not stressed are also often left out, such as 'bana' for 'banana'.

★ Similar sounds may be substituted: for example 's' for 'sh'.

★ Words containing several syllables are altered so that the syllables become very similar to each other. My younger son rather charmingly called a 'bunny rabbit' a 'bunny bunnit' at this stage.

GENERAL DEVELOPMENT

Your child's ability to manipulate and investigate objects develops even further sophistication now: she can unscrew a lid and open a door, turn the pages of a book a few at a time, and build a tower or train of three bricks. She can fit six pegs in a pegboard and fit a square and a circle into a formboard. She shows an interest in matching two similar objects, for example, putting together two cars which are the same; and she can now throw a ball – although it may well go in the wrong direction.

She also has increasing control over her body. She walks with a heel and toe gait, and can start and stop walking safely. She can squat to pick up a toy, and climb onto a large chair and turn round to sit. She has a much clearer understanding of her own body size in relation to spaces, and will be able to work out whether or not she could fit into a particular box.

On the social front, she is increasingly interested in imitating everything she sees adults do, and loves to pretend to read a book, make tea, and do all the myriad things she observes happening around her. She has an intense desire to find out what these things are all about, and an absolute determination to discover as much as she can about the world.

ATTENTION

In terms of attention span, you won't notice many differences between the seventeenth and eighteenth months, and the nineteenth and twentieth. She will still intersperse short periods of intense concentration with the more usual quick shifts of focus, and it will still be impossible to guide her attention away from something she is really engrossed in.

The only difference you might see is that by eighteen months she will be able to accurately locate the target of your gaze at a distance, and she will therefore show an increasing interest in following your focus of attention.

LISTENING

There really isn't any significant development at this stage from seventeen and eighteen months, although your child is likely to be ever more interested in listening to speech – partly because she's finding it ever easier to make the crucial link between a sound and where it comes from.

Play

Investigative, interactive and pretend play are all developing quickly now, and all help your baby in her quest to discover more about how the world works. Because she's learning so fast, it's very important that she has a wide range of both toys and situations – and remember that she will enjoy playing by herself as well as with a partner. It is very important that you are sensitive to what she wants at a particular time. She will usually make it very clear when she wants you to join in!

INVESTIGATIVE PLAY

You'll notice that your baby's control over her body, manual dexterity and eye–hand co-ordination is increasing quite dramatically, and this enables her to make lots of exciting discoveries. She can relate objects more accurately to each other now, carefully placing a cover straight on a doll's bed, and she will probably also show an interest in linking different parts of an object together in more complex ways: for example, fitting pictures into very simple inset jigsaw puzzles. She will learn how to place bricks so that they balance, which pieces of a puzzle are too big or too small, and how turning them round may help.

She will now use objects as they are intended to be used, banging drums and pushing vehicles. She will be more persistent in her games, and more dextrous: she can now build a small tower of bricks that doesn't immediately topple over. She'll still enjoy fitting and sorting things and will also still get lots of fun out of filling and emptying containers. I find it fascinating that many of these activities which involve relating two objects together, appear just at the time that she begins to link two words together.

She begins to enjoy playdough now, although rather than actually making something she will have fun patting, pulling and twisting it. Similarly, she'll enjoy sitting in a sandpit, particularly if there are other children to look at, but she won't yet play or build with the sand.

Scribbling with coloured pencils or crayons continues to be a firm favourite, particularly as she can now imitate vertical strokes. Water is still a fun, if messy, plaything. Anything that makes a good noise will please her, and she'll be keen to show you all the new games she's discovered. This is a really great time for playing together.

INTERACTIVE PLAY

The interactive rhymes and language games that she's been learning over the past few months continue to play an important part in her playtimes, but whereas she used to value the safe, predictable repetition, she'll now love variation and even chaos brought into them. She will find it hilarious if you

The Toy Box

The following are a few ideas for play material you could add to her Toy Box at this stage. Remember though that babies are adept at finding their own ways of playing with different materials. Don't become frustrated when a wonderful toy you have bought is used in a completely different way to that you had envisaged.

PRETEND PLAY

Although she can use objects symbolically – for example, pushing a box along and pretending it's a car – realistic toys will encourage her a great deal.

★ Dishes and pretend food
★ A toy vacuum cleaner
★ Small dolls
★ Doll's pram, bedding, bath and towel
★ Toy vehicles

INVESTIGATIVE PLAY

★ Objects that float and sink, and more containers for water play
★ Very simple inset jigsaws
★ A screw toy
★ A pegboard with pegs of different heights
★ Playdough

pretend to get things wrong, as she is now very much an equal partner, indeed often taking the lead. For instance, you will find that she loves games in which the two of you take it in turns to change roles, such as hide and seek, run and chase.

All these games are wonderful for maintaining joint attention, but things like taking turns imitating each other, copying

The Book Shelf

By now, your child will probably really enjoy opening and closing books, and helping you to turn the pages, looking at the pictures as she does so. As before, looking at books needs to be a lovely interactive time where you both enjoy physical closeness, so let her lead, turning the pages as she wishes to, and give her as much time as she wants to look at everything. (Remember to *tell* her what the pictures are, rather than asking her!)

She will still enjoy lots of the books she already has, particularly those with interesting textures, those which make sounds, and those with interesting features such as flaps which can be lifted.

When choosing a book for her remember:

★ The content of the book should relate to her everyday experiences.

★ She will love simple, bright pictures containing quite a lot of detail and the pictures can now be of children doing familiar things, rather than simply pictures of objects. She will get a lot out of stories involving little sequences of familiar events, like going shopping or to the park. Those which lend themselves to lots of little sentences containing two important words, like 'Doggy's barking. He wants dinner. Here's his dinner' are perfect for her level of understanding.

★ She'll really enjoy repetition.

There are very many wonderful books which meet these criteria. The following are examples of those which do so beautifully.

★ *Where's the Cat?*, Sheila Blackstone and Debbie Harter (Barefoot Books)

CONTINUED

- ★ *Cats Sleep Anywhere*, Eleanor Farjeon and Anne Mortimer (Frances Lincoln)
- ★ *Spot Stays Overnight* (and other Spot books), Eric Hill (Puffin)
- ★ *Peek-a-Boo!*, Jan Ormerod (Bodley Head)
- ★ *Rock-a-Baby*, Jan Ormerod (Bodley Head)
- ★ *Pass the Parcel with Pig*, Jo Lodge (Bodley Head)
- ★ *Come On Daisy!*, Jane Simmons (Orchard Books)
- ★ *Little Kipper 5: Hissss!* (and other Kipper books), Mick Inkpen (Hodder Children's)
- ★ *Jump Like A Frog*, Kate Burns (David and Charles Children's)
- ★ *Miffy*, Dick Bruna (World International)
- ★ *Noisy Farm*, Rod Campbell (Puffin)

each other's facial expressions, or copying actions with a teddy or other soft toy, are particularly good.

PRETEND PLAY

Pretend play now begins to dominate interactive play. She will love to imitate what she sees you and other adults doing, although she'll probably stick to short single actions like pushing a sweeper along or pretending to use a dustpan and brush. Both boys and girls will also now like to play with small dolls or stuffed animals, feeding and bathing them and taking them for walks in a buggy, and will want to involve other people in these games increasingly frequently.

She will still play at mimicry throughout this time, and it can be extremely amusing to see yourself imitated reading, writing, cooking, and doing lots of other things. Every little idiosyncrasy is likely to be there!

TELEVISION AND VIDEOS

The same three important rules apply as in the previous age band.

★ Don't let her watch for more than half an hour a day. There is so much she needs to be doing at this very important age, in terms of play, having real experiences, and above all, interaction with other people. She will get none of this from the television.

★ If you are very keen for her to enjoy a programme or video, never leave her to watch it alone. Always watch it together so that it becomes an interactive experience.

★ Remember that she is just learning about the world and what objects are for and why people do what they do. She doesn't know, for example, that trains don't talk, and could well believe that they do, creating considerable confusion!

Children's videos are so visually attractive that they will watch them for many hours a day. I have seen many who have, with very serious results.

> Three-year-old Billy was causing great concern to his parents and playgroup leader. He interacted very little, even with his mother, his language development was extremely delayed and his play was bizarre. He had no idea of what to do with the toys, and just lined them up or twirled them round. I found that he had been watching videos for over six hours every day, from the age of a year. He had, of course, missed out on all the wonderful developments in play and interaction which have usually occurred by now. We made big changes to his life, mainly in terms of banning television altogether and establishing the BabyTalk Programme, and ensuring that he had lots of appropriate life experiences. Although he made steady progress, and went to school at four and a half with the skills expected for his age, I don't feel that he will ever reach his full potential, and am still concerned that he might have some social difficulties in the future.

Summary

To summarise, by the age of twenty months, your baby is likely to:

★ Imitate sounds such as those made by fire engines, planes or animals.
★ Copy little phrases like 'here we go'.
★ Point to a doll's hair, ears and shoe if asked.
★ Have a spoken vocabulary of anything between ten and fifty words.
★ Imitate two- or three-word sentences and some of the sounds she hears around her.
★ Understand the meaning of some words which are not names, such as 'eat' and 'sleep'.
★ Know what the words 'you' and 'me' refer to.

Cause for concern

Below are circumstances in which it would be advisable to seek professional advice about your little child's development. (Please remember, though, that many children progress at slightly different rates.)

If you are in any doubt about your baby, even if the reason for your concern is not mentioned here, do take her to see your health visitor or GP as soon as possible.

At twenty months it would be advisable to seek a professional opinion if:

★ She is not yet using any words.
★ She seems to have difficulty following a little sentence like 'Your shoes are in the kitchen'.
★ She doesn't want lots of attention from you.
★ She doesn't want you to play with her.
★ She doesn't often look around to see where sounds are coming from.

The Baby Talk Programme

Hopefully, you and your baby have been enjoying your daily playtimes together for some time now. Keep it up! Not only are you providing her with the very best possible opportunities for language learning, but you are also doing great things for her emotional development. Nothing gives a child more confidence than the knowledge that

> **Half an hour a day is still crucial**

Charlie was the third of three brothers who were all very close in age. I first saw him when he was three years old and had been brought to see me because he was only speaking in two- to three-word sentences. His mother was in despair, as he managed to wreck all the children's play activities. He even spoiled those he loved the most, like water games, which were now forbidden because of all the floods he had caused.

I was immediately struck by how unhappy Charlie seemed: he was white and tense, and hardly ever smiled. I talked to his mother about the importance of giving Charlie some of her undivided time, although I well understood that it was not going to be easy for her. However, with the help of friends and relatives, she managed to find a little time for Charlie almost every day and the effect was amazing. When I saw him two weeks later, he looked like a different child. His head was held high, there was colour in his cheeks, and he was a happy and confident little boy. His language was developing very quickly, and his mother told me that the naughty behaviour had almost stopped. Within four months, there were no worries about Charlie!

she has the regular undivided attention of a beloved adult. Little children who do not receive this tend to put huge amounts of energy into trying to obtain it and, sadly, they would often rather attract attention by doing things which are forbidden than not attract it at all.

THE SETTING FOR YOUR DAILY PLAYTIME

I can't stress this enough: KEEP IT QUIET! Your child's ability to select what she listens to and tune out everything else is still not well established, and could be completely lost without these quiet times. Check that television, music, radio and telephone are all off, and remind anyone in the house that you are only to be interrupted in the case of a dire emergency!

> **Turn the phone off in your quiet room**

I was very puzzled a while ago when the mother of a little girl called Zara reported that the extremely rapid progress she had been making on the BabyTalk Progamme had slowed down. Zara's mother assured me that she was following the programme to the letter, so I decided that the best thing would be to go to see them at home. I found that the next-door neighbour had music on so loudly that it was clearly audible in the room Zara and her mother played in. Zara's mother hadn't noticed it, as it was not at a level that would cause difficulties for an adult, but as soon as Zara and her mother moved their playtime to another part of the house, rapid progress resumed.

It makes a big difference to your child's attention development to be regularly in an environment in which there are not too many distractions so there is now a balance to be struck between having enough toys around so that she can move rapidly from one to another if she chooses to, and having so many that the environment is distracting. I tend to have plenty there for the child to choose from, but I make sure that there is lots of floor space for her to play on, and that the toys are arranged so that she can easily see what is there without needing to tip them all onto the floor. Make sure that you have toys which give her opportunities for both investigative and pretend play, including things like shape sorters, bricks, puzzles, dolls, noise-makers and a few books.

> **Space out your toys so she can see what's there**

HOW TO TALK

Some subtle and important differences in the way you need to talk to your child emerge over this period, because this is a time at which she can increase her understanding of words incredibly fast. She needs lots of play experiences, so that she learns what objects and events are all about, and she needs your help to understand the relevant words, so that she can then come to use them herself.

There is a huge amount that you can do to help at this stage, and be assured that this help will stand your child in good stead for the whole of her life.

★ Be aware of her attention level
It is crucial that you remain very sensitive to your child's level of attention development, which now fluctuates between rapid shifts of focus and prolonged and rigid concentration on objects or activities of her own choice. It isn't difficult to see what is happening once you are aware of these stages.

★ Don't impose your own agenda
Never try to direct her attention at this stage. If you try to shift her focus, particularly when she is concentrating intently, all

> **Never try to direct her attention**

that will happen is that you will both become very frustrated because she simply cannot comply. You just need to wait. I remember how frustrated I was by my elder son posting bricks down a cardboard tube for what seemed like ages when I was dying to show him a wonderful new toy, but you really can't force a child at this age to concentrate on your choice of toy.

It's a good idea to give running commentary, but don't be surprised if you feel that she is not always really listening to you. Remember, however, that the more exactly you can relate your speech to what is in her mind at that moment, the more likely it is that she will be able to listen.

★ Follow the focus of her attention

The amount of time in which you and your child share the same focus of attention is of paramount importance for her language learning, and she needs to lead this focus for the great majority of the time. Of course you can now sometimes draw her attention to something interesting, particularly outside your playtime, but during this concentrated time together let her be the leader.

There has been a great deal of research into how a shared focus of attention affects children, and the studies clearly demonstrate that a child is most likely to acquire new words if an adult follows her attention focus. For example, an American study undertaken in 1983 found a very strong relationship between the amount of time that the mothers of twelve- to eighteen-month-old infants shared their infant's focus of attention, and the size of the infants' vocabularies later.[4] Another study of eighteen month olds in the UK, carried out in 1993, made very similar findings: the infants' rate of word learning increased significantly when an adult followed their attention focus.[5]

So try to work out what is actually in her mind, and make a comment on that. Does she want the object named – 'It's a hippo' – or does she want you to do something with the object: 'Let's make teddy jump'? Or is she interested in what is happening, in which case you might explain 'It broke'? Babies are very skilled at communicating with gesture and facial expression so it's not usually difficult to work out what they're thinking. Go with the flow, allowing her to move her attention focus from one thing to another as often as she wishes. This won't go on for ever, and she will reach the stage when she is ready and able to accept adult direction much more quickly if she

> **Watch her face to work out what she's thinking – and then make an appropriate comment**

Naseem's family were in acute distress at his failure to use any words at all by the age of nearly two years. When I watched him playing with his father, I saw that his father was delivering a non-stop stream of questions and directions: 'Come and look at this, Naseem. What colour is it? How does it go? Right, let's look at this one then. How many bricks has it got in it? What shape is it? Say triangle.' Naseem was busy ignoring all of this, frequently turning his back on his father, and his father was becoming more and more frustrated. He was convinced that Naseem would only learn to speak if he was asked to do so, and to play by being told what to do. He took a great deal of convincing that the reason Naseem didn't yet speak was that he did not understand more than a few words.

Once I showed him how to help Naseem to increase that understanding, he worked very hard at changing his interaction style. It took him about a month, but as soon as he managed it, Naseem's progress very quickly convinced him that he was doing the right thing. I was delighted when he told me how much he and Naseem were enjoying their playtimes together. Four months later, Naseem's language development was considerably in advance of his age.

is allowed to go through these preceding stages at her own pace.

Remember, it is vital that you avoid questions and directions entirely in these playtimes, so always just comment on what she is interested in here and now. If you ask her a question, part of her mind is on working out the answer, or indeed on deciding whether or not to answer at all. Similarly, if you give her a direction, part of her mind is on deciding whether or not to follow it. Comments cause

Avoid questions and directions

her no stress, and are very much the easiest and most attractive kind of speech to listen to. I have found that some fathers, in particular, find it very difficult to do this, slipping very easily into questions and directions. With practice, however, most thoroughly enjoy going into a different mode once they see how much their child enjoys it.

★ **Help her to continue to enjoy listening**

It's important to make sure that your baby continues to enjoy listening to sound in an environment which makes it easy for

> Noisy toys and nursery rhymes make listening fun

her. There is noise almost everywhere we go now – in shops, restaurants and even in the streets – and your playtimes are possibly the only occasion for her to listen properly. So continue with the activities you've been building up over the last few months.

★ Play with noise-makers such as musical instruments or containers which make different sounds when shaken.

★ Tell or sing her rhymes. Not only do they help her to learn that listening to voices is fun, but it has been found that children who have been exposed to lots of nursery rhymes are better readers later. The strong rhythm and high level of repetition enable children to understand a great deal about how syllables and words are constructed, which they can easily translate to the written form later on.

★ Show her where sounds come from whenever the opportunity arises. As you open a box at her request, for example, you could show her where the clicking sound originated – *if* she is interested.

★ Help her to crack the language code.

It is vital that you continue to use short simple sentences, to help her to link words with their meanings. It is so much easier, for example, to recognise the key words in a sentence like 'Car's on the table', than in 'Let's put all your cars on the trans-porter and then pretend that the table is the seaside and that's where we are taking them'. This is rather an extreme example, but I'm frequently surprised at the long and complex sentences some parents use with sixteen-month-old children.

You can use lots and lots of new words. She can learn to understand as many as nine new ones a day, as long as you put them into short sentences which make it clear what the key word is and exactly what it refers to. So when you think you may be using a word she does not know, put it into a little sentence which has only one important word in it, such as 'Here's a hedgehog', or 'It's huge'. Do make sure your sentences are grammatical though. For example, 'Daddy's gone to work' is, and 'Daddy work' is not!

One big change in the way you can now talk to your child is that she is likely to understand little sentences containing two important words. So use lots and lots of sentences with two key words, like 'Your shoes are in the kitchen', 'Teddy wants his dinner', 'Your fingers are sticky' and 'Johnny's in the park'.

Keep your sentences short!

Keeping to this length of sentence is very important indeed, so don't be tempted to gallop away into long sentences yet! I've seen many children in the clinic where exactly this had happened, and whose language development, having started well, slowed right down.

Rachel was an enchanting little blonde girl who came with her family to see me when she was nearly two. She looked the picture of health, but her mother had convinced herself that Rachel must have some terrible degenerative illness, because she had been acquiring new words very fast indeed up to two months previously, but her progress seemed to have stopped very suddenly, and she had only acquired two in the last few weeks. When I listened to Rachel's mother talking to her, I realised what had happened. She was using enormously long sentences, like 'Oh look! There's a sweet little tiny shopping basket which would be just right for a picnic if we made this plasticene into lots of little sandwiches and cakes and fruit.' Rachel alternated between looking bemused and switching off entirely. It emerged that her understanding of speech had developed very rapidly in the preceding weeks, and her mother was convinced that she 'understood everything' and could now be spoken to like an adult. As soon as she went back to speaking to Rachel in short sentences which were within her level of understanding, Rachel's rapid rate of language acquisition returned. When I saw her at two and a half, she was understanding and using speech like a three year old.

★ Continue to make play sounds

Play sounds help your child to focus her attention, to enjoy listening to voices, and give her the opportunity to hear speech sounds separately rather than in a rapidly changing stream of speech. Her games will often lend themselves very well to such play sounds now:

> **You can learn a lot from 'splish splosh', 'der der' and 'moo'!**

- ★ 'Splish splosh', 'drip drip' and 't t t t t' work very well with water games.
- ★ 'Crashshshsh', 'brmm brmm' and 'der der' naturally accompany games with cars and trucks.
- ★ 'Baa baa', 'moo moo' and 'miaow' really liven up games with toy animals.

★ Speak slowly, loudly and tunefully

This is still the kind of speech your baby will find the most easy and attractive to listen to. It helps her to focus on your speech and is also enormously helpful in sorting out which sounds go where in which words.

Marcus was brought to my clinic at nearly four because only his mother could understand what he said, and school was on the horizon. He was clearly very intelligent, and immensely keen to communicate. It emerged that his understanding of speech was fine, and so was his spoken vocabulary and sentence construction. The problem was his speech sounds, which were in a state of total confusion. They were nearly all there, but Marcus was quite unsure of what went where in which words. His mother was probably the fastest speaker I have ever heard. I had to do a double-take at times to try to work out what she had said if it was out of context. Slowing her speech down so that Marcus could begin to notice which sound went where was the most important part of the BabyTalk Programme for him. When I showed his mother the appropriate speed for her speech to him, within an hour he had begun to use some sounds in the right places.

★ Use lots of repetition

Repetition is still very important indeed, so use the same words both in different sentences and in different situations. This is essential both in helping your child to understand the meaning of individual words more fully, and also in enabling her to hear the sounds many times so that eventually she will be able to recall them accurately.

> **Repetition clarifies words for her**

- ★ Use the same word in lots of different little phrases and sentences, for example, 'There's the elephant. Elephant's huge. A huge elephant'.
- ★ Labelling games are still useful and fun. Babies at this age love repetitious ones like 'Teddy's nose, Teddy's ears, Teddy's eyes. Sally's nose, Sally's ears, Sally's eyes' and so on.
- ★ Some daily activities also lend themselves well to repetition: for example, 'Pants off, shoe off, sock off' at bedtime, and 'wash your hands, wash your face, wash your feet' at bathtime.

★ Use names a lot

Your baby is still building up her vocabulary, and needs to hear the names of objects many, many times. So make a point of using names rather than pronouns. It would be better, for example, to say 'Let's put the book on the table' than 'Let's put it on there'.

> **Tell her the names of things**

I'm often asked if it's a good idea to use baby words like 'tummy' and 'horsie' at this stage. The answer is a resounding yes. These have become consistently used variations in nursery speech and indeed in nursery rhymes, because they make it so easy for the baby to notice the sounds in them and also to say them. Compare, for example, saying 'Tummy' with 'stomach'. Doesn't 'gee gee' stand out more easily than 'horse'? Don't worry, they won't stick for ever. Your baby will soon use the adult forms.

★ **Repeat what she has said back to her**

As we know, little children often don't pronounce words in the adult way, largely because they cannot remember which sounds go where. They need to hear them over and over again, until eventually they can recall them correctly. Repeating back to her correctly will help her enormously at this stage.

> Repeat what she says back to her – but *don't* sound as if you're correcting

A word of caution, however. It is vital that you are extremely careful that it never sounds as if you are correcting her, so the golden rule is always to start with a 'yes'. If she says 'nana', you could say 'Yes, it's a banana. Would you like the banana?' Her two-word sentences can also be a little confused, and again, the most helpful thing you can do is to say them back to her correctly, as part of the natural conversation. If she says 'Car Daddy', you could say 'Yes, that's Daddy's car'. That way you don't sound as if she's done something wrong. My colleagues and I have seen many children whose communicative attempts have been corrected, and who consequently made fewer and fewer such attempts.

Three-year-old Anna's mother was extremely keen for her to 'speak nicely'. She responded to most of Anna's early words by looking her firmly in the eye, and slowly and deliberately repeating each syllable she had said. I remember Anna being delighted at coming upon a little elephant in the toy box. Wanting to share the discovery with her mother, she held it out and said 'efant!'. Her mother, rather than affirming the communication Anna had made, looked at her with an expressionless face, and very slowly said 'e-le-phan-t'. Anna's disappointment was palpable. She dropped the toy, and made no further attempt to share her discoveries with her mother. Once again, the change in the whole relationship between Anna and her mother was a joy to see once the mother altered her response to Anna's communications.

★ **Repeat what she means back to her**

It is still very important to reflect back the meaning of her communications when she communicates only partly verbally, which still happens a lot. She needs you to show that you understand what she is trying to tell you. So always focus on her message, and not on the way she is communicating it. She might point at the sky for example, saying 'eeeooow', and showing by her facial expression and body language that the plane she can see is of huge interest to her. She wants you to share this excitement, showing by your facial expression and the enthusiastic tone in your voice as you say 'Yes, what a big plane!' that you too find it very interesting. The more responsive you are as a communicative partner, whatever form her communication takes, the better her future language development will be.

> **Respond to her message**

★ **Show her what you mean**

It is still very important that you help her to know exactly what you mean, by using gesture and adding language at the exact moment you are doing something, for example saying 'I'm pouring the tea, and in goes the milk,' as it happens.

> **Fit the words to the actions**

SOME 'DON'TS'!

★ **Never comment on the way she has said something, or the fact that she has said it!**

> I don't know who was more frustrated, Umar or his parents. He was a long-awaited first child, living in an extended family, and the apple of everyone's eye. Almost every time he spoke, an adult joyfully reported it to some of the others, in front of him. This had made him very self-conscious, and he had stopped talking. His powerful desire to communicate was clearly in conflict with a strong feeling of self-consciousness. As soon as his family realised what the problem was, and only shared their excitement about his prowess out of his hearing, Umar began to talk happily and constantly.

★ Continue to avoid negative speech

Your baby's explorations are still very likely to involve danger-ous activities like trying to climb the chimney, and investigat-ing your prized ornaments. You will have to move her away bodily, and it's still important not to accompany this by the kind of speech none of us likes to listen to such as 'Stop it', 'Don't touch', or 'Put that down at once!' You want her to feel that your voice is something she very much wants to listen to.

★ Questions

The golden rule is: Never ask her a question unless you need to know the answer. There is no point in 'What's that?', or 'What does the cow say?'. If she knows the answer already, you have added nothing to her knowledge, and if she does not, you just make her feel uncomfortable.

Don't ask questions!

Christopher's frantic parents brought him to see me when he was two and a half. It emerged that he had started speaking early, to the delight of all the family. He had then had a series of ear infections in his second year, which are very likely to have affected his hearing. He did what many children who have this problem do: he began to concentrate on looking and handling and to engage less in conversation, because he found it stressful in the noisy environment he shared with his older brother and sister. As soon as his parents noticed that he was speaking less, they did what most concerned parents do, and began to try to get Christopher to speak by asking him endless questions like 'What colour is this?', 'What does the cow say?' and 'What's this?'. Christopher knew perfectly well that they knew the answers to the questions, and began to feel increasingly pressured. As a result, he spoke less and less, and the whole situation had become a vicious circle. Once the circle was broken it was amazing how rapidly Christopher's language development flourished. I saw him recently at the age of five, and was very pleased to hear that he is doing exceptionally well in school.

If you are a father doing the programme, it is likely that you will find this difficult. In my experience, this is always the hardest thing for fathers to do. I have known many who were doing all the rest of the programme beautifully, but could not resist the temptation to ask questions to get their little children to say words. Believe me, your little child will come on more quickly if you can bring yourself to resist this temptation!

I know it's very difficult, but please try to make sure that nobody else asks your child questions of this kind. This is very important. One of the central principles of the BabyTalk Programme is that it is based entirely on input, with no demands at any time for output. If we talk to children in the right way, they will look after their own talking.

OUTSIDE YOUR HALF HOUR A DAY

★ Talk to her a lot! Tell her about whatever is going on.
★ Involve her in lots of different activities, like visiting friends, going to the park or the shops.
★ Make a game of naming her body parts as you wash her, and her clothes as you dress her.
★ If you can manage it, talk to her as much of the time as you can in the same way as in your half an hour playtime.

20 to 24 months

An overview

Your toddler will be co-operative for much of the time, thoroughly enjoying some newly acquired skills and making life easier for you. He'll actively help to dress and undress himself for example, and wash his hands without much help. He can at last feed himself with a spoon without making much mess. He can amuse himself for up to half an hour now if you are busy, which is quite a boon, and loves to do little errands for you too, like fetching or putting away something. There's still a very long way to go to true independence though. He can become very anxious if you leave him at this stage, and very demanding of your attention. He may discover sudden needs for food and drink at bedtime to postpone his separation from you, and all his new-found independence can disappear very fast if he is tired or unwell.

Please note that the developmental stages described here are averages only.

All babies develop at slightly different rates, and often progress in one area can result in a temporary delay in another. Do not get worried or depressed if your child does not appear to be doing everything at exactly the time periods mentioned here. For further information, see Cause for Concern, page 210.

His increasing sense of self leads him at times to start to engage in battles of will with you. He may refuse food, or try to resist wearing a particular garment. He may now continue to insist for some time, which can require heroic diplomacy.

He still loves his outings, the more so if he has plenty of time to stop and chat and look at everything. He's likely to be happy to hold your hand, but watch out for sudden dartings off.

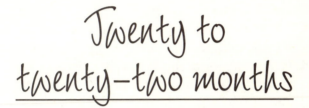

Twenty to twenty–two months

THE DEVELOPMENT OF LANGUAGE

Many little children are now really taking off both in terms of understanding and use of language, although there is a very wide variation in language abilities in this age group. Conversation skills are well established, and conversation with this age group becomes an absolute delight. Adults often feel very much that the child is an equal partner, in that he takes as big a role as the adult in maintaining the conversation by means of clear turn-taking. He also takes an equal part now in terms of repairing any breakdowns in communication, and seeking or giving further information to clarify a topic. His mother might say, for example, 'We'll see Mary later', and he may reply 'Mary house?' He becomes extremely persevering in engaging others in conversation, and is virtually impossible to resist.

Understanding of speech continues to develop rapidly. This is greatly helped, as we have seen, by the little child's increasing knowledge and understanding of the sequences of events within all his daily routines. He now understands these in much more detail than he did previously, when he only had an awareness of the broad outlines. He knows and anticipates now, for example, not only the point in the day that he will be dressed, but also the sequence in which his clothes are put on him. Similarly, he may be aware of the transaction of money after going round the supermarket, and the events around packing and unpacking the shopping. This knowledge helps him to attach meaning to new words extremely easily. The name of a new garment, for instance, or the word 'money', would readily be understood in the context of those he knew already. Similarly, he would understand the word 'soap-dish' without difficulty, once he was aware of the purpose of soap, its slippery qualities and tendency to disappear into the bath water.

An extremely important development is that he is now coming to understand much about the ways in which language is used. He knows, for example, the situations in which it is appropriate to use greetings, and when he is being asked for clarification.

He also now has some understanding of what other people know, which is very vital information for the initiation and maintenance of conversation. He realises, for example, that when he refers to his brother by name, everyone in his family knows exactly who he is talking about, but that the doctor or somebody he has just met does not, and needs to be told. Even adults have problems with this at times. I recently rang up to find the exact whereabouts of a stately home I wanted to visit. When the phone was answered, I said: 'Could you tell me exactly where you are, please?' The reply came back: 'I'm standing by the telephone.'

The number of words the little child recognises now grows at an ever-expanding rate, and several may be added every day. By the time he is twenty-two months, he is likely to recognise the names of all the objects in his home which have relevance to him.[1] He also shows increasingly good understanding of sentences containing two important words. You may notice him responding with alacrity to instructions like 'Get your hat from the cupboard'. He may even be able to follow a little series of three simple instructions. 'Open the cupboard, take out the ball and give it to Daddy' might for example be managed at this time. The little child also shows a new ability to identify objects which are not referred to directly: for example, something referred to by place as in 'the one by the cooker', or by a pronoun as in 'give it to him'.

This is also a time of rapid expansion of **speech** vocabulary, although as before, there is still a huge gap between understanding and use of words. As we have heard, understanding can increase by several new words every day, and production simply cannot keep up with this. At the beginning of this time period, he is likely to be understanding as many as two hundred words or even more, and only using somewhere between ten and fifty of them. Children with vocabularies at the top end of this range may already be linking words and imitating two-word sentences.

Most other children now begin the rapid expansion in spoken vocabulary, producing more new words every week. Those who have not usually begin this now, very quickly catching up. This rapid increase in spoken vocabulary tends to last throughout this period. The new words he acquires are now of more varied types, and include more verbs, and some adjectives like 'fat' and 'thin'. This enables him to produce many more two-word sentences of a wide range of different kinds. It's interesting that infants show great consistency in these early sentences, most of which are often key action words combined with names, such as 'Mummy come', 'go sleep' or 'Bye Bye Daddy'. He sometimes puts a stress on the important word to make quite sure he is well understood, saying for example, 'Daddy *gone*'.

Your child's increased spoken vocabulary and range of types of words now enables him to widen considerably the range of ways in which he uses language, although again there are wide variations in this. He begins for the first time to try to tell other people about interesting events he has seen or experienced. He doesn't have quite enough language to do this entirely verbally, and often has to supplement words with gestures and pantomime, filling in the gaps with babble. It can be quite a problem working out what he means at times, particularly if he is excited. In this new situation of talking about events which are not present, he may begin to use some past tenses, although often not entirely accurately. You may for example hear something like 'He goed'.

Question forms begin to come in now, such as 'Where dat?' A friend of mine reported that the first question her granddaughter asked was 'Where sink?'

He also begins to use negatives now, usually at the beginning of the sentence, for example 'No drink' meaning 'I don't want a drink'.

Another big step forward is that he recognises that words can be used to stand for whole categories of object, such as animals or clothing, and to use them in this way.

Although he has so many more words now, babble has not entirely disappeared, and is used at times as 'padding' between true words when he can't quite produce the whole string he would like to.

GENERAL DEVELOPMENT

Your child's ability to move around and explore his environment is developing apace, enabling him to acquire the experiences he needs for language to continue to develop meaningfully. His increasing control over his body means that he can now concentrate more fully on what he is doing and learning, rather than on how he is going to reach a particular object, and how he will handle it when he does so.

In terms of mobility, he can now run smoothly, and even walk backwards. He can squat on his haunches, and lean forward to pick up a toy without overbalancing. He can now also throw a ball without falling over and kick it on request. He walks upstairs holding the handrail, and can propel a 'ride-on' toy, using his feet to propel himself along the floor.

Manual dexterity and hand-eye co-ordination are developing fast as well, enabling him to explore objects to his heart's content. He thoroughly enjoys these new-found abilities. He can hold a pencil with thumb and two fingers to scribble, and for the first time can turn the pages of a book singly and skilfully. His eyesight is now as good as that of adults, and he can thread a shoelace through a large hole. He can fit shapes into a three-hole form-board after a demonstration, and build a tower of seven bricks.[2] The first idea of number sometimes begins to develop now, as he acquires a vague idea of the difference between 'one ' and 'many'.

Your child now very much enjoys being shown what to do with toys, and will pull an adult to show her a toy. He will imitate the adult's actions with the toy: for example, he will pull a train after being shown how to do so.

He has as yet no concept of playing with other children, but will happily play alongside them. He certainly has no idea at all about sharing, and will protest vigorously if another child grabs his toy!

A little role play starts at this time, and he may, for example, pretend to be his mother writing a letter or his father going shopping.

ATTENTION

You are likely to see him often giving very concentrated attention to what he is doing or watching now. This attention is still entirely 'single channelled' in that its focus totally absorbs him. You will find now, though, that he can almost always listen to meaningful language added in a fun way to what is happening, and so increases his enjoyment. A game of 'Where's Johnny gone?' as you pull his jersey over his head, for example, would receive his delighted attention, whereas 'come on, let's get you dressed so we can go out' will not. This can seem puzzling to parents, but the difference is that in the former case, that which the baby is thinking about, doing and interested in are exactly the same thing, and in the latter they are not!

LISTENING

If you have been following the programme, your child is likely now to be able to choose what he wants to listen to, and continue to do so for as long as he wishes. He still, however, needs a much bigger difference between the background sound and what he is listening to than an adult does to be able to do this, and he is also still relatively easily distracted. The proviso 'what he wants to listen to' remains very important: this ability to listen selectively still only relates to his chosen focus of attention and not to someone else's.

He will have built up his understanding of the meanings of most everyday sounds now, for example those connected with domestic routines, like the vacuum cleaner and the voices of many people in his life.

Twenty–two to twenty–four months

THE DEVELOPMENT OF LANGUAGE

From the age of around twenty months, his communications become more frequent and diversified, and there are some interesting and important developments. Your child begins to use language to express his feelings, rather than doing so by crying or fussing. He might say firmly, for instance, 'Johnny cross'. He also starts to initiate conversation by using a name, for example, catching his mother's attention by calling out 'Mummy'. Even more importantly, he now begins to try to tell others of his experiences by an eloquent mixture of babble, words, gesture and pantomime. Questions also begin to appear in his conversation for the first time, such as 'Where Daddy?'

Your child now begins to attach meaning to words more and more rapidly, and there are a number of factors which enable him to do this:

As in the previous time period, his increasing **understanding** of 'how the world works' in terms of the meaning and sequence of his daily activities helps him to understand more and more of the language he hears around him. When out shopping with his mother, for example, he is now likely to anticipate the whole sequence of events from the items of food going into the shopping trolley to appearing on the table. As a result, it wouldn't be difficult for him to deduce the meaning of the word 'tomato' in the sentence 'These tomatoes will go with the egg you are having for tea'.

Another factor that helps him to link words very easily with their meanings is that he begins to be able to fit them into categories. At this stage, he understands and fits new words into broad categories such as body parts or clothing.

Another interesting little step is that he now identifies many more toys, people and animals by name, showing that he now really does understand that words can represent not only objects, but also representations of objects.

His increasing understanding of the ways in which language is used – for example, when it is appropriate to use a greeting or when to give information – coupled with his now good knowledge of the 'rules' of conversation, are also of great help to him in working out the meaning of new words. Hearing the word 'cheerio', in a context in which he usually hears 'bye bye', for instance, makes it easy for him to know that the new word is a variant of 'bye bye'.

All this rich knowledge about how the world works and the ways in which language is used enable him to learn the meaning of words increasingly efficiently and rapidly, which is quite a remarkable feat considering that he only joined the party less than two years ago.

By the time he reaches the age of two years, he can usually understand quite long and complicated sentences, and the meaning and reason behind them. He would understand, for example, sentences like 'When Mummy comes home, we'll play hide and seek' (and remember it when the time came) and also the reason behind his father saying 'I'll close the window to keep the rain out'.

All this amazingly rapid increase in understanding is way ahead of his ability to use language, although this, too, is making great strides. The rapid expansion in **speech** vocabulary continues, and by the time he is two, your little child may be using as many as two hundred words consistently, or even more. By that time, he uses many different kinds of words: more verbs (like 'swimming' or 'playing'); adjectives (like 'big ' and 'small'); adverbs (like 'quickly' and 'slowly') and some pronouns, although these tend to be confused at this stage: for example 'Her gone'. This word variety helps him greatly in putting together more and more little two-word phrases and sentences like 'Joey slide,' 'going quickly', or 'Mummy jumping'. He is now generating grammar. He usually refers to himself by name, to ensure that there is no confusion, as in 'Johnny biscuit'. Names, however, are still the words used most frequently by most little children at this stage.

He begins to use negatives like 'no' or 'not want', and for the first time, his use of negatives now extends into denial. He might for example tell you 'no drop' meaning 'I didn't drop the plate'. He also extends his use of questions, enquiring for example, 'Where Daddy go?'

He begins to copy three-word sentences at times, and by the age of two, may even put some together himself, such as 'Johnny want drink'. He has now truly begun to use not only words, but also grammar.

These little phrases and sentences still often have some words missing at this stage, but usually convey his meaning pretty clearly.

Yet another little milestone is that he can now give both his first and second name if he has been taught to do so.

The 'babble drift' – the process in which the sounds not in his mother tongue cease to appear in the little child's speech – is now complete, but his pronunciation is still quite a bit at variance with that of adults. He continues to replace difficult to say sounds by easier ones, for example, 'tat' for 'cat' and 'tair' for 'chair'. Clusters of sounds are still reduced, as in 'tep' for 'step', and sounds and syllables which do not have a stress on them omitted as in 'bella' for 'umbrella'. Interestingly, he can clearly detect these substitutions in the speech of others. You will find that if you mispronounce a word in the way in which your little child does, you will get a very funny look indeed, and he may even try to correct you, continuing to use his version of the word.

This considerable increase in the ability to use language results in a huge enthusiasm for conversation. Your child now expects to engage adults in conversation, and perseveres determinedly if he doesn't get a response. A busy adult may find him or herself subject to pulls, pushes and very persistent and repetitive vocalisations. The little child is also extremely keen to repair any breakdown in communication, and will go to great lengths to be understood by means of alternative words, if necessary supplemented by gesture and pantomime.

Once again, intellectual and language processes are developing in parallel. Of particular importance at this stage is the continued development of concepts and categories. This results in the child's ability to use meaningfully the words relating to those concepts, such as rough and smooth, wide and narrow, and to understand that words can refer to whole categories such as clothing or animals.

GENERAL DEVELOPMENT

There are many developments in motor ability at this time, all of which help in your child's world exploration. He can climb on a chair to look out of the window, and walk upstairs two feet to a step. Other motor skills at this time are those of walking backwards while pulling a toy, and picking up a toy from the floor without falling over. He can now throw a ball overhead, and sit on a small tricycle and propel it with his feet. The great paediatrician Arnold Gesell coined a wonderful phrase about the two year old: 'He thinks with his muscles'. He comments on the total interdependence of motor and mental activity at this stage, describing how the two year old 'talks while he acts and acts while he talks'.[3]

Manipulative skills are also developing fast. The little child can pick up tiny objects with a very fine grip, like pins and thread, can make a train of three bricks, and can turn the pages of a book singly. His eye-hand co-ordination now enables him to insert shapes into a simple form-board, not only when it is facing him, but also when it is turned at an angle.

He is becoming a little more independent now in terms of daily living skills, and by two years can remove most of his clothing, wash his hands with little help, and feed himself well with a spoon which he manages not to turn over.

By the time he is two years old, as Gesell also comments, he has an emotional life of considerable depth and complexity, and can show considerable sensitivity to the feelings of others. He likes things to remain the same as, after all, it is not long since he learned to anticipate the pattern of his days. Change needs to be gradual and gentle.

ATTENTION

There is little difference in attention development from that of the last two months. You may wonder why he is still so difficult to direct when he can now concentrate so beautifully on what he's doing when he wants to! Don't worry – it won't be long before he moves into the next stage, in which he will be able to shift the focus of his attention with your help, and to follow your directions. Please resist the temptation to try to bring this about before he's ready. Although it is probably just possible now, it really does all happen by far the best and earliest when you allow him to progress through the stages at his own rate.

LISTENING

The little child now lives in a world in which most of the sounds he hears are meaningful to him, and which he can locate easily. Listening is now a big source of pleasure in his life, as he loves not only voices speaking and singing to him, but increasingly has fun playing with noise-making toys.

Be aware still, though, that he will still find listening very difficult if there is much background sound. You may, for example, find yourself ignored in noisy settings like the supermarket for this reason!

INVESTIGATIVE PLAY

Your child is now really into investigation; his passion to understand the world is boundless. He loves to explore different materials, and in doing so learns a great deal about their properties. Water play delights him still, and will continue to do so for some considerable time to come. He loves to pour

A little girl of four, named Melissa, was brought to my clinic recently because she had not been accepted into the school of her parents' choice, which had a selection test even at this very early age. I found that her mother was extremely house-proud, and as a result had very much limited the kind of play she allowed Melissa to engage in. She had never been allowed to play with water, sand, clay or playdough, and certainly not with crayons or paints. Scissors were also forbidden, and Melissa had not been able to spread play materials such as bricks around the floor, or to move the furniture about in any way. As the result of all these restrictions, Melissa, who was a much loved and beautifully cared for child, had lacked experience to the degree where her concepts, and consequently her understanding and use of language, were well below those to be expected at her age. Melissa caught up with her age level in terms of language skills within six months of starting the BabyTalk Programme, but I felt very sad, as I was sure that had she been able to have a wider range of experiences earlier, her attainments could have been considerably higher than this.

water from one container to another, and to find out what floats and what sinks slowly and not so slowly. As we have said before, this play is wonderful for building up concepts such as quick, slow, closer and further, first and last, to which language can so readily be attached. Children who do not have these experiences, or only to a very limited extent, are at a very great disadvantage.

Clay and playdough are still very much enjoyed at this stage, and the child begins a little basic manipulation when he approaches the age of two, banging clay with a cutter or roller. For example, he now enjoys still more scribbling with a fat crayon or pencil, and will do so for longer spells, marking the paper more heavily.

Sand is also popular now, and rather than just sitting in it as he did at earlier times, the little child now likes to tip it into a truck or wheelbarrow.

Throwing games are fun too, and lend themselves well to turn-taking, now often with several people.

The little child's increased manipulative ability and longer concentration span now enable him to enjoy toys that need more effort and finer control of his hands. He likes to try to put giant beads onto a lace rather than a rod, and to do very simple jigsaw puzzles rather than just simple inset form-boards. He loves toys that fit together, and particularly enjoys those which are graded, like sets of Russian dolls or barrels.

Matching and sorting continue to be of great interest too, and he much enjoys games like large picture dominoes, colour matching games and large beads.

He also now begins to show interest in construction toys, as long as these are large and very easy to fit together: for example, large interlocking bricks or stickle bricks. He doesn't try to build anything yet, but his enjoyment in manipulating the materials and finding out how they go together will stand him in very good stead a little later on when he does.

He has a much more sophisticated idea of cause and effect now, and relishes toys like a jack in the box or other pop-up toy, where his actions can result in such a dramatic effect.

INTERACTIVE AND PRETEND PLAY

The very favourite play of children of this age is 'helping' adults in their daily activities and re-enacting them in play in an attempt to find out the meaning of all that they do. You will find that your little child watches you intently, and later shows in his play that he remembers what you were doing when he imitates the activity. This is still usually single actions like putting potatoes into a pan. The little child will also re-enact many of these activities with his teddies or dollies, and very much enjoys adults joining in this play.

His increasing knowledge of 'how the world works' is also shown in his appropriate use of objects and materials. He now, for example, correctly places both the doll's pillow and cover, and puts knife, fork and plate on the table. He loves toys that represent implements used by adults, such as a toy iron and ironing board.

He also loves to play with model people, objects and animals, such as a farm or zoo with animals, or a garage and vehicles. A simple doll's house can be very much enjoyed at this time. These toys will stand the little child in good stead for a long time to come, as he will be able to play with them with increasing complexity.

Adults have a very important role in all his play now. In terms of manipulative and investigative play, he loves an adult to show him ways in which his toys can be used, but then likes him or her to withdraw while he then tries out for himself what he has been shown. Little children at this stage can benefit most from this kind of adult intervention when they have mastered the basic skills, and the adult is showing them a variation. For example, once he has learned to thread beads, being shown how to make a pattern with alternate colours could be an interesting development.

Adult involvement in pretend play is also very much welcomed. Turn-taking is still found to be great fun, and can become a lovely part of this play, for example in games involving feeding teddies and dolls, or taking turns to be the shopkeeper and the shopper. In both this and imaginative play, the adult can make helpful suggestions like showing him where the furniture goes in a doll's house, or helping to set up the materials for a shopping game.

Rhymes and songs are still very popular, and will continue to be so for a very long time to come. The little child at this stage loves those involving actions, such as 'Row, row, row your boat', or 'The wheels on the bus'. He particularly relishes rhymes in which the words relate to people or objects he knows, made up to go with traditional songs with a familiar tune.

As in the previous time period, your little child likes to play on his own at times, although he usually wants to be near his parent, and is likely to cry if he or she leaves. Once again, considerable sensitivity is needed to recognise when he wants the adult to join in and for how long, and when he wants to get on with his explorations and activities by himself.

There is still not yet any real play with other children. Two toddlers may be engaged in pretend play side by side, but the only interaction is likely to be the occasional grab at one another's toys.

TELEVISION AND VIDEOS

The three rules of earlier times still hold.

★ It is important to limit your little child's viewing to half an hour a day.

★ It is also very important that you watch with him, so that the experience becomes an interactive one, and you can help to relate what he sees to his own experiences.

★ Do make sure, too, that the content relates to the world as he is coming to learn about it and not about events which do not really occur, as was discussed in the previous chapter. His limited experience of the world makes him still unready for those.

Now that he is able to follow a little story, programmes which depict children and animals in situations he would

The Toy Box

The following toys and play materials would make good additions to your little child's toy box at this stage. They are again divided into those likely to be used for investigative and for imaginative play, but as at earlier times, he may think of ways of playing with them that you would never have thought of!

INVESTIGATIVE PLAY

★ More containers for water play, such as squeezy bottles and different shaped containers
★ Simple rolling pin or cutter for playdough
★ Truck or wheelbarrow which can go in the sandpit
★ Giant beads and a lace
★ Russian dolls or interlocking barrels
★ Large picture dominoes
★ Colour matching game
★ Large interlocking bricks
★ Some new noise-makers, such as more musical instruments or filled containers which make new interesting noises
★ Jack in the box or other pop-up toy

INTERACTIVE AND PRETEND PLAY

★ Shopping bag
★ Iron and ironing board
★ Washing-up bowl and brush
★ Zoo with animals
★ Farm with animals
★ Garage and more vehicles
★ Doll's house and furniture

The Book Shelf

It's now very important indeed to establish a routine when you share a book with your little child on a daily basis. This could be part of your daily playtime, at bedtime, or whenever it conveniently fits into your day.

I can't overestimate the importance of this from this time onwards. The extent to which books are shared between adults and children in the pre-school years is the best predictor of reading success later. It isn't the early teaching of reading which achieves this, and in fact too early teaching can have a strongly adverse effect. It is the sheer enjoyment in books that matters, as they become part of a lovely interactive situation.

When we looked at the results of our follow-up study, we found that some of the children who had extremely high spoken language skills disappointingly had only average reading ability. We thought that this was likely to be because they had rarely shared books with an adult before they went to school. Sadly, very many children now arrive at school in this situation, some of them not even aware of how to open a book, that the text runs from left to right, and that the story continues from one page to another.

Regarding content, your little child will certainly still enjoy those books added at the previous age band. He will continue to love those to which you can attach lots of 'play sounds', such as those about animals and vehicles: these are wonderful for helping him to acquire a very early appreciation of the fact that sounds can be represented in books. This is a vital realisation, which will lead him towards that crucial ability later to associate sounds with their written forms. 'Play sounds' are also very helpful in helping him to become aware of the separate sounds within words, which is essential for later reading.

Rhyme books are great now. The resulting awareness of sounds and ability to rhyme is a very important precursor of reading. In fact, inability to rhyme is a marker of poor readers.

His increasing understanding of language, and longer attention span, now make it possible also to enjoy simple stories. Reality is still very important in terms of these. He is not yet ready for fantasy, as he is still building up and consolidating his knowledge of the world, and could easily become confused. As before, the best stories are those which relate to his own experiences, as we have seen how much that helps him to attach meaning to words. These predictable patterns and sequences of activities help to reinforce his knowledge of 'how the world works', particularly as you can talk to him about how the events in the stories relate to his own experiences. When he understands the basic sequences of events, it is very easy for him to attach meaning to any new words that come into the sequence. It is interesting that children use more correct sentences when talking about routines with which they have become very familiar.

As before, repetition in the stories is found to be highly enjoyable.

Made-up stories about himself, possibly around photographs, are still enormously popular, and he would find it huge fun to match the photos to the real objects in his home.

Some of the many wonderful books which meet these criteria are:

★ *A First Picture Book of Nursery Rhymes*, Elizabeth Harbour (Puffin)
★ *The Oxford Nursery Book*, Ian Beck (OUP)
★ *So Much*, Trish Cooke and Helen Oxenbury (Walker Books)

CONTINUED

- ★ *Barnyard Banter*, Denise Fleming (Red Fox)
- ★ *Going to Playschool*, Sarah Garland (Bodley Head)
- ★ *Humpty Dumpty and Other Rhymes*, Maureen Roffey (Bodley Head)
- ★ *Everyone Hide from Wibbly Pig*, Mick Inkpen (Hodder Children's)
- ★ *The Jolly Postman*, Janet and Allan Ahlberg (Viking Children's)
- ★ *Cat is Sleepy*, Satoshi Kitamura (Andersen Press)

recognise can be fun. As with books, repetition is good, and series where the same characters do and say the same or similar things can be much enjoyed.

Summary

To summarise, by the time he is two, your little child is likely to:

- ★ Understand quite long and complicated sentences.
- ★ Use around fifty words.
- ★ Link two words together, and occasionally three.
- ★ Use words (pronouns) such as he and she, him and her, but with some mistakes.

Cause for concern

Below are circumstances in which it would be advisable to seek professional advice about your little child's development. (Please remember, though, that many children progress at slightly different rates.)

If you are in any doubt about your child, even if the reason for your concern is not mentioned here, do take him to see your Health Visitor or GP as soon as possible.

At two years it would be advisable to seek a professional opinion if:

★ You notice that he doesn't seem to understand the names of lots of everyday objects, such as furniture or cutlery.
★ He never links two words together.
★ He doesn't often show intense concentration on an object or activity of his own choice.
★ He doesn't want to help you in your activities.
★ He doesn't show any pretend play.

The Baby Talk Programme

HALF AN HOUR A DAY

I hope that you and your little child are now enjoying your playtimes so much that you would only give them up in a dire emergency. You will be continuing to do a great deal for his emotional security and life-long confidence as well as providing him with the very best possible language learning situation. As his play skills develop in this time, you can also continue to boost his confidence by affirming and admiring what he can do and gently helping him to do more difficult tasks so that he doesn't become frustrated. This can be like treading quite a fine line.

> Shaun came to the clinic with his father at twenty months of age, as he had not yet begun to use any words. For some reason, his father thought that not only did children of this age not need to be talked to much but also that they should be left to find things out by themselves. While the two of them were playing together, Shaun found a screw toy which was just too tight for his little hands to manage. He tried and tried, with no success, and within a few ▶

minutes, he was weeping with rage and frustration. I couldn't resist intervening, and the moment I slightly loosened the nut for him, Shaun was all smiles, and learned a lot from the toy.

I also remember, however, a little girl called Antonia, whose mother couldn't bear her to experience any frustration at all, and solved all Antonia's problems before she knew she had them, talking all the while on her own agenda. I vividly remember, for example, Antonia playing with an inset jigsaw puzzle, and as soon as she had a piece in her hand, her mother was showing her where it went. This was nearly as frustrating for Antonia as Shaun's father's non-intervention was for him. These children both blossomed once their parents learned the knack of talking to them on the child's agenda rather than their own, and giving them an appropriate amount of help with their play activities.

THE SETTING FOR YOUR ONE-TO-ONE PLAYTIME

Please ensure that noise and distractions have not crept back. Check that there is no significant noise coming in from the surroundings and that you are very

Keep the room quiet

unlikely to be interrupted. Your little child still needs to experience times when listening is very easy and lots of fun.

As you have done before, have a selection of toys available so that your little child has a wide choice of materials for both investigative and pretend play. It helps to

Make sure all the toys are working and complete

keep them in the same places so that he can readily find what he wants, and make sure that they are all assembled and complete. Little children at this age have no tolerance at all for the jack in the box that doesn't pop

up, or the puzzle with a piece missing.

Arrange the toys so that there is a clear area of floor and some surfaces for him to play on. A floor and walls covered with pictures and toys, however attractive, can actually be over-stimulating, and make it difficult for him to focus.

★ **Share the same attention focus**

It is still vital that you and your little child continue to share the same focus of interest and attention, and it is likely that this will be very well established by now through your habitual awareness of his focus of attention.

Your little child will now much more often let you know very clearly what the object of his interest is, often by means of speech, which removes much of the guesswork needed at earlier times. When he points and smiles and says 'Dere cat', for example, there is little doubt about what is interesting him. He will also be quick to let you know if you haven't worked out correctly what is in his mind. If, for example, you responded to 'Teddy drink' by offering teddy a drink, and he actually meant that he wanted you to hand him teddy's cup, he would soon show you by elaborate pantomime what he actually meant.

Perhaps the most important change at this time is that, due to his rapidly expanding world knowledge and command of language, what is in his mind is not always the 'here and now'. He loves to try to tell you about exciting things that have happened, often over and over again. This can happen rather suddenly. My daughter, aged twenty-one months, was totally enchanted by her first visit to the zoo, and told everyone she came across: 'Mummy giraffe ... baby giraffe ... and dicky bird said hallo.'

Your little child may also start to talk about events which are to happen in the future – usually at this stage the very near future such as later in the day. Do join in these conversations, and don't worry for a moment that because you are now not always talking about what is happening at that moment you are not following his interests – you are. You can now expand a little on what he has said, and add a little, to help him to recall more of what has happened. If, for example, he was talking about some children he saw playing in the park, telling you all about it in a mixture of little sentences and longer ones padded out with jargon saying, for example, 'Johnny hit ball. All fall down', you could say: 'Yes, Johnny hit the ball. He fell down. His mummy picked him up. We all went home for tea.'

At other times his mind will be on what is going to happen in the near future. He may say, for example, 'Tom go park. See bunnies.' Again, you could expand on this by reminding him of other things he might see in the park, such as flowers, and the swing and slide. These conversations now provide opportunities for him to hear and come to acquire more complex grammatical forms such as past and future tenses, which of course don't occur when you are talking about the 'here and now'. They also enable you to use, and him to follow, more complex constructions, like 'If it's raining, we can't go to the park'.

At this stage, very carefully used rhetorical questions can help him to think through and remember events. 'I wonder what we'll see in the park today?', for example, may stimulate lots of memories of past visits to the park. Be sure to answer your question yourself if he doesn't answer.

By the time he's two years old, you may well find that nearly half your conversations will be about past and future events, and at this stage, this is very helpful to his language learning.

Another form of non-concrete topic you will find yourselves talking about is that of feelings, which is another new departure. 'Mary's got ball. Johnny cross', for example, could lead to a very interesting conversation.

As your joint experiences and conversations about them increase, your little child will come to know, as we all do, what knowledge we can expect our conversational partner to have. Knowing, for example, that he and his mother have been amused by a particular jack in the box, he can safely assume that the mention of 'popped up' will make her laugh, whereas another adult who had not seen the toy would need much more explanation. The more that the adults around have followed the little child's focus of attention, the more quickly he will be able to make the right assumptions about what other people know which is so important in conversation. You can see how important your daily playtimes have been in all this. I

> When Sara came into the room the first time we met, she said 'He bigger and bigger and bigger and broke!' It took me a long time to work out that she and the other children in her playgroup had been blowing up balloons until they burst. She didn't realise that, as I hadn't been there, I didn't know that she was talking about balloons.

have seen many children in the clinic for whom this has not happened, and it makes conversation very difficult indeed.

It is important that you are very much aware of the moment when he switches out of these conversations back into the 'here and now'. Never ever try to keep them going, however much you are enjoying them. At this stage, the little child's mind can change direction quite suddenly.

This is a time of transition in terms of attention development. There will still be times when his attention switches from one thing to another very rapidly. As before, make it clear to him that that is fine, and again, as before, comment on each focus of interest, however rapidly this changes.

At other times, and probably more of the time now, he will give long spells of very focused attention to objects or activities which have caught his interest. As you have done before, give a 'running commentary' which relates as closely as possible to what is actually in his mind: for example, 'What a big car! It's going up ... up ... up ... the slope ... it's at the top ... and down it comes.' This close matching of your speech to his attention focus is the only way in which your speech will be listened to, and is clearly the best possible way in which he will learn language.

It is still very important, as before, to avoid directions entirely. As we have seen, his attention level now makes it possible for him to listen to directions which are an inherent part of the game such as 'Where's your hand?' while dressing him. These are fine in daily living activities now but in your playtime, a 'running commentary' is still what he listens to most easily and with the greatest

> **Avoid directions entirely**

enjoyment. He experiences you as adding to his pleasure in what he is doing, instead of interfering with his activities. (Of course, if he shows an interest in scribbling, there's nothing wrong with saying 'Get the crayons from the shelf'. That is still following his interest.)

Please don't be tempted to try to get him to shift the focus of his attention at this stage. He is just reaching the stage when he will be able to do this at an adult's request, but it will soon be very much easier for him, and it is much better to wait for him to reach this point.

It will now not be long at all before you can do this, but at this stage, it is very easy to hinder the development of a little child's attention. If he is intent on something, and you try to make him shift his attention focus, you can still actually 'split' his attention by causing him to make rapid shifts between one focus and another. If this happens a lot, the result can be a child who has extremely scattered attention.

An English study on the effects of joint adult and child attention was carried out in 1986. The authors point out that adults are better at changing attention focus than children are.[4]

An associated finding in an interesting study in Canada showed that children whose mothers were intrusive in their

I have seen many in the clinic, up to seven or eight years old, whose attention is just like quicksilver, and who go through the contents of several toy boxes in the space of half an hour, failing to learn or benefit from any of the materials in them. I saw a little girl called Dana in a nursery only recently. Her nursery worker had noted that at times Dana was now able to follow adult direction, and she was deeply frustrated that the child did not always do so. As I came into the room, she was holding Dana's head and trying to make her focus on a counting task. Each time she took hold of Dana's head, the little girl's eye gaze flicked immediately in a totally different direction. I don't know which of the two of them, Dana or the nursery worker, was the more frustrated.

play had lower language levels than children whose mothers allowed their children to play as they chose.[5]

Do bring in lots of new words now, while following his interests, of which you are likely to be very much aware. He will absorb them up at a great rate. Use all kinds of words, and don't be worried about using long or complicated ones. As long as you are using them in that situation, he will find it great fun. I used the word 'catastrophe' recently to a little boy of rising two, as his aeroplane fell out of the air. He laughed delightedly, and tried to imitate me.

★ **Help him to continue to enjoy listening**
A quiet background is still the most important factor in this, but it is still important to give your little child opportunities to find listening easy, enjoyable and a lot of fun. Try to put one or two new noise-makers into his toy-box, such as dried peas in a tin, or musical toys, so that he will be encouraged to play with them.

Songs and rhymes are still very much enjoyed, so take any opportunities to bring these in. Dancing to music is also now a lot of fun.

It might be fun too, to include in your toy box at this stage, books where you could use different voices, for example, soft and loud ones for the different characters, as well as those to which you could add 'play sounds'.

Drawing your little child's attention to the sounds made by his chosen activity can also be interesting for him, such as the sound of the bubbles when he's involved in water play, or the squelch made by clay or playdough as it is handled.

★ **Continue to use short sentences in your playtime**
By the end of this age period, you are likely to have noticed that he understands a great deal of what you say. As a consequence, you will naturally start to talk to him in considerably longer

Two-and-a-half-year-old Susie had been sent for repeated hearing tests because she left out so many of the unstressed sounds and syllables in her speech, which can, of course, happen when a child has a hearing loss. Susie's hearing was found to be fine, and everyone was very puzzled about her speech problem. When I heard the way in which her mother was speaking, and particularly when I discovered that it was nearly always very noisy at home, all became clear. Susie's mother was speaking in enormously long sentences and, as well, her voice was extremely quiet. Poor Susie just hadn't had a chance to notice all the little quiet sounds and syllables, as she was having to work very hard to follow the meaning of what her mother was saying. As soon as her mother realised what was causing the problem, and changed the way she spoke, Susie's speech began to improve, and within a very few months was normal for her age.

sentences. It's fine to do this now outside your playtimes, but it is very helpful to limit the length of sentence you use within them.[6]

Try to use sentences that contain not more than three important words, such as 'Johnny's going to the park later'. If your sentences get much longer than this at this stage, your little child will take longer to sort out the sounds within each word. He is also likely to fail to notice all the little words in your sentences, as he's busy focusing on following their meaning.

> **During playtimes, use sentences with not more than three important words**

Continue to speak a little slower and louder than you would to an adult, with lots of tune in your voice. This is still the most attractive kind of speech for little children to listen to, and the one which makes it easiest for them to hear and notice exactly what is in each word in terms of speech sounds.

Pause between sentences, to give him time to take in what you have said.

Do continue using names rather than pronouns. You may think he knows them all already, and you may be right, but this

> Patrick was recently brought to me because his speech was not at all clear. He was one of a wonderful family of eight children, whose mother managed to give all her children plenty of attention. Not surprisingly, she spoke at high speed, and never seemed to pause to take a breath. Once we managed to establish that she had a little time with Patrick on his own and, in this time, used short sentences and paused between sentences, his speech rapidly improved.

will certainly do no harm. It may help him a lot if he is not yet sure of how the sequence of sounds goes within that particular name, or doesn't know it as well as you think he does.

> **Speak a little slower and louder, with lots of tune**

★ Expand a little on what he has said

At this stage, the most helpful thing is to say back to him what he has said with a little expansion. For example, if he said 'Mummy go', you could reply 'Yes, Mummy's going to work', or if he said 'Want drink' you could say 'You want a drink? Here's a drink'. Similarly, if he said 'Teddy fall', you could say 'Yes, teddy's fallen' or if he said 'Daddy goed shops' you might say 'Yes, Daddy went to the shops'.

Perhaps not surprisingly, doing this is well known to relate to increased length of sentences later on.[7] [8] [9] It is extremely helpful in giving him information about grammatical structures, and also in maintaining joint attention. (Do be very careful that you never ever give him the impression that you are correcting him. Keep to that golden rule of always starting with a 'yes'.)

> **Never give the impression that you are correcting**

If there are words he says in such a way as to make it difficult for other people to understand them, it's very helpful to put them into several little sentences, to give him opportunities to hear what sounds are actually in them. One of my children at this stage said 'bit' for 'biscuit', and got quite cross when not everyone understood what he meant. I made a point of using lots of little sentences containing the word, like 'Nice biscuits', 'Biscuits for tea', 'I like biscuits', and so on, and it was not long before he noticed all the sounds in the word. Again, be extremely careful that you never ever give him the impression that you are correcting him.

★ Show him what you mean

It can still be very helpful to use gesture so that your little child knows exactly what you are referring to, particularly when you think that you may be using a new word. It also helps to show

> **Use gestures alongside the words**

him exactly what you mean: for example, showing him how a toy goes 'round and round' as it does so, or telling him 'We'll open the drawer and put the pencil in', as you do so.

★ Continue to make play sounds to go with things that happen

Play sounds continue to serve a number of very useful purposes, so keep them up. They enable the little child to hear separate speech sounds, for example 'sshshsh' as you are

> **Add play sounds to pictures in books**

sweeping, or 'gugug' as water runs away, and they still give him that all-important message that voice is great fun to listen to. At this stage, it's particularly helpful to add them to appropriate pictures in books, giving him an early message that there can

be links between sounds and pictures, which will stand him in good stead for when he later makes links between sounds in their heard and written forms.

★ Continue to use lots of repetition

Repetition continues to be very important for the same reasons as in the previous time period. As you know, the little child still needs to hear words many, many times, so he can eventually recall all the sounds in them accurately enough to say them correctly.

Mark had had a very long and serious illness, and had as a consequence missed out on a great deal of play and language experience. I went to see Mark in school, and the following conversation which he had had with his teacher was reported to me:-

Mark: I want to see Mrs G (another teacher).

His teacher: Mrs G is busy.

Mark: I want to see Mrs B (another teacher).

His teacher: Mrs B is busy.

Mark: I want to see busy.

Mark was showing clearly that he had not heard the word 'busy' in enough different contexts to know what it means, and even what kind of word it is, referring to it as if it were a name. He will only be able to learn the full meaning of that word when he has heard it in many contexts, such as 'Mark's busy with his bricks', 'Daddy's busy cooking the dinner', or 'Mummy's busy writing'.

He has also now reached a period of very rapid increase in his understanding, and the more different contexts a word is heard in, the more quickly it is fully understood. For instance, a little child might only have heard the word 'dog' when his family dog appeared. He would take very much longer to realise that the word applies to a large number of four-legged animals who share certain characteristics than a child who had heard the word used to refer to other dogs in other settings and situations.

The number of different contexts the word is heard in is also important in helping the little child to form concepts. Different sentences such as 'Dog's eating', 'He's chasing the dog', 'Dog's too hot', 'Dog's very friendly' and so on, also help to give him a clear picture of what kind of animal this is.

Children who only hear words in very limited contexts can fail fully to understand their meanings.

Repetition is particularly helpful at this stage when you are using what you think may be a new word. This is great fun to do a

> **Repetition is very helpful when using new words**

lot now, and you can quickly enrich your little child's vocabulary. The more different little sentences you put these words into, the more quickly he will come fully to understand them. You might, for example, say something like 'Teddy wants cocoa. Cocoa for teddy. Here's teddy's cocoa.'

★ Say back to him what he means

There will still be lots of times now when you know exactly what he means, but he hasn't the language to express it fully verbally, and needs to use lots of gesture and pantomime, padded out with babble. Saying back to him what he means to say is still of the greatest help to him. For example, he may be looking out of the window, waving his arms about excitedly, and saying 'Birdie, birdie, birdie!' and you could say 'Yes, there's lots of birds. They are all flying. They're flying together.'

SOME 'DON'TS' FOR THIS PERIOD

However tempted you are, never ask him to say or copy words or sounds, and make sure that nobody else does. One of the most important principles of the BabyTalk Programme is that we look after our input, and we can rely on our children to look after their output. If your little child mispronounces a word, gets his sentences in a muddle or leaves out sounds or syllables, he just needs to hear the word or sentence clearly many, many times. He never benefits from a message that he has not said something right.

It remains very important indeed that you never comment on how he has said something or on the fact that he has said it. This, as he very well knows, is not part of normal communication, and only serves to make him feel self-conscious. As before, always respond to his communications, in whatever way he makes them.

> **Never make him feel self-conscious**

QUESTIONS

As we have seen above, it can now be helpful to ask a few rhetorical questions, when talking about something that has happened or is going to happen, in order to help him to recall events more easily. We want him to be listening intently to what you say, rather than trying to work out the answer to a question. Please limit the number of these questions to a few per conversation, and always answer them yourself if he does not soon show a sign that he is going to do so.

> **If you know the answer to a question, don't ask it**

As before, don't ever ask him 'test' questions, in order to get him to answer. If you are in doubt about whether to ask a question, ask yourself if you know the answer. If you do, don't ask the question. He knows that this is not natural communication, and will just become stressed if he does not know the answer.

OUTSIDE YOUR HALF HOUR

★ Keep his routines consistent.
★ Make sure that he is talked to a lot, about all the routines and experiences of his day.
★ Share a book with him every day.
★ Include him in the conversation: whenever you can explain to him what is happening.

2 to 2½ years

An overview

By this stage your toddler is really becoming a little child. Her interest in the world and all the people in it continues to be insatiable, and her passion to try out activities she's seen adults do can lead to some wonderful family moments. Wanting to find out about planting bulbs, for example, led one of my sons to 'plant' his bricks all over my flowerbeds!

You'll find that she's still extremely emotionally dependent on you, and may now set up prolonged rituals at bedtime to keep you with her. My daughter managed to persuade me to read her no less than three books and tell her three rhymes every bedtime at this stage.

Please note that the developmental stages described here are averages only.

All babies develop at slightly different rates, and often progress in one area can result in a temporary delay in another. Do not get worried or depressed if your child does not appear to be doing everything at exactly the time periods mentioned here. For further information, see Cause for Concern, page 240.

She still needs constant supervision. This is a very common age for accidents because the powerful drive to investigate is not matched by experience of the world. It can also lead to behaviour which is less than acceptable. Her joy at marking paper with paint, for example, may lead her to 'paint' walls, floor and furniture given a chance.

She'll start to assert herself more now, and may have full blown tantrums if she is thwarted, which can be embarrassing in the supermarket. She can be quite frightened by the strength of her own feelings, and really needs the adult to be decisive, making it clear gently but firmly what she can and cannot do. Your diplomatic skills will also be called into play when she shows a huge determination to succeed all by herself at a task like a jigsaw puzzle, and you know that she will need a little bit of help if she's not to become frustrated.

Two to two and a quarter years

THE DEVELOPMENT OF LANGUAGE

At the beginning of this age period, the little child is already able to **understand** quite long and complicated sentences. Her ever-increasing knowledge of the sequences of events in her daily life, and of the way in which words fall into categories, now enable her understanding to increase faster and faster and more and more efficiently. Knowing, for example, that there is a category of names for clothing enables her to understand a new word like 'vest' very easily in the context of dressing. Her experience of ball games and knowledge that things move at different speeds would enable her to understand the word 'slowly' readily in that context. All the events of her daily life are wonderful learning situations now.

She is very interested in small parts of a whole now, and understands smaller and smaller subcategories, such as 'eyebrow' and 'knee' in terms of body parts, or 'collar' and 'buckle' in terms of clothing.

The little child's ever-expanding acquisition of concepts enables her to attach names to them with ease, and she now comes to understand words such as 'bigger', 'smaller' and even 'one' and 'lots'.

She understands many more verbs now, and may point correctly to pictures of children doing different things.

Very great changes are also happening in terms of the use of **speech**. Spoken vocabulary is often around two hundred words at the beginning of this time, and now continues to increase extremely quickly. Some little children add as many as ten new words a day. At the beginning of this period, most are using mainly two-word sentences, with the occasional one containing three. The two-word sentences most often consist of the names of people or objects, together with some action words: for example, 'Baby sleep', or 'Ball gone'.

Some pronouns such as him and her are coming in now, but they are often confused at first. Sentences like 'Him sleeping' are common.

Your little child often talks to herself at this stage, chattering away about what she is doing as she plays, and coming out with sequences of little sentences which are not addressed to anyone in particular. It's as if she's practising putting words together. As Gesell puts it, she tends to 'talk while she acts and act while she talks'.[1]

Although, as we have seen, she understands most of the rules about starting, maintaining and repairing conversations, when she becomes involved in one, her contributions can be quite disjointed, particularly outside the one-to-one situation, and the adults still have to do most of the work. She is often most fluent when she is talking about interesting things that have happened to her, but at this stage, usually talks of them in the present tense. 'Go park', for example, could mean that she went to the park earlier. She can also use these little sentences to ask for help with her personal needs: for example, 'Wash hands' or, as my daughter often said, meaning just that: 'Sticky fingers'!

The little child now begins to use more and more three-word sentences. These are constructed in a number of ways. Some are expansions of the two-word sentences that she has been using for some time. 'Janey car', for example, might now become 'Janey big car'. Two-word phrases can also be put together, again often those she has been using for some time. 'Mummy wash' and 'Wash hair', for example, might be combined into 'Mummy wash hair'. Others may be constructed from single words, such as 'Me want dinner', or 'Teddy hit ball'. The little child's speech is still telegraphic, but will gradually become less so over the next few months. Word order will also be correct more often. Pronouns, too, are more often used correctly, and she will begin to refer to herself as 'I'.

She begins to ask more questions now, and a new departure is that she will enquire 'What's that?'. She also starts to use more and more questions like 'Where Mummy?' or 'What dinner?' to get information and attention. If they don't work, however, she'll still pull and grab to get her meaning across.

As always is the case, all this progress is linked to development in other areas.

GENERAL DEVELOPMENT

Your child can now walk in any direction, and even on tiptoe. She can rise from a kneeling position without using her hands, climb onto a piece of apparatus with considerable agility, climb on a chair to reach an object, and even now stand on one foot. This greatly increased control makes it still easier for her to concentrate on what is happening and being said, whereas balance and control of her body used to take a great deal of her attention.

She has more sense of herself as a separate person now, and of the needs and feelings of other people. She likes to assert her independence by doing tasks such as hand washing with the minimum of adult help. (At other times, particularly when she is tired or unwell, she will revert to extreme dependence.)

Social contacts with other toddlers are still few and brief. She does, however, show the very beginnings of co-operation in that she may begin to share her toys occasionally.

ATTENTION

A child at this age may show an important development in attention at about this time. She is for the first time able to be directed by adults, but only in certain circumstances.[2] The spells of intensely focused concentration will continue for some time, but at times when her attention is not so engaged, she can respond to your voice drawing her attention to something, and change her focus to that. Her attention is still totally single channelled, and it is essential to recognise that she cannot listen while she is doing something: she has to stop what she is doing, and won't be able to resume it until she has stopped listening.

Maurice was four years old when I first saw him, very handsome, and big for his age, but very delayed in his speech development.

He emptied two toy boxes item after item in the space of a few minutes, listening not at all to his mother's suggestions for play. He then fixated on a train, pushing it round and round a track, and again clearly was not listening to her at all. His mother reported that this behaviour was typical, and that she was at her wits' end trying to get through to him.

Fortunately, attention will develop as soon as appropriate changes are made to the child's environment. As soon as Maurice's mother understood and recognised the attention stage he was at and, as a result, made sure that he experienced one-to-one quiet times with her in which she talked about his focus of attention, he began to make progress. When I saw him three weeks later, he was able to stop what he was doing and listen to his mother, and was also understanding much more of what was being said.

She is also extremely easily distracted, and an extraneous noise or other event will stop her listening to you.

Many children whose environments have not enabled their attention to develop do not reach this stage for many years, and continue to fluctuate between spells of extremely short attention span interspersed with those spells of inflexible focus in which they cannot listen at all to what is being said. This can easily continue into primary school or even later, with disastrous effects on educational progress.

LISTENING

It is likely that if you have been following the BabyTalk Programme, your little child's ability to listen to whatever she wishes to and tune out what she doesn't will now be well established in all environments provided that they are quiet.

Her knowledge of the origins and meaning of the sounds around her will be very extensive now, and one important new departure is that she will now be able to ask what causes a particular sound when she encounters something new. She'll be able to let you know too, if she doesn't like a noise she hears!

Two and a quarter to two and a half years

THE DEVELOPMENT OF LANGUAGE

In terms of **understanding**, the little child now recognises the meaning of many more verbs, and can point to pictures of children doing a wide variety of different things when they are named for her.

She also understands questions better, and will respond appropriately to 'Where?' questions, either looking towards the object named or trotting to fetch it.

She now recognises an increasing number of categories that names can belong to, such as those of food, cutlery and family members. She knows, for example, that family members have names such as 'Grandma' and 'Sister' and this makes it very easy for her to associate meaning with a new name, such as 'Aunty'.

Her greater understanding of the world is shown by the fact that she can also now identify objects by their use, identifying correctly, for example, 'the thing you eat' or 'the one you wear'.[3]

The little child's developing and more secure concept formation enables her to understand the words associated with concepts, such as some colours and words relating to size, like big and little. In terms of number, she may have a concept of two or even three by the end of this time period.

Her greatest achievement at this stage is to understand language without the support of clues, such as the time of day, or the actions of other people. She really does understand the words. You may notice, for instance, that she goes for her shoes as soon as you mention that you are going shopping, whereas before, she did not do so until you had got out your shopping basket.

In terms of **speech**, there are equally important developments. The little child now uses language in an even wider variety of different ways. She is much more skilful in both asking and answering questions, and in expressing her feelings. She also now uses language in order to assert her independence. Whereas previously she might have pushed away the hand of an adult who was trying to wipe her sticky fingers, she may now announce firmly 'Me do it'. Another very significant extension of her use of language is one which we as adults use throughout our lives, that of discovering the meaning of new words. 'What dat?' may now refer to a word, and not only a real object.

She now begins, for the first time, to use the little grammatical markers which make meaning so much clearer, such as 'ing' added to a verb to mark the present tense, or an 's' added to a word to denote that it is the plural form.[4] The clarity of the little child's communication is also enhanced by her use of prepositions (such as 'in' or 'on'), and by her use of more accurate forms of words, such as 'no' instead of 'not' in a sentence like 'no more dinner'. At the same time, word order is coming more and more into line with that of adults. She appears to be noticing more and more about how adults construct grammatical sentences.

Your child asks more questions now, and makes clearer what she actually wants to know. She now asks 'Where?' questions, and those which require a 'yes' or 'no' answer, such as 'Susie hat?'

There is a steady increase in the extent to which she talks about the past and the future.

Although she is making enormous strides in terms of verbal communication, she only joined the party a short time ago, and still has a long way to go in terms of becoming a really skilled conversationalist. She may appear to be one in your daily playtimes, as this is the situation in which she can use all her communication skills most easily, but in most other situations, she still needs a lot of help. There will be many times when she doesn't respond to conversational overtures, even when these take the form of comments. The main reason for this is that her attention is still single channelled, and in the general situation, she is not always sharing joint attention with an adult. This makes everything much more difficult for her.

The speech-sound substitutions discussed in the previous chapter, such as substituting an easier sound for a more difficult one, like 'wabbit' for 'rabbit' continue for the moment for most children.

GENERAL DEVELOPMENT

Again, this progress in language development is made possible by developments in other areas. The little child's control over her body increases still more. She can now jump using two feet together, and climb over as well as into nursery apparatus. She can at last kick a ball, albeit gently and lopsidedly. She also begins to be able to pedal a trike, another great achievement which can lead to a lifetime's enjoyment. She can push a toy along with good steering.

Her eye-hand co-ordination is improving rapidly. She can complete a simple jigsaw with accuracy, and build a tower of eight bricks. She can add a chimney to a train made of bricks, and copy a bridge of three bricks. Her pencil control is better too, and she can copy a cross. She can also match primary colours, and sort objects according to whether they are big or small.

Socialisation continues apace. The little child will now join in play with one other person. She is often co-operative, and if she refuses to do something, you can now begin to bargain with her. You could say, for example, 'biscuits after lunch; not now', and find that she accepts this. This is another example of the way in which she is not always thinking about something in the here and now. She is likely to be willing to help to put things away, and to have a very good try at dressing herself, even if she does tend to put some of her clothes on back to front. She may now feed herself with a fork as well as a spoon, wash and dry her hands without much help, and go the bathroom alone.

ATTENTION

Your little child is likely to be able to accept your directions a little more easily now, but still only when her attention is not intently focused on what she is doing or watching. This emergent state of being able to accept direction needs to be handled with great care and considerable sensitivity. If, as we have mentioned before, you are so delighted that your child can follow directions that you begin to give her many more of them, both you and she will be frustrated, as her ability to follow them is still extremely limited.

When you have a real need to direct your child, there are several important rules to follow.

★ If you want her to stop doing something and come to the table, for example, she needs plenty of warning. Expecting her to change activity suddenly can be a rich source of tantrums in the 'terrible twos'.
★ She can only take in a direction when she is focused on you, and not when she is busy.
★ It is best if a direction is made to add to the fun of an activity, such as a game of 'Here comes the aeroplane' as you approach her mouth with a spoon.
★ It helps if the direction comes immediately before the event, for example, 'and next your trousers on' just before this happens in a familiar dressing sequence.

One amusing fact is that she now starts to give herself directions. You might, for example, hear her say 'put it on there – and now put that on' as she plays with her bricks.

LISTENING

Your little child's ability to listen easily in quiet environments is likely to have been well established for some time now. If at any time she doesn't seem to listen as well as she did previously, do have her hearing checked.

Infections of the ear, nose and throat are very common in pre-school children, and when as often happens, they result in even a mild hearing impairment, this can set back listening even in children who have had no earlier problems. These hearing impairments can vary from day to day and even from hour to hour, and listening consequently becomes difficult and confusing. The little child is likely therefore to focus on looking and touching rather than on listening.

Both investigative and pretend play really flourish during this period, and the latter now develops into true imaginative play.

Your child will now love you to be involved in her play for much of the time, and very much welcomes suggestions that can help her to extend the range of both kinds of play. (It's still very important, however, to be sensitive to the times when she really wants to 'do her own thing'.)

INVESTIGATIVE PLAY

The little child's explorations of play materials and toys and what she can do with them now knows no bounds. Her increasing control of her body and improved eye-hand co-ordination enables her to make impressive leaps in this.

She is likely to continue engaging in many of the activities she enjoyed in the previous age band, but in more dextrous and sophisticated ways.

She can now kick and catch a large ball, but may find a box easier to kick. Many children also find at the beginning of this age period that they can pedal a tricycle for the first time, which they usually find very exciting.

Your little child can build a tower of eight bricks competently, placing each very carefully on top of the last. She becomes more skilful at handling crayons and pencils, making more positive marks, and can imitate horizontal strokes. She begins to enjoy other drawing materials, such as chalks and paint. She can string beads with more dexterity, and now for the first time tackles scissors. If she is shown how to hold them, she can snip paper, and loves doing so. She is quicker in her manipulation of toys which represent tools, like a screw toy or hammer peg, and will play with them for longer than she did previously.

Little children of this age are immensely interested in matching and sorting. These activities give her valuable knowledge of the world of materials, by enabling her to compare different sizes, shapes and colours, and to develop many concepts like full and empty, rigid and bendy. She not only likes to compare different objects which are the same, but now also enjoys matching small objects to pictures.

Most children of this age love puzzles, and will persevere with them for much longer now.

PRETEND PLAY

Pretend play flourishes throughout this age period. This stage is characterised by a passionate interest in the domestic activities the child sees around her, such as housework and gardening. This reflects her powerful drive to understand what it is that adults do, and the meaning of doing these things. She watches intently for quite long periods, and begins to remember and imitate what she has seen, delighting in bringing these actions into her play. (You may notice at times at the beginning of the time period that she doesn't always get it quite right. I remember a little girl in my clinic playing at setting the table, and solemnly putting the napkins on the chairs!)

This play shows great developments now. At an earlier stage, she used objects in single actions, like pretending to brush her hair, or drink from a cup. She now remembers not only single acts, but whole sequences, and might, for example, sit down, pretend to put on her glasses, and pick up the newspaper. She might re-enact a whole washing-up sequence when playing with water, fetching the plates and cutlery, washing them, drying them and putting them away, or put a hat on a dolly, place her in the buggy and take her for a walk. All this mimicry is extremely important in helping to distinguish herself from other people by becoming more and more aware of how it feels to be doing what they do, as opposed to what she does.

Another development is the changing roles of teddy and dolly. At an earlier time, the little child brought dolly or teddy into the play, but they were passive partners in the games. They now become active.[5] Teddy may, for example, hand back her cup for another drink, or dolly jump up to catch the ball.

Your child loves adults to be involved in this play, and to help her to extend it by modelling for her actions which she can incorporate into her own play sequences. You might suggest, for instance, that dolly might like a drink after her bath, or you might suggest giving her a kiss as she is tucked up after putting her to bed.

IMAGINATIVE PLAY

Real imaginative play, in which the child not only re-enacts events she has seen, but starts to combine them in new ways to create a story, begins to emerge at the beginning of this time period, and then really flourishes, particularly if the child has a sympathetic adult partner who responds to their inventiveness with interest, and who contributes to the imaginative and pretend sequences in their play.

Your child is beginning to experience herself much more as a separate person, and to understand the feelings and needs of other people. As a result, she increasingly starts to imagine that she is another person, and to enact imaginative sequences of events which are not merely what she has observed. She is most likely to take on the role of her mother or father or other people she most frequently observes in her daily life, and when she does so, dolly or teddy often become her. While pretending to be her mother, for example, she might pick up her shopping bag, put teddy in the pram, and pretend to go to the shops. These imaginative sequences all help her to find out what it is like to be that person, and to do the things they do.

Role reversal – for example, taking it in turns to be the shopkeeper and the shopper – is very much enjoyed. She is again trying by experience to understand the meaning of their different activities and how it feels to be engaged in them.

The little child also enjoys prolonged imaginative play with models, and plays more extensively and imaginatively with a doll's house and furniture, or zoo or farm animals. She may also pretend to feed a picture of a doll. By the end of this age, she may even invent people: for example, other shoppers in a shop or imaginary people visiting a zoo.

Her constructions become so elaborate that she may want them to remain in place overnight so that she can continue her game the next day!

Do keep to the rules of earlier times.

★ Limit the time your child spends watching television or videos to half an hour a day.

★ Watch with her so that you can discuss what you see together.

★ It's still important not to confuse your child with fantasies such as flying trains or talking animals: your child still has a long way to go in terms of understanding how the world works.

★ The same criteria apply to choosing videos and television programmes as to choosing books. She will still love familiar characters doing the kind of things that she does, and she will adore repetition in terms of getting to know the same

The Toy Box

The suggested additions to the little child's toy box are divided into those which are likely to encourage exploratory and pretend play, but as at all the other age bands, your little child may surprise you with the ways she thinks of using the toys.

INVESTIGATIVE PLAY

★ Different sizes and colours of paper
★ Paint and brushes
★ Chalks
★ Plastic scissors

★ Pedal tricycle
★ Picture lotto
★ More puzzles
★ More boxes

PRETEND PLAY

★ Till and money
★ Cooker

★ More gardening or housework equipment

The Book Shelf

Please continue to share a book every day with your little child. Nothing, as we have seen, stands her in better stead for reading later on.

Do not, whatever you do, try to teach her to read at this stage. The essential thing as before is that you and she share a lovely time together as you introduce her to the magical world of books. She will absorb so much vital information: such as the fact that you read from left to right, that words relate to pictures, and above all that books are enormous fun.

Your little child will still love stories about the familiar sequences of events in her daily life. These can lead to discussions about past and future events just as sometimes her play does, giving wonderful opportunities for you to give her a rich language input.

The stories can be a little longer now, and are preferably illustrated by bright pictures which are true to life. She'll enjoy those which contain a lot of detail. The best books combine an interesting story with very attractive pictures.

Your little child will very much enjoy certain characters who appear in several books. They will soon acquire the comfortable familiarity of old friends. She'll enjoy discussing their feelings and motives, as well as their activities.

She will particularly love stories about herself, and adding to your book of photographs and the stories you tell around them will be much relished.

Rhymes are still hugely enjoyed, and very helpful to her: as we have seen they are a very vital precursor to reading. Make sure that you use a lively voice and emphasise the rhythm in these.

CONTINUED

It is helpful if the content of the stories lends itself to large numbers of sentences containing three important words, for example, 'Grandma lost her hat', or 'He blew out the candles'.

She is likely to be very interested in concepts like big and small and one and many, and would love books in which these are illustrated.

There are many wonderful books that meet these criteria, some examples of which are shown below. (She doesn't need huge numbers of new books at this time, as she loves the frequent repetition of familiar stories.)

★ *Ella and the Naughty Lion*, Anne Cottinger and Russell Ayto (Mammoth)
★ *The Pop-up Potty Book*, Marianne Borgardt and Maxi Chambliss (Orion Children's)
★ *Usborne First Experiences*, Anne Civardi and Stephen Cartwright (Usborne)
★ *All Join In*, Quentin Blake (Red Fox)
★ *Oh Where, Oh Where*, John Prater (Bodley Head)
★ *As Quiet as a Mouse*, Hilda Offen (Red Fox)
★ *Za-Za's Baby Brother*, Lucy Cousins (Walker Books)
★ *Eat Your Dinner*, Virginia Miller (Walker Books)
★ *Oliver's Vegetables*, Vivian French and Alison Bartlett (Hodder Children's)
★ *I Like It When...*, Mary Murphy (Mammoth)

characters and seeing them enact familiar sequences of events.

★ Rhymes and music will have a powerful appeal, and so will humour at this stage, particularly of a slapstick variety.
★ Again, as in books, she will enjoy programmes which include the kind of concepts which interest her, such as those of size and number.
★ She will enjoy little stories, and as when she is being read to, will like to hear a lively voice and dramatic rendering.

Summary

To summarise, by the time she is two and a half years old, your little child is likely to:

★ Use as many as two hundred words, or even more.
★ Talk to herself about what is happening.
★ Ask 'what?' and 'where?' questions.
★ Put three words together.
★ Refer to herself as 'me' or 'I'.

Cause for concern

Below are circumstances in which it would be advisable to seek professional advice about your little child's development. (Please remember, though, that many children progress at slightly different rates.)

If you are in any doubt about your child, even if the reason for your concern is not mentioned here, do take her to see your Health Visitor or GP as soon as possible.

At two and a half years it would be advisable to seek a professional opinion if:

★ She is not showing an increase in the number of words she is using.
★ She still mainly uses single words rather than two together.
★ You often can't understand what she has said.
★ She does not seem to want you to play with her.
★ She does not show any pretend or imaginative play.
★ She doesn't seem to understand what you say to her unless you make it very simple.
★ Her attention span is still very short most of the time.

The Baby Talk Programme

Do make sure that this is not lapsing. I hope that you are enjoying your daily playtimes so much that there is no question of that. They will continue to do so much for your child, not only in terms of her language development, but also for her play, attention, and emotional development.

The fact that you are providing the best possible setting for her to increase her understanding of language has particularly great implications for her emotional development. Many studies both in the United States and in the United Kingdom, examples of which are given below, have shown that a very high proportion of children with delayed language development have emotional problems.[6][7][8] This is hardly surprising, as it is not difficult to imagine the frustration of being unable to understand what is being said, or to make yourself understood.

The connection between language and emotional development is of particularly great importance at this age, often referred to as 'the terrible twos'. Children at this age are beginning to perceive themselves as independent people, and in the process to assert themselves, frequently kicking against the traces by refusing to do

> **Explain why she can and can't do things**

what they are asked. Much of the inevitable frustration can be avoided by explaining to the child why she cannot do something, and negotiating with her. (It really is best to avoid saying 'no' unless it is absolutely necessary.) Clearly, you can do this much more easily with a child with good understanding of speech, and conversely, children who have limited understanding often just feel they live in a world where adults arbitrarily prevent them doing what they want, and make them do what they don't. It isn't difficult to see how easily behaviour problems can arise from this.

Children's interaction with each other is also affected by the degree to which they can understand and use language. An interesting American study found that children's popularity was predicted by the level of their understanding of speech.[9]

Four-year-old Dan was brought to see me because he was only talking like a two year old. His mother reported that she was extremely distressed at Dan's inability to make friends. She had tried to help by having other children home, and taking them out on interesting trips, but the day always ended in fighting and tears. Once Dan and his mother started on the BabyTalk Programme, Dan's language skills quickly began to catch up, and his mother noticed that he and other children began to discuss what they were going to do, and to negotiate and establish rules instead of fighting. Dan's popularity began to improve as soon as this started to happen, and six months after I first saw him, both his language and social interaction were normal for his age.

As we have said before, the undivided attention of a beloved adult does a huge amount to make a little child feel affirmed and therefore confident, and relieves her of the

Teddy, aged three, was so tense when I first saw him that he gave the impression that he might explode at any moment. His movements were so tremulous that his co-ordination looked very poor. He and his mother were in a vicious circle, in which his behaviour was becoming worse and worse in an attempt to gain her attention, and she was becoming so frustrated with this that she was cutting off more and more from him. The difference in Teddy was astonishing once he realised that he was to have a daily playtime with his mother, however he behaved. His naughty behaviour began to diminish after just a few days.

enormous stress of trying by any means (often, sadly, by being naughty) of obtaining it. I have seen many children who have calmed down to an amazing extent when they started on the BabyTalk Programme, even before they had had enough input to increase their understanding of speech.

There is much you can do now to enrich and enhance your little child's play. She is at the stage when adult suggestions sensitively given can do much to help her make imaginative leaps in her pretend play, and also to find out many wonderful ways in which play materials can be used.

The highest number of children are referred to Speech and Language Therapy at this age, and I am always sad when I see the ones who have not been played with. Their experience is already so much more limited than those who have had the benefit of an adult who was interested in their play and showed them how to do things.

Mandy was a charming little dark-haired girl. She clearly had lots of toys at home, as she knew basically what they were for, but the way in which she played with mine was extremely limited. She approached the doll's house, for example, and just piled the doll's-house furniture into it at random. The dolls were just pushed around, and there was no real play at all.

Scott had been left in the care of many different child-minders, none of whom had really played with him. He handled the toys listlessly and without any evident enjoyment when he first came to the clinic, and clearly did not expect any adult involvement in his play. I saw him again two weeks after his mother had established a daily playtime with him, and the difference in him gave me great pleasure. Scott handed his mother toys several times, looking at her expectantly, and avidly took up the play ideas she gave him. The two of them were clearly beginning to have real fun together.

Regular playtimes together build up a bank of shared experiences which provide wonderful conversational topics.

These conversations do so much for the little child's language development and her understanding of the world.

Your little child's attention is now likely to be moving into an interesting new stage, as we have seen. Adult awareness of this and of how to help does much for her development, and this help is best given in this one-to-one setting. (Conversely, lack of awareness can be a huge source of frustration both to adult and child, leading to many tantrums. If you don't recognise, for example, how totally single channelled your child's attention still is, and expect her to answer a question when she is busy, you may interpret her failure to do so as lack of co-operation.)

THE SETTING FOR YOUR ONE-TO-ONE PLAYTIME

Do make sure that the setting is still quiet and that you are unlikely to be interrupted.

> **Make sure it's still quiet in your playtimes**

Make sure that the toys are intact, and are kept in the same place so that your little child knows exactly where they are and doesn't need to be distracted by searching for them.

Have a clear area of floor or table top so that she has plenty of room to play. Some of her pretend play may need a considerable amount of space. She may want it to be left up overnight now.

HOW TO TALK

★ **Continue to share her attention focus**
The importance of you and your child continuing to share the same focus of attention throughout your playtime cannot be underestimated. The ways in which this happens, however, and the nature of that focus is changing now. As children get older, more and more of their conversation is not about the ongoing situation, but instead is about experiences she has had, and plans for the time ahead. This is very helpful for lan-

guage development, as it enables the adult to use, and the child to understand, lots of more complicated sentences, such as 'When we get to the park...' or 'While we were out shopping, we saw...'

> Two-year-old Andrea came to my clinic for the first time the day after she had been taken to a restaurant. She had clearly found it very exciting, and wanted to play-act this new experience, but her problem was that she was very unclear about the sequence of events. She play-acted paying the waiter (me!) as soon as she arrived, and then handed me the bread rolls. The whole play sequence was chaotic, and it was plain that nobody had explained to her either before or after the event what it was all about.

Talking through past experiences is also very helpful for her in terms of becoming very clear about the sequences of events in her daily life.

Children who have not been given these conversational opportunities show clearly in their play that they are not at all clear about the meaning and purpose of many of their experiences, and consequently live in a very confusing world.

Do make sure that these conversations about non-present events are always initiated by her and conclude the moment her attention switches. Let her govern entirely how much of your conversation is about the here and now in your playtimes.

These conversations are likely to be quite extensive now, and to include discussions about feelings and motivation as well as actions.

Do bring in lots and lots of new words. Don't be afraid of extending her vocabulary in this way. As long as you are following the focus of her interest, she will absorb them extremely easily. As before, always show her exactly what you mean by using gesture

Always follow her focus of attention, but bring in lots of new words

and relating what you say to exactly what is happening at that moment as we discussed in the last section. You might say, for example, after building a tower of bricks, 'It's toppling over! Oh dear, it toppled over' as it does so.

This shared attention focus, as we have said before, is the most vital precursor to all subsequent communication and cultural learning. The authors of an interesting English study[10] discuss the way in which the skills of shared attention at this stage are the precursors to understanding the thoughts and feelings of others at four to five years of age, so accomplishing a 'meeting of minds'.

★ **Help her to develop her play**
Your little child is almost certain to want you to join in her play, as you have been having so much fun together.

As you have done before, when you are playing together, make sure that you keep mainly to a 'running commentary' which is related to her immediate focus of attention, as this is still a wonderful language learning situation.

We have heard how your little child is now likely to be just moving into the stage when she can be directed by an adult in some situations. It is better not to do this at all in your play session yet, however, because the optimum learning situation is still to follow her choice of activity. I have seen many children whose parents became very directive as soon as they noticed that their little child was able to follow their directions at times.

Nigel was brought to see me at four years old because his speech was very unclear. He approached the toy box, and as soon as I began to speak, put his hands over his ears. When I later saw him playing with his parents, it became clear why this had happened. They both – and sometimes at the same time – gave Nigel streams of directions like 'Come and look at this', 'Now do this jigsaw', 'Finish it' and 'Right, now build the bricks'. The whole family was becoming increasingly cross.

It can now, however, be enormously helpful to make some suggestions in order to help her to extend her pretend play. If you were playing together – for example, at going to the doctor

---

– you could show her the prescription pad, or if you were in the role of shopkeeper, show her how the scales work.

It's also very helpful to show her all the different ways in which play materials can be used. It could be fun, for example, to show her how you can build a double tower once she is adept at building a single one.

It's best, when showing her a new activity, to start it and then to withdraw and let her try it out for herself. She'll let you know as soon as she wants your further involvement.

As you have been such a rewarding play partner, your little child is now very likely to look to you to make suggestions, so picking the right moment to do so is unlikely to cause any problems at all. You will be much too aware of her attention level to make a suggestion when she is deeply engrossed in something. Make sure that your suggestions are just that, and never turn into directions. If she doesn't show interest in your suggestion, never persist with it.

> **Make suggestions to develop her play**

The benefits of avoiding directions in play are strongly supported by research findings. A Canadian study, for example, found that a group of children whose mothers showed a high level of intrusiveness into their children's play had significantly lower language attainments than did a group whose mothers followed their children's lead.[11]

★ Help her to continue to enjoy listening

It's still important that your little child continues to have lots of experiences of finding listening easy, attractive and lots of fun.

Repetitive rhymes and action rhymes such as 'The wheels on the bus' and 'Bumpy road' are great for this and, as we have heard, also give her an awareness of rhyme and how sounds are put together to form words that will help her later with learning to read. She will still love rhymes made up about herself that go with a traditional tune.

Something else, which is great fun at this stage, is to make a joke out of coughing and sneezing. She'll love that and find it quite hilarious.

There is still much you can do in terms of the way you talk to her which will ensure that she enjoys listening to you.

I hope that keeping your voice lively and tuneful is by now the natural way you speak to her, and that you also speak a little slower and louder than you do to an adult. This still makes your speech very easy and attractive to listen to for her, so do keep it up. Similarly, a little pause between sentences helps her to listen easily to what you have said.

> **Help her to continue to enjoy listening**

As before, it is often great fun to draw her attention to sounds made by something which is the focus of her attention, like the sound made when you open or close a box.

She will still enjoy listening to 'play sounds' very much, so don't stop these yet.

★ Say back to her what she means

Your little child now has a great deal to say, but still has not quite enough language to say it with. As before, when she mispronounces a word, make a point of using it in several little sentences, for example, 'Yes, it's a gorilla. Gorilla's huge. A huge gorilla!'

If her sentence is muddled or incomplete, you say for her what she wanted to say. If she said for example, 'Daddy goed work', you could reply 'Yes, Daddy went to work'. This is of great help to her in terms of the development of her conversational skills, so take every opportunity of doing it.

> **When talking back, always start with a 'yes'**

As before, it is *extremely* important that you always make this part of the natural conversation. The golden rule is still always start with a 'yes'.

You may now run into what can be a very distressing situation where you don't understand what she has said. Just make sure that she feels this is your fault. I usually say something like 'I'm sorry, I didn't quite hear that' and, if necessary, I encourage the little child to point and show me in any way she can what she means.

★ Keep your sentences short in your playtime

The best way to speak to your little child in your playtimes continues to differ from the way in which you speak to her the rest of the time. Her understanding is extensive now, and you really can chat away outside these times if all has gone well. Your little child herself, however, is likely still to be mainly using two- to three-word sentences which are a bit telegraphic, and she's also likely to have lots of immaturities in her pronunciation. These can easily combine, as we've heard, to make little children at this stage quite often difficult to understand, particularly for people who do not know them well.

To help her through this stage as quickly as possible, it is very helpful to keep your sentences short, in your playtimes, while bringing in lots and lots of new words. Try still to limit some of your sentences to those containing not more than three important words such as 'Teddy's fallen off his chair', 'On your chair, Teddy', 'Don't fall off again'.

> **Don't let your sentences get too long**

> I saw a very bright little girl called Mary in my clinic recently. Her vocabulary and the way she was putting sentences together was fine, but I found her very difficult to understand because she had lots of confusion in her speech sounds. Her mother could understand her perfectly, and didn't realise how difficult it was for other people. She was talking to Mary in very long sentences, and it was evident that all Mary's attention was taken up with following the meaning of them. Once she began to give Mary a clear model of what she was trying to say, and to speak to her in short sentences for part of the time, Mary's speech very quickly became much clearer.

★ Continue to use repetition

Repetition is still very helpful, particularly when you think you may be using a word she doesn't know. Bringing it into several different little sentences will very quickly establish her understanding of it. You might say, for example: 'I'm slicing. Slicing the potatoes. There: slices of potato.'

★ Extend what she says

We have already talked about the fact that it is enormously helpful to give your little child a clear model of what she meant to say, when either her words or her sentences are not quite clear. Do continue to do this.

It is now extremely helpful, at other times, to extend what she has said, as you did in the previous section, adding a little more information. You might, for example, reply to 'Mummy went shops' with: 'Yes, Mummy went to the shops. She bought some new shoes.'

> **Expand a little on what she has said**

Both of these responses are wonderful for building up your little child's understanding. They give her lots of information about both grammar and the meaning of words in the form easiest for her to take in.[12] [13] [14]

Do remember the golden rules at all times when you do either of these. Always start with a 'yes', and never ever give her the impression that you are correcting her in any way.

'DON'TS' FOR THIS AGE PERIOD

As before, make absolutely sure that nobody *ever* corrects your little child's speech, or asks her to say or copy words or sounds. I hope I have shown you how our role as adults is to talk to little children in the most appropriate way, and they will then look after their own talking. Not only is there no need to ask them to say or copy sounds or words, but as we discussed earlier, doing so can make her inhibit her speech. We don't want to give her the message that we don't like the way she speaks.

QUESTIONS

A few questions are now permissible in addition to the rhetorical ones we have discussed before, such as 'That was fun, wasn't it?' which are a nice way of letting the child know that you are giving her the conversational floor. It's good now to include some which can help her to remember sequences of events. Saying, for example, 'Something came after the big swan, remember?' might help her to remember that she also saw some cygnets. Do limit the number of these questions, and always answer them yourself if she doesn't.

Never ask her questions in order to get her to answer. This again is not part of normal communication, and she knows this very well.

Again, limit the amount of 'negative' speech that you use. You will still need to move her bodily away from or towards things, and there is plenty of time later to explain why some things are forbidden, and others that she must do whether she likes it or not.

In particular, try to limit your use of the word 'no' as far as you can. We as adults don't like to hear it, and neither do our little children. Doing this can itself limit the number of tantrums you encounter.

OUTSIDE YOUR HALF HOUR

★ Always talk through her daily routines.
★ *Explain* to her why she cannot do certain things and must do others.
★ Help her to join in your conversations by telling her clearly what is being talked about.

2½ to 3 years

An overview

Your little child will be full of charm at this stage. He will be amenable, helpful and affectionate for much of the time, and altogether a great delight. At other times, however, he will still have violent tantrums if he's thwarted, and can be very difficult to distract at this stage.

His drive towards independence continues apace, and he no longer demands your attention on quite such a moment to moment basis. He can eat skilfully now, and will play for longer spells and at a wider range of activities. He can be difficult to entertain at times, though; you may find that you go to a lot of trouble to set up an activity, and then have to clear it away a few minutes later when he suddenly loses interest.

Please note that the developmental stages described here are averages only.

All babies develop at slightly different rates, and often progress in one area can result in a temporary delay in another. Do not get worried or depressed if your child does not appear to be doing everything at exactly the time periods mentioned here. For further information, see Cause for Concern, page 269.

He still has no sense of danger, and that constant watchfulness on the part of adults is still much needed, particularly when he is in the vicinity of potential hazards like gates and ponds.

Outings will still be a great joy to him, and can now be longer and further afield. He'll start to enjoy parent and toddler groups very much now.

Your little child will still be very emotionally dependent on you, and can be very jealous of siblings at this stage.

Two and a half to two and three-quarter years

THE DEVELOPMENT OF LANGUAGE

The number of words the little child **understands** continues to increase very rapidly in this time, and as a result, he can follow more and more complex sentences. He comes to recognise not only virtually all common object names and action words, but also most common adjectives such as 'thick' and 'thin', 'tall' and 'short'. He also begins to understand prepositions, and will look in the right place for an object he has been told is 'in' or 'on' another object. This enables him to follow long and complicated sentences from the words alone, without the help of clues given by the situation. He no longer needs to see his father's library books to know that he and his father are going to the library.

The amount of information he can take in, in one sentence, is still limited to two important words. You could ask him to fetch one object from another room, for example, but if you asked him to fetch a cup and a spoon, he would almost certainly only bring you either the cup or the spoon.

The little child is making important advances in realising what information other people already have and what is new to them, which is vital for the development of the ability to converse with a wide range of people outside his immediate family. He is aware, for example, that the milkman knows that he likes both milk and orange juice, and the postman knows that he gets regular postcards from his grandma, but that each does not have the information of the other.

His use of language in **speech** is also developing very fast. He begins to use lots more grammatical markers now, although with considerable inaccuracy at first. He begins, for example, to use verbs like 'can' and 'will', and a variety of forms of the verb 'to be', such as 'is', 'are' and 'am'. Mistakes like 'him is going', however, are frequent at this stage.

He starts to use the words 'the' and 'a', again not always in quite the right places yet. You might hear, for example, 'a car's going' or 'I want a biscuit tin'.

A final 's' to indicate plurals comes in more often now, and pronouns like 'he' and 'they' are more often used accurately. The little child also begins to use 'can't ' and 'don't' in the middle of sentences, as in 'I can't do it' or 'I don't want to go to sleep'.

These developments not only serve to make the little child's sentences less telegraphic, but also enable him to use language in interesting new ways. He begins to use it imaginatively, making up little stories like: 'The train came out of the tunnel … and it went up the hill … and it fell over.'

He also names and talks about what he has scribbled, stating, for example, that what looks like a tangle of string is in fact a train track. He can also give more information, including telling his first and second name, and correctly answering the question 'Are you a boy or a girl?'

If his conversational partner doesn't understand him, he may not only repeat what he had said, but may also change it to help his partner to understand his meaning.

A development that looms very large in the lives of parents now, is that many little children begin to ask 'why?' by the end of this age period. They soon realise the great power of this little word both in obtaining information and in keeping the conversation going and, as a result, the frequency with which it is used tends to rise rapidly!

GENERAL DEVELOPMENT

As always, these advances in language and communication development occur alongside those in other areas.

The little child's control over his large body movements continues to improve. Not only can he jump with two feet together, but he can jump down from a bottom step. He can pedal his tricycle more easily, kick a ball a little more forcibly, and march in time to music, which he finds a lot of fun.

His improved hand-eye co-ordination and hand control enable his investigative and manipulative play to develop quite considerably. He can match geometric forms such as a triangle and a square, and fold a piece of paper in half. He recognises tiny details in pictures, and loves to point them out to an interested adult.

The little child can do much more for himself now. He can use a spoon and fork together, and remove and put on simple articles of clothing. He needs little help with this, even undoing and doing up his buttons himself.

He will imitate a long sequence of actions he has seen an adult carry out, and usually does so correctly. He might, for example, pour a cup of pretend tea, then add 'milk' and 'sugar', and finally stir it.

By the end of this age period, he will start occasionally to join in play with other children, in games like kicking a ball, or chasing games.

ATTENTION

Your child's attention development has not changed greatly from the last age period. He still has many spells of intense concentration on objects or activities of his own choice, in which he cannot listen to an adult at all. As in the last age period, he can in some situations shift his attention focus from what he is doing to listening to an adult speaking to him, and then return to his original focus, but never when he is deeply engrossed.[1] He can still only focus on one thing at a time, and is still, therefore, a very long way from the ability which we as adults take for granted and operate without thought: of doing and thinking about several things simultaneously.

He is still highly distractible. Even if he has stopped what he was doing in order to listen to you, he will immediately cease to do so if something else occurs, such as a sudden noise, or someone coming into the room.

As in the last time period, if you need to talk to him about something which is not related to his immediate focus of interest, choose your moment carefully.

Give him warning of a change of activity, saying, for example, 'We'll have to fetch Tim from school in a minute'. Wait until his attention is focused on you before you speak, if at all possible, and if you have to give him a direction, do so immediately ahead of the task, saying, for example, 'Coat on' as you hold his coat out to him.

LISTENING

It is likely that your child will have no difficulty in listening in a quiet environment now. It is still much more difficult than for an adult, however, to listen in noise, so don't be surprised if he still responds to you markedly less well in a noisy environment.

Two and three-quarters to three years

THE DEVELOPMENT OF LANGUAGE

There are further important and significant developments in the little child's **understanding** of words by the time he reaches the age of three. By this time, he fully understands a wide range of prepositions, verbs and adjectives, and can even identify people by the actions they are engaged in, replying correctly, for example, to questions 'Which one is sleeping?'[2] By the time he reaches the age of three, he is fully aware of the meaning of different question forms, and responds appropriately to 'why?' and 'how?'.

The number of words he can take in, in one sentence, also increases, which is a very important step forward. Whereas at the beginning of this time he could only cope easily with sentences containing two important words, such as '**Teddy** wants his **hat**', or 'Your **shoes** are **upstairs**', by the end of this time period, he can follow and remember a sentence containing three key words, such as 'Give the **big ball** to **Daddy**'.[3]

Another important advance the little child makes now is that he comes to understand meanings that are not stated directly – a considerable intellectual achievement. He knows by the time he's three, for example, that 'in a minute' means that he has to wait for something, but not for very long.

He has acquired many concepts now, about animals, people and toys. He knows not only about their colours, shapes and sizes, but also more importantly, about what they do, and how they interact with each other and with him. As a result, simple stories which relate to his everyday life become meaningful, and he can follow them with great enjoyment.

The little child knows still more about what knowledge other people have and what is new to them, and might say to a stranger, for example: 'That's my baby in there. He's called Joey.' He would be well aware that family members would not need to be given this information.

He really listens to the answers to his questions now, particularly the 'why' ones. He also makes the very interesting discovery that the answer to his 'why' questions can be responded to with another 'why', and that this can continue for a very long time!

Equally big changes are happening in terms of his use of **speech**. By the age of three, the little child may be using sentences containing up to three or four important words or even more, like 'Mummy went shopping to buy trousers for work', or 'Daddy's going to London in the car later'. He even joins two together now, which is a great new departure. He may use conjunctions such as 'and' or 'because', saying something like ' We went to the park and I dropped my tractor', or 'Daddy was cross 'cos I spilled my juice'.

His sentences are rarely telegraphic now, but many still contain a number of errors in grammar. After all, he has not been using these markers very long at all. Verbs are frequently still inaccurate, and sentences like 'he wented out' are common at this stage.

He may use more correct plurals, both regular and some irregular, such as 'trains', 'houses', and 'children'.

One quite sophisticated development is that he starts to use 'tag' questions like 'isn't it?' or 'doesn't it?', saying, for example, 'smoke comes out of the chimney, doesn't it?' (You realise just what a complicated grammatical system we have when you listen to a learner talker!)

All these new skills now enable the little child to use language freely to relate interesting experiences he has had in the recent past, and to describe in lots of detail what he sees in pictures. He can also begin to tell little stories, although these are usually limited to one or two sentences at this time. He might say, for example: 'The car went down the road, and met a tractor. They had a big crash.'

The little child's ability to take part in a conversation also develops remarkably in this time At the beginning, as we saw, his contributions were quite disjointed, and adults were having to do most of the work in keeping the conversation going. Quite a lot of his speech was not even directed at a speaker at all. But by the time he is three, the situation is very different. The little child can initiate a conversation with ease, saying, for example, 'Listen Mummy', or 'I want to tell you...'. Turn-taking in conversation is very well established, and by the end of this time, he can even handle interrupted turn-taking: he'll wait, for example, for his mother to complete what she was saying after breaking off to answer the phone.

He is very well aware of his conversational partner's intentions, and understands, for example, whether he is being asked a question or to clarify what he has just said.

By the time the little child is three, language really is becoming the vehicle for thought, as it will be for the rest of his life. He talks to himself a lot when he is not having conversations with other people, as if he is practising putting his thoughts into words. Rather than just describing what he is doing, as he did at the beginning of this time, by the time he is three, he will be using speech to clarify his concepts and ideas. He may for example, say something like: 'These are all big ones ... They're Johnny's. These are little ones, they're for the baby.'

He can now use speech to express his problems as well as for expressing his feelings and needs. He might say, for example, 'I can't do it', 'I lost the ball', or 'I was frightened'. He also uses speech when he wants to resist doing things. Sentences like 'I don't want to', or 'I won't' may be heard.

Words can also help him to think about his behaviour, and how it is regarded by other people. He is keen for approval, and will ask questions like 'Is that right?'

By the time he is three, he has fully realised the huge value of asking questions in the pursuit of information, and may do so endlessly, sometimes driving the adults in his life to the point of exhaustion. His interest in this wonderful world is boundless, and he now has the key to finding out all about it!

Some of his questioning may at this time seem like a game, particularly when he asks streams of them, but it is usually the outcome of a genuine wish to understand and to clarify the meaning of words and information.

Speech is also used for humour now. He may relish telling little jokes like 'Why did the chicken cross the road?' 'To get to the other side!'

GENERAL DEVELOPMENT

Once again, the little child's increased control over his body and the fact that many motor activities, such as walking and running, are carried out automatically and without thought, mean that he can give less attention to this and more to conversation and question and answer sessions.

He can walk upstairs with alternate feet to a step, and backwards and sideways holding a toy. He can throw a ball overhead and catch it between extended arms, and can at last kick a ball forcibly, which pleases him very much. He can pedal his tricycle, not only in a straight line but also round wide corners. He seems altogether much more aware of his body in relation to his surroundings knowing, for example, what size of space he can fit himself into, and how to climb under and over obstacles, ducking to go under a barrier or clambering over a low fence.

He uses his hands more skilfully now. He holds a pencil near the point, with two fingers and thumb, and attempts for the first time to draw a person, producing a circle and two lines to represent legs. He is likely to be able to copy a circle, match six colours and name one, and count by rote to five.[4]

The little child can copy a bridge built from bricks, and build a tower of nine to ten bricks. He can fold paper twice, cut more skilfully with scissors, and put lids on and take them off containers with considerable dexterity.

An interesting development is that he begins to combine play materials. He will play with cars and bricks together, for example, making a road or a garage for the cars. He may put a driver into the engine of a train, or parcels into a lorry.

He is well versed in the routines of daily life now. He can help to set the table, and pour from a jug with little spilling. He drinks from an open cup with few accidents, and can dry as well as wash his hands with little or no help. He is more skilful at dressing himself, but may still put his shoes on the wrong feet.

He is still most likely to play alongside other children, although he is becoming much more interested in them and what they are doing. He does, however, begin to play with them a little more, and awareness of the rules of turn-taking in play begins to emerge. He learns, for example, to wait for his turn on a swing or slide, and to kick a ball.

The little child will play alone for short spells now, but needs to be constantly watched, and to know that an adult is nearby. He loves to involve adults in his imaginative play.

ATTENTION

There is little change in the little child's attention development during these three months.

LISTENING

His knowledge of the meaning of the sounds in his environment will be becoming ever more extensive, particularly now he can ask about the meaning of all those he hears.

Play

Both investigative and pretend play continue to develop and flourish in this time period.

In terms of investigative play, the little child's increased control of his body and eye-hand co-ordination enables him to do much more with the different play materials available to him. He develops much greater skills in using scissors and drawing materials, and is more adept at handling bricks and toys, such as a screw toy or threading beads. In the course of his investigations, he continues to learn a very great deal about colours, shapes, sizes and textures. Pretend play also really flourishes now, and includes very extensive role play in which he likes to reverse the roles, taking turns with an adult, for example, at being dentist and patient. Imaginative play continues to flourish.

Your contribution to his play is now extremely important. In terms of investigative play, it's very important that he is provided with appropriate materials, and his use of them, as before, can be greatly enriched if you tell and show him all the different things he can do with them.

The development of imaginative play is also greatly helped by enabling the little child to have different experiences such as visits to a farm or a zoo, as well as to the shops or the park. He will love to re-enact them later in an attempt to find out all about them.

He also needs time to watch others in his home engaging in activities such as cooking or gardening. It's wonderful for him, too, if adults playing with him take on all the many roles he asks them to, and as before, makes suggestions about how the roles could be extended. He could be shown, for example, how the librarian stamps the books, and perhaps even given a play stamp.

It is enormously helpful for the same adult to play with the little child on a regular basis. She or he will know all about the games which have gone before, and when an activity is being repeated or extended. She or he will also of course know about the real experiences the little child has had and wants to re-enact in his play.

INVESTIGATIVE PLAY

The little child now enjoys lots of very active play, such as pedalling his tricycle, and throwing and kicking balls. Sand and water are extremely popular, and he will play with these in more complicated ways, often using them as a background for a play activity rather than just investigating their properties as he did before. He will now, for example, enjoy sailing boats in the water, or making roadways in the sand for his cars and other vehicles. He enjoys large play equipment such as a swing and a slide in the park, under close adult supervision, and becomes increasingly interested in playing near other children.

He still loves matching, sorting, and grading colours, shapes, and sizes, and becomes increasingly skilful at doing so.

He starts to manipulate play materials more finely. His cutting with scissors is more accurate, and he becomes interested in copying an adult folding paper. He can do this vertically and horizontally, but interestingly, his visual perception is not yet mature enough for him to do obliquely.

He still loves to scribble with pencils, crayons, chalks and paint, and will tell you what his scribbles are meant to be. He attempts for the first time to draw a person, and produces a circle for the head, and two lines to represent legs.

Construction materials, like large interlocking bricks, are now used in a variety of different ways, such as for making roads and houses. Like sand and water, these materials are now being used as a means to an end rather than investigated in order to discover their properties.

PRETEND PLAY

This is really flourishing now, and is a delight to watch and to participate in. The little child will engage in very long sequences which represent very accurately the activities of adults he's been observing for some time. He may pretend, for example, to wash teddy's clothes, put them out to dry, iron them and then put them back on teddy.

He is still very interested in role play, and loves to dress up to make this more realistic. He will love to totter about on high heels being Mummy, or smoke a pretend pipe, being Grandpa. He would find a fireman's, nurse's or postman's outfit enormous fun.

He re-enacts less frequently occurring events now, such as going to the hairdresser, and brings more and more detail into his play. He might, for example, not only pretend to cut someone's hair when pretending to be a hairdresser, but also carefully brush the cuttings off his shoulders and remove his overall.

This role play helps him enormously in his understanding of the world. The discussions it often leads to, because they involve re-capturing memory and understanding sequences of events, also greatly help both his thinking and his conversational skills.

The objects the little child uses to represent others can be less realistic now. A piece of string would serve as a stethoscope, for example, or a piece of card a book. By the time he's three, he can do without any object at all. Imagination really starts to blossom. His extensive language skills now enable him to undertake considerable flights of fancy. He may have an imaginary dog at the end of a piece of string, or talk to imaginary passengers when he's pretending to drive a bus. He can even, at times, be unclear as to what is real and what imaginary. I was amused recently when a friend described how her little boy, Charles, frightened himself with his own imagined story. He started talking about how a little boy went walking in a wood, and how it grew dark and he became lost. Charles began to get quite frightened, until his mother reminded him that it was only a story, which she quickly steered to a happy ending. Many little children have an imaginary friend at this time.

He plays much more imaginatively with models, and begins to combine them in order to elaborate his play. He may, for example, build a long road for his cars, or a runway for his aeroplanes A tractor may be made to push a wagon, and a driver and passenger put into a bus or train. The train, for example, may break down and need rescue, or stop at many different stations, representing all the places he has been to. Farm and zoo animals may have all sorts of adventures, such as getting out and becoming lost and eventually safely returned to their homes.

Dolls and teddies are involved in much longer play sequences, and may, for example, be undressed, bathed, fed and dressed in night-clothes.

Glove puppets can be lots of fun now, and may take on distinct personalities, and again have all sorts of wonderful adventures.

He mostly plays alongside other children, but does begin to involve them in his pretend play, which then begins to turn into a social activity. Another child might be involved in a pretend tea-party, for example, and instructed to drink up his tea.

TELEVISION AND VIDEOS

As you have done previously, please limit your little child's television or video watching to half an hour a day, and preferably watch with him so that you can discuss what he has seen, and give him any necessary explanations.

Your choice of programmes can be determined by the same principles as apply to your choice of books. He will very much enjoy those in which characters who become familiar do the kinds of things that he does himself, and will still relish lots of repetition of both scenes and activities. He will like some imaginative stories but, as with books, be careful that he does not become frightened.

Rhymes and music will continue to appeal, as will slapstick humour, and he will also enjoy programmes which address the kind of concepts he is interested in now: those of size and colour.

The Toy Box

As before, the suggested toys and play materials are divided into those which may encourage investigative and imaginative play, but once again, your little child may surprise you in the ways he thinks up of using them.

INVESTIGATIVE PLAY

★ Small ball
★ Small bricks
★ Rollers and cutters for playdough
★ Large outdoor play materials such as a swing or slide
★ More construction materials

PRETEND PLAY

★ Boats for water play
★ Play people to go with doll's house and garage
★ Model vehicles and people – which can be used in the sand pit
★ Farm and animals
★ Airport and planes
★ Dressing-up clothes
★ Shoes or other items of clothing belonging to the adults in his life
★ Train and track with driver and passengers
★ Crane
★ Glove puppets and finger puppets

The Book Shelf

Your little child will certainly continue to enjoy the books from the previous time period. He will still love to go through the same books over and over again, and there is, therefore, no need to add large numbers of books at this stage.

As before, *please do not be tempted to teach him to read yet.* Tell him about the pictures, and read him little stories. When he initiates it, talk to him about the characters and events in the books, and how they relate to his own experiences. These conversations will often be about past and future events, and give wonderful opportunities for language input.

It is still the shared enjoyment of books that matters, and as we discussed in the last section, your little child is learning a great deal about how books work in terms of the conventions of print, for example that we read from left to right, and that pictures and those marks on the page stand for real objects. All this vital groundwork means that at the right time, he is likely to learn to read extremely quickly and easily. Conversely, many children who are taught to read before they are ready are put off books for life, and have a huge struggle learning to read. All that matters at this stage is that the two of you have fun together.

Your little child will still love books which relate to the experiences of his daily life, and to talk about how the characters feel about them. He will also very much enjoy books which encompass the kind of concepts he is now interested in: such as those of size, number and colour.

His language skills now enable him to follow a simple story, and his grounding of knowledge about how the world actually works is now adequate for him to differentiate between the real and the imaginary to a sufficient

CONTINUED

extent to enable him to enjoy some fantasy now. Now at last, he can find stories about animals and vehicles who do the kind of things that he does great fun, secure in the knowledge of what they do in real life.

Bring in lots of drama by using a lively voice, and perhaps using different voices for the different characters. He'd find that great fun. (You can, by the way, still change the words of the stories a little at this stage, if you think they are too long for his attention span or that a change of wording would help his understanding.)

Be careful that your little child doesn't become frightened by imaginary events. Make sure that you always help him to know what is and what is not real by discussing this, and if he does become frightened, change the story, particularly by ensuring a happy ending.

Again, there are many wonderful books which meet the criteria for this stage, some of which are suggested below:

★ *Butcher's Cat, Runaway Orange*, Felicity Brooks (Usborne Publishing)
★ *Arthur's Chicken Pox*, Marc Brown (Red Fox)
★ *Ellie's Shoes & Ellie's Breakfast*, Sarah Garland (Red Fox)
★ *Cockatoos*, Quentin Blake (Red Fox)
★ *Nearly But Not Quite*, John Prater and Paul Rogers (Red Fox)
★ *The Wide-mouthed Frog*, Keith Faulkner (Madcap)
★ *Mole's Summer Stories*, Richard Fowler and Jonathan Lambert (Andre Deutsch)
★ *Fuzzy Yellow Ducklings*, Matthew Van Fleet (Dial Books)
★ *I Love You, Blue Kangaroo*, Emma Chichester Clark (Andersen Press)
★ *The Baby Who Wouldn't Go to Bed*, Helen Cooper (Corgi)
★ *When Martha's Away*, Bruce Ingman (Mammoth)
★ *Harry the Dirty Dog*, Gene Zion and Margaret Bloy Graham (Red Fox)

Summary

To summarise, by the age of three years, your little child is likely to:

★ Listen with great enjoyment to stories.
★ Understand little instructions with three important words, like: 'Open the box, take out the car, and give it to Daddy.'
★ Talk about what is happening in a long monologue.
★ Take part in a conversation about something that has happened.
★ Give his full name.

Cause for concern

Below are circumstances in which it would be advisable to seek professional advice about your little child's development. (Please remember, though, that many children progress at slightly different rates.)

If you are in any doubt about your child, even if the reason for your concern is not mentioned here, do take him to see your health visitor or GP as soon as possible.

At three years it would be advisable to seek a professional opinion if:

★ He frequently doesn't seem to understand what you have said.
★ He often shows that he is not aware of what other people know already. For example, he may start talking to a stranger about 'Johnny' (his baby brother) and not realise that the person he is talking to has no idea who Johnny is.
★ He often says things that seem to you to be irrelevant.
★ He still uses sentences of only two or three words.
★ He doesn't use any little grammatical markers like an 's' at the end of a word to mark a plural.
★ He never asks questions.

* ★ He shows no interest in stories.
* ★ He shows no interest in playing with other children.
* ★ People outside the family find him difficult to understand.
* ★ His attention span is still very short most of the time.

The Baby Talk Programme

HALF AN HOUR A DAY

Make sure that you are keeping up your daily playtimes. As we have said earlier, they are of immeasurable benefit to almost every aspect of your little child's development. He still needs you to be very much aware of his attention level, and as we have seen in the section on play, you can do a great deal to enhance his development in this area. In particular, your regular availability as a play partner is a wonderful gift to your little child. His emotional development will also, as before, benefit

Guy was brought to see me at the age of three because there were concerns that he would not be able to make himself understood in the playgroup he was about to enter. It transpired that Guy had three extremely talkative sisters, and throughout his life had had very few opportunities to spend time alone with one adult. As a result, he had very few opportunities to engage in any kind of extended conversation, and had not learned the basic rules like how to start a conversation, or to take turns. He constantly interrupted other members of his family, which made them very cross, and often didn't listen to their replies, which made them even crosser. Once we established daily one-to-one playtimes for him with his mother, Guy quickly began to learn these skills. He entered the playgroup three months later, and settled in without any problems.

immensely from this undivided attention from you, in which you facilitate and support his explorations, and boost his confidence by encouraging and praising him. These times, too, give you opportunities for discussing your daily lives, including any prohibitions and necessities to conform. Explaining the reasons for these is the most powerful way of minimising tantrums.

He's at the age when little children sometimes test out the rules by deliberately silly behaviour, like refusing to do something or claiming they can't do something you know they can do perfectly well. If you do have to reprimand him, try always to criticise the behaviour and not your little child. It's much better, for example, to say 'That was a silly thing to do' rather than 'You're a silly boy'.

These playtimes will also give you an opportunity to answer his endless questions for as long as he wishes to continue with them. It can be difficult to do this in the hurly burly of everyday life, but he will learn so much from being able to pursue an enquiry for as long as he wishes to. They give him wonderful opportunities to practise his newly acquired conversational skills, which is really important.

Yet another reason why these playtimes can be so important for some little children is that it is a common age for a new baby to come upon the scene. Feelings of jealousy and displacement can be very greatly alleviated by these times alone with one adult, and it's worth ensuring by hook or by crook that they continue. Wait until your partner gets home and can mind the baby, or bring in a friend or relative for half an hour a day if necessary. The emotional aspect of this is the most important at this time, but there is also no doubt that it is difficult, if not impossible, to give two children the best possible language input even if they are at the same age and stage. You will be aware that this is because of the need to follow the focus of attention of each child.

Please do not underestimate in any way the enormous benefits of having a sibling for the rest of his life. Even in terms of language development, conversations between child, parent and sibling are often the situations in which the parent can most easily help the little child to take part in a three-way conversation, which is a very important skill.[5] Children eventually need to learn to communicate competently in many settings other than the one-to-one.

Do not be tempted to turn these playtimes into teaching sessions. This temptation can arise because your little child is now likely to be showing interest in concepts such as colour, number and shape, and many adults think that teaching these puts their child at an educational advantage. Do not waste your precious time together doing this. Bring the names of these concept names into the conversation as they arise naturally, by all means, such as in 'the blue car and the yellow car' as you play with cars, or 'the long brick fits next to the short one' as you build with bricks. New words to describe these concepts, such as 'huge' or 'tiny', could be found very interesting now. Telling your little child concept names in this way conforms to the golden rule of following the child's focus of attention. They will be interesting and meaningful for him, and will consequently be learned effortlessly. A teaching session set up on your agenda would be infinitely less effective and could be very frustrating both for you and for your little child.[6]

I have seen many children who could name lots of colours and shapes, and who knew the alphabet and recited it like automata, but didn't know what the objects were that they were describing, or what to do with them. Their parents had taught them these concept names almost to the exclusion of normal conversation.

Conversations which arise naturally out of the situation, as opposed to teaching situations, are also enormously helpful in enabling the little child to acquire that vital understanding of what prior knowledge different people have, and what they need to be told in order to join in the conversation. A discussion, for example, about how you will tell various people about the new baby would reinforce for him the fact that they don't already have that knowledge; and talking with him about how you both told Grandma about the lovely afternoon you'd had swimming, would again remind him of what she previously

Toby, a three year old, was brought to see me because his language development was very delayed. His most frequent phrase was 'I can't'. His mother had had the notion that children acquire skills much more quickly if they are taught them, and she had spent hours a day trying to teach Toby to walk when he was five months old, and had started to teach him the letters of the alphabet and the names of colours, numbers and shapes before he was a year old. Toby had become an extremely aggressive and frustrated little boy, whose development was showing delay in most areas. Once his mother started to move from her agenda to his, following his interests and commenting on them instead of teaching him, she was interested to find that he quickly relaxed and started to learn. His behaviour soon started to improve as well, and his language development caught up with his age level within a few months.

I first saw Tom when he was nearly three. He had an uncle with learning difficulties and his parents were so anxious to ensure that Tom would not be the same that they spent every available moment teaching him to count and to say the alphabet. Like Toby, he hadn't the least idea what these letters and numbers meant, and because of all the time the teaching had taken, he had missed out on a huge amount of play and conversational experiences. He said very little spontaneously, and instead, because he understood little of what was said to him, frequently echoed back what he had heard. His attention was at the fleeting level and he showed hardly any pretend play. Happily, he also made huge progress very quickly once his parents stopped teaching him and became aware of his attention focus.

knew and did not know. We all need this information to a high degree if we are to communicate successfully with each other.

These conversations also help him to understand clearly the different ways in which we all use language, such as commenting, questioning and requesting clarification. These will all crop up, and will be very easy for the little child to recognise in this situation.

There could be days when shared activity, such as housework or dealing with the laundry, can be an excellent time to spend together, particularly if there is a new baby and your time is very limited. Do make sure though, that you are alone together, and the room is quiet.

Your playtime can be particularly important if your child has experienced a distressing event like the split up of his parents or the loss of a family member. It is so important that he has the opportunity to talk about the event and how he feels about it and to ask you questions about it. In particular, it also gives you the opportunity of reassuring him that what has happened is in no way his fault, which is something that little children often tend to assume.

THE SETTING FOR YOUR ONE-TO-ONE PLAYTIME

This does not differ from that of the previous age period. As he did then, your child will need to have a wide variety of toys and play materials available, including those for investigative and for imaginative play now. As you did before, make sure that they are intact, and are kept where your little child can easily find them. He may well want to combine different toys and play materials now, like using bricks to make a road for his cars, or people to put in a train, so do keep this in mind when you assemble his toys.

Make sure too that there is adequate floor and table space for him to play, and if possible let him leave constructions like roadways or runways up overnight.

> When my son was three, he and his friend Paul spent a whole afternoon building a farm, with walls and houses for the animals, and were delighted with their effort. Unfortunately, Paul's father was very house-proud, and did not allow the boys to leave their construction up, insisting that they dismantled it almost immediately after completing it. At the end of the afternoon, when I arrived to collect my little boy, both children were in tears.

★ **Continue to share his attention focus**

Although, as we have said, your little child can now, in certain situations, follow a direction from you, it is still very much better in your playtimes always to follow his attention focus. You will find that you are now having lots of conversations about interesting things that have happened to him in the recent past, and things you are planning for the near future, but as before, always let him determine entirely how much you talk about the here and now and how much about non-present events. Both are wonderful for his language development, so don't worry; just let him be the decider.

Always stop a conversation as soon as his attention switches to something else, whether this be another topic of conversation about past or future events, or whether

> **Continue to follow his focus of attention**

Maria's mother spent lots of time playing with her, but very much wanted the two of them to complete each play activity and tidy it away before starting on the next one. I watched the two of them thoroughly enjoying a tea-party game one day. After a while, and just after her mother had introduced another character, Maria lost interest in the game, and moved towards the paints. Her mother insisted that she sat down at the tea-party again, but it was clear that she was neither enjoying it nor listening at all to what her mother was saying to her, instead constantly looking towards the paints. They both started to have so much more fun together once Maria's mother recognised the problem, and let Maria lead the play.

Three-year-old Lucy had the opposite problem. Her parents both played with her at the same time, and wanted her to complete a large number of activities in the limited time they had with her while her baby brother was asleep. Poor Lucy had barely completed an activity when it was whisked away, giving her no time to admire the result of her efforts.

---

it is about something in the here and now. (If it is the latter, as before, comment on what is happening.)

Although your little child is becoming so competent in many ways, his attention is still entirely single channelled. He still really can only think about one thing at a time, whereas it is very likely that many thoughts not connected with the here and now go through your mind in the course of your playtime. I have seen so many parents who did not understand this, and complained about their children's concentration.

Conversing with your little child will become much easier for you as this time period progresses. You will find that he is doing much more of his share of the work. Many of your conversations are likely to be extensive now, and to include not only discussions about things he and other people have done, but also the reasons for doing them and the feelings associated with them.

The opportunities for a rich language input are boundless. You can use as many new words as you like now, and do not be frightened of doing so. As long as they are used in the context of his interest and attention, he will very quickly come to understand them. As before, repetition is very helpful when you think that a word may be new to him. Put the word into several different little sentences, such as: 'It's a tarantula. Look! The tarantula's running. What a big tarantula.'

You can also use a wide variety of grammatical structures. Don't worry now about simplifying your sentences, just use whatever sentence form seems appropriate. Your little child is acquiring these grammatical markers very fast now, and again, as long as they are used in the context of his chosen focus of attention, he will rapidly increase his knowledge of them.

Use lots of new words

HELP TO DEVELOP HIS PLAY

Playing regularly with your little child is now of the very greatest help to him. As we have seen, both investigative and pretend play are developing enormously and there is much you can do to him with both. In terms of investigative play, the first essential is to provide him with lots of appropriate materials, such as different materials for drawing, like chalks or different colours and sizes of paper, and more toys which can be used with water, sand and playdough. These could include different sizes and shapes of containers, or pastry cutters. Your little child will very much appreciate you showing him what exciting things can be done with all these materials, like what fun it can be drawing with white chalk on black paper, or drawing round his hand or foot. Of course, you will pick the moments when he looks to you for such suggestions, which he surely will. He's likely to try to do more difficult things now, like cutting and folding paper, or building more complicated structures, and often a little help, tactfully given, can be very welcome. As you did before, you will find it best to extend the skills he has already. When he can cut relatively skilfully with scissors, for example, you could show him how doubling the paper over before cutting makes an interesting shape. As before again, it's best to show him an activity or extension to an activity and then retreat, leaving him to have a try himself. He will not hesitate to let you know when he wants you to be involved again.

There may also be opportunities to help him understand turn-taking in play, even at this early stage. By the end of this time period, he is likely to enjoy matching games such as picture dominoes and colour matching games, and learning to take turns becomes a natural part of the game.

You can be of just as much help to him in terms of his imaginative play. Again, providing materials such as dressing-up clothes or some of your old clothes or shoes can stimulate wonderful games. You will also be much in demand as a participant in role play. You are likely to find yourself in all sorts of roles relating to all the different experiences he has now, like going to the dentist, or the hairdresser, as he seeks to find out what these people do and why they do it. He will love to reverse the roles with you too. As before, you can help enormously to extend the play by adding in suggestions like showing him how the barber sweeps the hair clippings from the floor, or how the dentist makes the water whirl round in the basin. (Of course, you will never persist if he is not interested in your suggestions.)

When he plays with model toys, such as a farm or zoo, you can also help to extend his play in similar ways, suggesting, for example, that a tractor breaks down and it has to be fixed. (It's important to make sure, however, that such suggestions are within his experience, and are, therefore, meaningful for him.)

When he starts to combine materials, like making a road for his cars out of bricks, you will also find opportunities to elaborate the game, like adding traffic lights or a crossing in this instance.

Your little child may bring pretend people into his play by the end of this time period, and will be delighted if you join in with his imagination. You could even help

Help him to extend his play

him to extend the personalities and events of these people, and, of course, be very interested in the activities of his imaginary friend if he has one.

★ Make sure that he continues to enjoy listening

It is still very helpful to ensure that your little child has plenty of opportunities to enjoy listening, particularly to voice. Those repetitive rhymes and action rhymes we've been talking about for so long are still wonderful for this, such as 'Ring a roses', 'Row your boat', 'Here we go round the mulberry bush' and 'The wheels on the bus'. These are still enormously enjoyed. He'll relish silly songs and chants now, like 'Silly Billy' and, as before, jokes made around coughing and sneezing. Exaggerated expressions of surprise and horror will

Keep lots of tune in your voice

also amuse him mightily.

Please continue to speak to him a little slower and louder than you would to an adult, with lots of tune in your voice. This is still the most attractive kind of speech for him to listen to. Keep your play sounds up too, for example, saying 'der der' and 'brm

brm' as you play with vehicles. He won't be too old to find these great fun to listen to for some considerable time yet.

★ Don't let your sentences get too long in your playtimes
As we have seen, the little child now understands an enormous number of words of all kinds, and lots of grammatical structures. There is still, however, a limit to the amount of information he can deal with in one sentence. This limit is still three important words by the end of this age period, which actually gives scope for quite long sentences, like 'Grandma is going on a bus to the shops'. It's helpful to keep your sentences to this length within your playtimes, as this will help his understanding to develop as fast as possible.

There is another important reason for limiting your length of sentence in your playtime. The little child is also beginning to use lots of the little grammatical markers, such as 's' at the end of a word to mark plurals, and all the different forms of verbs. This is really no small task to sort out. Think of all the variations of the verb 'to be' for example, which include 'am', 'is', 'are', 'were', 'will be' and so on.

The more he is enabled to notice all these variations, the more quickly he will acquire the ability to use them accurately, and we can best give him this help by limiting the length of the sentences we use to him. When we use long sentences to little children, all their energy goes into following the meaning of them, and they do not have much chance of noticing these grammatical markers. Many of

> **Don't let your sentences get too long**

these are, in fact, in the unstressed part of the word and very quiet. It would be easy, for example, to miss the ending of the word 'walked' in a long sentence.

★ Say back to him what he means
As we have discussed above, your little child is busily noticing and beginning to use lots of the little grammatical markers which make the meaning of what we say so much clearer for our listeners. It is still very helpful indeed, when you notice that

your little child has not got a sentence quite right, to say back to him the correct version. If he said, for example, 'We wented to the park' you could say: 'Yes, we did. We went to the park. We went this morning.'

Please remember the golden rule when you do this. Make sure that your response is always part of the natural conversation, and never gives him the impression that you are correcting him. Start with a 'yes' to ensure this.

Your little child will still almost certainly be mispronouncing some words, as we do not expect the whole speech-sound system to be in place until the age of seven.

As before, it is very helpful to say back to him clearly words he has mispronounced, in several short sentences. For example, if he said 'It's a big simney', you could say: 'Yes, it is big. It's a very big chimney. The chimney nearly reaches the sky.'

This gives him the best possible chance of noticing all the sounds in words and the order in which they come, which is all he needs to help him eventually to be able to say the words correctly.

Again, always remember the golden rule and start with a 'yes'.

★ Expand on what he says

We talked in the last section about how helpful it is to expand on what your little child has said. Do this lots now. He might say, for example, 'The clown had a funny hat', and you could say, 'Yes, he did. It had a bobble on the top. The bobble waggled about and made us laugh.' You are very likely to find that these expansions lead to very interesting conversations now.

'DON'TS' FOR THIS AGE GROUP

Never correct his speech, and make sure that nobody else does either. As we have said, his pronunciation is likely to be immature for some time yet. This is largely because he has not yet noticed where every sound goes in every word, and also that he hasn't quite attained the necessary fine co-ordination of tongue and lips to enable him to produce the more difficult sounds or blends of sounds. Correcting the little child does not in any way help with these, and only serves to give a message that we don't like the way he speaks, which we certainly do not want to do. As we have said before, the most helpful thing is to enable him to hear us saying the words clearly.

The hundreds of children who have been treated in our clinics for unintelligible speech have never had any idea that they had a problem. They just thought they came for a thoroughly enjoyable playtime. In fact, of course, we were talking to them in such a way as to enable them to notice all the different speech sounds and where they go in words, which was exactly what they needed. The only problem we had was in persuading children to come out of the room at the end of the session!

★ Don't set out to teach him

Providing that you spend time with your little child, and follow his agenda in terms of your activities, your little child will acquire vocabulary, grammatical structures, concepts and the rules of social interaction effortlessly and naturally.

Were you to set the agenda and decide to teach him specific words or concepts, his learning would be nowhere near as fast, as these would be so much less meaningful and interesting for him. I have seen many children who were in a state of considerable confusion about colours, shapes and numbers because their parents had set out to teach them. The children had picked up their parents' anxiety for them to learn, and this of course had the result that they found learning difficult. Conversely, I have seen other children who knew every colour by the age of two because they were particularly interested in them and their parents had noticed this and used the names incidentally while following their child's lead in play.

QUESTIONS

You are likely to find yourself asking more of the kind of questions we discussed in the last section, which are designed to help the little child remember the sequences of events he has experienced. The question 'Do you remember what the dentist did after you got out of his chair?' for example, could lead to a useful recapitulation of the events of the morning. It's still important to limit the number of these questions, though, and always to answer them yourself if he doesn't. For example, if

> An enchanting three year old called Mike was brought to our clinic because he was having difficulties putting words into sentences. His mother was asking him a constant stream of questions designed to force him to put words together, like 'Is that a big bus or a little car?' and 'Are these your black socks or your white gloves?' Mike steadfastly refused to answer, and was becoming more and more inturned, ignoring the presence of other people altogether. As soon as his mother began to turn most of her questions into comments relating to his focus of attention, he became the greatest fun to play with. He had lots of imaginative ideas, and a wonderful sense of humour.

that particular sentence were greeted with a silence, you could say: 'He gave you your coat and a sticker to put on it.'

It's fine to ask a question if you do not know the answer

Once again, never ask questions in order to get your child to answer. This really is very, very important.

It's fine, of course, to ask questions to which you do not know the answer such as 'Would you like milk or juice?' This kind of question may now include those asked in order to clarify what's in your little child's mind, such as 'Do you want teddy to have the next turn, or me?'

Again, the golden rule is that it is fine to ask a question if you do not know the answer.

OUTSIDE YOUR HALF HOUR

★ Let him do things for himself whenever possible (but be there to help if he is becoming frustrated).
★ Explain to him why he must and cannot do things.
★ Give him lots of opportunities to watch you and other adults carry out domestic routines such as cooking and gardening.
★ Talk him through his daily routines, telling him what is happening.
★ Let him use large play equipment in the park.
★ Give him opportunities to play near other children.
★ Give him opportunities to act out his experiences: for example, going to the hairdresser or the dentist.

3 to 4 years

An overview

This is an absolutely delightful age, and in many ways a relatively easier one for the adults in the little child's life.

She will be very competent at managing her daily life now, largely independent at feeding and dressing herself. She is also much more aware of other people's feelings and needs, and can be sympathetic both to other children and to adults. All these things can be discussed with her now – she is full of conversational charm!

You'll find her affectionate and confiding, and very much wanting to please you. She will love to help you around the house or garden, and will even make efforts to keep her surroundings tidy!

Please note that the developmental stages described here are averages only.

All babies develop at slightly different rates, and often progress in one area can result in a temporary delay in another. Do not get worried or depressed if your child does not appear to be doing everything at exactly the time periods mentioned here. For further information, see Cause for Concern, page 303.

An important landmark is that your child may now be happy to visit the homes of other children without you, and to be left at a playgroup, as long as she knows exactly when you will be coming for her.

She loves to play with other children, and you will find that when she has a playmate you will be interrupted much less than you were formerly. She will stick at activities for much longer, and you won't often now find that you set up an activity which is abandoned after just a few minutes.

Three to three and a half

THE DEVELOPMENT OF LANGUAGE

At the beginning of this age period, as we have seen, the little child **understands** a wide range of verbs, adjectives and prepositions, and can follow sentences containing three important words, like 'Teddy's on the biggest chair'.

She has begun to understand the meaning of indirect comments like 'in a minute', and has acquired considerable awareness of what other people do and do not know already, which helps her to converse with a wider range of people.

By the time she reaches the age of three and a half, she also understands words which are much less commonly heard, like 'delivery' and 'horrible', and can follow sentences containing four important words – like 'Baby's yellow cup is in the kitchen' – another big step forward. She begins to understand and enjoy similes such as 'rain like rods' or 'shoes like plates' and even metaphors like 'under the weather' if she has heard them used.

Most of the little child's understanding, however, is still strictly literal. I was amused recently by a story a friend told me. She had taken her little boy Charles to her grandmother's house, and her grandmother opened the door to them, saying:

'I'm having such a fight to put on my duvet cover.' Charles fell about laughing, saying, 'You can't fight with a duvet cover.' He was still giggling about it the next day.

You will find that your child's great interest in and awareness of words means that it is no longer possible for you to change the wording of a song or story without being greeted with strong protests.

She does not always listen fully to the answers to her questions, being more interested in how they fit in with her own thoughts. You might, for example, be giving a detailed explanation, in reply to her question, of how bulbs develop into flowers, only to be greeted with the response 'There are lots of flowers in the park'.

At the beginning of this time her **speech** features sentences containing three important words or even more, like 'Mummy's gone to work in the car'. She may also use language for humour, having discovered that jokes make people laugh, and telling them frequently, although not always understanding them.

Sentences will be joined together with 'and' or 'cos' (because), such as 'I went shopping and bought a balloon', and 'I dropped it cos it was hot', and she is beginning, too, to use some grammatical markers like an 's' at the end of words to indicate a plural, and some correct past and present verb forms such as 'went' and 'go'.

By the time she's three and a half, she will have started using more complex sentences with many more correct grammatical markers, including more correct past tenses like 'cried', present tenses like 'going', and more plurals both regular and irregular, like 'babies' and 'women'.

At this stage she now uses the pronouns 'I', 'you', 'we', 'she' and 'they' correctly, and the word order in her questions is correct too. She will now say, for example, 'What are you doing?' rather than 'What you are doing?' as she would have earlier. She uses a variety of negative forms now, including 'can't' and 'won't' and links many more sentences together, including by 'but' 'if' and 'then'. For example: 'I want that one, but it's too hot', 'We'll go out if it stops raining' and 'I'm going on the swing, then I'm going on the slide'.

These developments enable her to use language freely to express herself, and she now does so clearly and in considerable detail. She would have no difficulty, for example, in asking for 'The big cookie with the chocolate on the top'.

She may also, at times, respond to other people's conversations. I noticed a little boy in a supermarket recently listening intently to two other shoppers' conversation about a dog. As he passed them, he piped up: 'I've got a doggie. He's called Rusty.'

At the beginning of this time period, language has begun to be truly a vehicle for thought, enabling the little child to solve problems and to make plans. She has also become a skilled conversationalist: initiating, maintaining and repairing breakdowns in conversation. By three and a half she has developed more strategies for initiating conversation, with opening questions such as 'Do you know what?' She is much more able to communicate with strangers and her peers, thanks to her much greater knowledge of what they do and do not know previously, and how to fill in the gaps in this knowledge. She is very well aware of the conventions of conversation, for example, knowing when she is being asked a question or to clarify something she has said.

One amusing feature is that when playing with a partner, she now at times talks alternately to herself and her partner. She might say to herself, for example, 'I'm putting this here,' and then turn to her partner and add 'and you put that one there'.

She can participate in pretend conversations, and switch from one kind of voice and way of speaking to another, using a deep gruff voice for a giant, for example, and a high piping one for a little child.

GENERAL DEVELOPMENT

As always, language is not the only area in which there are great advances and developments.

The little child at this age loves vigorous outdoor activities, at which she is becoming a lot more proficient. She can kick a large ball, and can also throw a small one several feet. She can hop, jump from a second step, and runs very smoothly now, not needing to stop before going round wide corners. She can also run while she is pushing or pulling toys along.

Her improved hand-eye co-ordination and hand control are now also reflected in new skills. By the time she is three and a half, the little child can cut along a line fairly straight with scissors, and trace a double diamond. She can copy the letters V, H and T.

She becomes still more independent in caring for herself, and can eat with a knife and fork, and wash and dry her hands, arms and face.

She relishes adult approval, and will try to conform to the household rules, for example by helping to tidy up her toys, and sharing them with others.

ATTENTION

An important development occurs at or near the beginning of this time period in terms of attention. For the first time, the little child becomes able to shift her attention focus from what she is doing to someone speaking – by herself.[1] She no longer needs an adult to cue her by calling her name, but instead she will notice that someone is speaking, and shift her attention from what she is doing in order to listen. This shift of focus is not quick: she often takes some time to register that someone is speaking and stop what she is doing to listen. The more she is concentrating on what she is doing, the longer she takes to shift her attention focus and the more quickly she returns to what she was doing previously.

LISTENING

It is unlikely if you have been following the programme that your child will have any difficulty selecting what she wants to listen to and maintaining focus for as long as she wants to. Even if she has had a hearing loss, the programme will have minimised its effects, by giving her plenty of opportunities to listen to speech in a quiet environment, and to hear speech which is easy and attractive to listen to.

Three and a half to four

THE DEVELOPMENT OF LANGUAGE

The amazing fact is that your child will basically have mastered language by the end of this time period. In the space of only four short years, she will have acquired a vocabulary of thousands of words which she can both understand and use, and all the basic sentence types that there are in the language. She will continue to increase her vocabulary throughout her life, as we all do, and will find more and more complex ways of putting sentences together, but she is now already a fully verbally communicating human being.

The little child's **understanding** of speech now becomes extremely extensive. By the time she reaches the age of four, she knows the meaning of many thousands of words, including all the basic types such as nouns, verbs, adverbs, adjectives and prepositions. She understands words which are infrequently heard, like 'liquid', 'forest', 'eagle', 'pasting' and 'woolly'.[2] Even more importantly, she now can follow sentences containing up to six important words, such as 'Let's put both the big teddies under the long shelf', or 'The big bricks are in the red box behind the door'. This means that there is very little everyday speech which she will not follow, and consequently she will be listening to and acquiring the meaning of new words and grammatical structures for much of the time, and not only when she is being spoken to directly.

This enormous increase in understanding is reflected in the little child's use of **speech**. By the time she reaches the age of four, the little child's spoken vocabulary is around 5,000 words. She has also acquired the ability to use all the basic grammatical structures of the language (although she still makes mistakes from time to time). All that remains for the future is to acquire more vocabulary, which we all do throughout our lives, and to come to use grammatical structures in more and more complex ways.

She uses many more mature grammatical forms now, such as negatives in the past tense like 'I didn't do it', and possessives like 'Teddy's coat'.

The extent to which she can use language to plan and problem solve is evidenced by her use of sentences like 'I think we'll let Tommy come too', and 'I want to play outside, but it's going to rain'.

The little child's speech is usually easy to understand now, despite some continuing immaturities. She is likely still to substitute an easier sound for a more difficult one, like 'tare' for 'chair', and to simplify difficult clusters of sounds as in 'sibble ' for 'scribble'. It may be another two years or even more before these are all correct. Some children do not pronounce the difficult sounds 'r' and 'th' correctly until they are seven years old.

The little child at this stage seems to revel in her new linguistic abilities, and becomes very talkative indeed. She can give coherent accounts of recent events and future plans, and can tell long stories in which fact and fiction are considerably confused, reflecting her difficulty in separating the two. She may make up wonderful excuses and fabrications which she comes to believe herself. She may assure you, for example, that a giant came down the chimney and knocked over her juice!

She can give more factual information now, including her full name and address.

Questioning is at its peak now. The questions she asks differ now from those of earlier times, in that rather than relating to simple cause and effect as in something like 'Why is that wet?', many now relate to her desire to understand both nature and the social world. Questions like 'Why did that lady give...?' or 'How do birds fly?' are now common.

Your child is a very skilled conversationalist now, helped by her greatly increased social awareness. She is very competent at initiating conversation by calling a name or using a phrase like 'I want to tell you something'; and finishing them by changing topic or starting a different activity. She notices straight away when her partner is looking puzzled, and quickly repeats or re-phrases unclear words or sentences before she is asked. Her timing of conversational 'turns' approximates to that of adults. She chooses, for example, an appropriate time to join in other people's conversations, waiting for a pause in which to do so, and keeping to the topic under discussion. She will continue to take turns for longer in a conversation, and may nod or say 'yes' to acknowledge what her partner has said. Her greatly increased social awareness even enables her to adapt her speech to suit different conversational partners. She would speak very simply to a baby, for example, and politely to an authority figure like a playgroup leader, being careful to use 'good morning' and 'please' and 'thank you' which may get forgotten at times at home and with her peers.

Her knowledge of what prior knowledge her conversational partners have is extensive, but not yet complete. She could still forget, for example, that her nursery teacher didn't know that she went to the sea at the weekend, and say something like 'and the waves got bigger and bigger', to the teacher's considerable confusion.

Language is used in still more different ways, and fulfils more purposes in a social context both with adults and peers. She can bargain – saying to another child, for example, 'You can go first on the slide, and I'll go first on the swing' – and negotiate: 'I'll give you all these bricks if you let me choose what we build'. She will also threaten, with statements like 'I'll take them all away if you don't let me have a turn'. She can use language to state rules, as in 'You put the counter on this square first', and even as a means of establishing an alibi, with a comment like 'It must have been Johnny: I was outside'. She also uses language to discuss her own actions and what she thinks of them. She can be critical of herself, saying, for example, 'That was silly'. She can also congratulate herself with comments like 'I did a lovely drawing today'.

The little child now loves to play with language. She adores jokes like: 'Why did the grass snake sniff? Because the adder 'ad 'er 'andkerchief!' Even before she understands the joke, she realises that it makes people laugh, and tells them often. She loves to use language to clown, for example chanting 'It's raining, it's pouring, the old man's snoring' repeatedly as she waves her arms vigorously in the shower. Malapropisms like 'It's roaring with pain' for 'It's pouring with rain' are considered hilarious.

GENERAL DEVELOPMENT

The little child is now becoming even more skilful in terms of the active outdoor activities she loves. She can now run to kick a ball, which goes in her chosen direction, can catch a ball bounced to her, and can begin to use a large bat. She can run on tiptoe, and turn sharp corners when she is running. She loves to climb ladders or trees. She can hop on one foot, skip and pick up small objects from the floor by bending from the waist. She can jump from standing or running, and can even turn a somersault. She is an expert bike rider now, manoeuvring at speed with considerable dexterity.

The little child now holds a pencil in the same way as adults do, realising that it is helpful to steady the paper with her other hand. She draws a person with head, legs, arms, eyes and trunk, and also a very simple house. She can copy a cross. She is able to fold a piece of paper three times and crease it, and build a tower of ten bricks. She may be able to count to ten by rote (although she is very far from understanding the concept of more than three as yet).

The little child can carry out still more of the tasks of everyday life. She is almost entirely independent in terms of dressing and undressing, only needing help with difficult fastenings. She can spread jam with a knife, and brush her teeth herself. She loves to go on little errands, such as to post a letter in the letter box.

By the time she is four, the little child tends to be a bundle of energy, active and exuberant, and finding it extremely hard to sit still. She tends to become very self-willed, and her behaviour tends to go out of bounds at times. She may be quite impertinent, saying things like 'I don't like you, and I won't do what you say'. She can, however, cope at times with not getting her own way.

The little child now becomes a considerable show-off, and loves to seize the floor by mimicry, jokes and teasing.

ATTENTION

Her attention is still single channelled. She cannot, until the very end of this time period or even beyond it, listen to some-one talking about something unconnected with what she is doing. (This is the stage necessary to cope with school, where of course children need to be able to listen to and follow instructions as they work.)

The little child still needs lots of warning when there is to be a change of activity, and time to make a shift of attention focus. It is still very helpful if any necessary directions are given not far ahead of what she is being asked to do. Instructions like 'Wash your hands before lunch' are still best given shortly before she is required to wash her hands.

LISTENING

There are no particular changes from the last time period.

Play

This is a wonderful period for play, which really flourishes in many ways now. The biggest change is that play increasingly becomes a co-operative social activity. The little child delights more and more in playing with her peers, although she will also still play alongside them at times. Her newly acquired skills in language enable her to discuss and agree plans and rules, and this allows her gradually to learn to co-operate with others. She learns to take turns, to explain herself, to listen to others, to negotiate and to understand their point of view – all of which are very important skills for life.

Individual differences in play preferences now begin to emerge more strongly, the precursor of adults' choice of leisure activities. Lifelong interests in art, music or science may begin at this stage.

Another important development is that creative play now begins to come into its own. This happens because the little child now has a good working knowledge of the properties of the toys and play materials available to him, and the language skills with which to think about them imaginatively and creatively.

THREE TO THREE AND A HALF

★ Investigative play

The little child still enjoys active outdoor play very much. She loves to ride her tricycle and to run, jump and kick balls.

She still also very much enjoys sand and water play, and likes to pour them to and from different containers at times. More often now, however, they are used as even more complicated backgrounds for play with vehicles and play people. The little child continues to learn a great deal about size, weight, texture and volume from these materials.

She starts to enjoy a wider range of modelling materials, such as clay or plasticene, and will use them constructively to make objects for her games, like food for a doll's tea-party, or structures like houses for her farm animals. She starts to experiment with them too, discovering, for example, that patterns can be made by pressing different objects on to them.

She now also enjoys using 'junk' materials constructively, building boxes and tubs into wonderful constructions, for example, both indoors and out.[3]

At this stage, the little child relishes being involved in real activities such as gardening and cooking. Her joy at producing biscuits or jelly, or watching the flower of a bulb she has planted is boundless. She will also marvel at silkworm or butterfly cocoons and the transformation of tadpoles into frogs.

★ Imaginative play

Pretend play, if the little child has opportunities, now develops into social play in which different children take different roles: for example, that of a shopkeeper and people taking turns to make purchases.[4] This occurs in short spells initially, as the children still have much to learn about how to organise and maintain such play. Co-operation is a very new departure. There is not yet much of a plot with a sequence of events – that will come later.

When there are no other children available, the little child will, as before, act out experiences she has had, like going to the doctor, and will still love adult involvement in such play. She may now also act out events from a story or television programme, such as pretending to be a runaway train or a monster. She still very much appreciates realistic 'props' like a shopping bag, till and toy money.

Pretend play with roadway, garage, and farm or zoo also becomes steadily more elaborate, and again will often now be enjoyed by two or more children at the same time. One child, for example, might be in charge of the farmer, and load up the tractor, while another will see that the animals are returned to the field.

Little children, at this age, start to enjoy playing competitive games such as very simple card games like 'snap', and board games like 'picture lotto'. Skittles and party games such as 'Pass the Parcel' are also much enjoyed, and the children become very interested in learning the rules (and enforcing them when necessary).

★ Investigative play

The little child's enjoyment in very active outdoor play continues strongly. By the time she reaches the age of four, she loves to test herself to the limit, jumping as high and as far as she can, and doing stunts like riding her tricycle in a standing position.

Her manipulation of creative materials is much more co-ordinated than it was earlier. She enjoys painting and drawing very much, and she now also loves to use many different media: for example printing with potato cuts and other materials; making rubbings and collages; cutting out and pasting.

She will use 'junk' such as yoghurt pots, lids, tubs, and boxes to create wonderful constructions like a fire station or a castle. Her interest in cooking and gardening is undiminished.

She likes to do more difficult puzzles now, and uses construction material like interlocking bricks to make much more elaborate structures. She also likes smaller construction materials, and will use them, for example, to make buildings to go with her airport.

Play with construction materials like bricks also becomes co-operative, and elaborate definite plans may now be made, for example to build a roadway, with several children collaborating in its building. Of course, there is not always harmony and agreement, and squabbles are not at all infrequent. Children at this age are often alternately co-operative and aggressive, both with each other and with adults. They can, however, show considerable sensitivity to others, particularly for siblings and playfellows who are in distress.

Co-operative games now become very popular, such as 'Follow my Leader' and 'O'Grady Says', as do simple card games and board games.

Materials like large boxes and large blocks are now very much welcomed, and can be transformed into a shop, a plane, or anything else needed for a game.

The interest in nature which began in the last time period is undiminished, and little children at this stage are fascinated, for example, by sprouting peas and beans, in watching bulbs flower, tadpoles and butterflies. They love to watch birds eating bird-food from a bird-table or feeder, and become greatly interested in caterpillars and spiders.

★ Imaginative play

Group pretend play really develops now. The little child makes many more social advances, and now engages in much longer sequences with definite outcomes. These may be sequences of events they have experienced, like going to the hairdresser or doctor, but now may also be from a book or television programme. Imaginary themes start to come in, such as stories of dragons or monsters. A decision may be made, for example, to have a pretend fire, rescue all the people in the building and put out the fire. This extended pretend play may at times include fantasy: for example, a fire engine coming from the sky to the rescue. This kind of dramatic play is much enhanced by dressing up, and the little child finds what fun it can be to act, changing her voice and movements to fit different characters.

A play house really comes into its own now, and can be used for all sorts of domestic play with opportunities to take many roles.

Dolls, too, are often involved in imaginary play, like being train passengers who experience a crash and are taken to hospital. Again, these play sequences may be lengthy.

TELEVISION AND VIDEOS

These really come into their own now that the little child has enough language to follow what is being said in them. They can be a good source of information, learning and sheer fun, as well as providing food for the imagination. As with books and play, little children now show more marked individual preferences, but certain programmes are very likely to appeal.

The little child will love stories, particularly about characters who become familiar to her by appearing in a series of programmes. She will love to follow sequences of events, particularly when she can predict what will happen next.

The Toy Box

Again, the suggestions for additions to the toybox are divided into those which are likely to be used for investigative, pretend and social play, but as always, your little child may use them quite differently from the way you had envisaged.

INVESTIGATIVE AND CREATIVE PLAY

★ Clay
★ Plasticene
★ Finger paints
★ Felt-tipped pens
★ Sponges for painting
★ Stamps and other materials for printing
★ Tissue paper
★ More difficult puzzles
★ Large boxes for outside constructions
★ 'Junk' such as tubes, boxes, yoghurt pots, pipe cleaners, shoe laces
★ Plants and bulbs
★ Bird table or feeder
★ Silkworm or butterfly cocoons
★ Tadpoles

IMAGINATIVE PLAY

★ Realistic dolls that can be involved in prolonged imaginative sequences
★ Play house
★ Model houses, trees and people for sand play
★ More dressing-up clothes, such as those for fireman or doctor
★ Hobby horse

CONTINUED

> ★ Farm or zoo board
> ★ Floor road map
>
> ### SOCIAL PLAY
>
> ★ Board games such as 'Snakes and Ladders', 'Picture Dominoes', 'Picture Lotto' and 'Ludo'
> ★ Simple card games such as 'Snap' and 'Happy Families'
> ★ Skittles

Imaginary events will be much enjoyed, but do remember that she still has a lot of difficulty separating fact from fiction, and may need some help with this. The word 'pretend' is a very useful one now. Remember, too, that her understanding is very literal in the main, and she could become very confused by figures of speech like 'The giant's legs were like tree trunks'.

Rhymes and music will be very much enjoyed, and she will love jokes and slapstick humour even more than she did previously.

As we have said, the little child tends to be extremely interested in nature at this time, and this is really where television and videos come into their own. They can enable the little child to have many wonderful experiences that are not possible either in her daily life or by means of other media. She can see many marvels: for example speeded-up flower opening or the transformation of a chrysalis to a butterfly. She can also see animals in their natural habitats in many different parts of the world. (Do watch with her, and be prepared to answer plenty of questions.)

Although at this stage, television and videos have much value to offer, it is still very important that you limit the amount of time your little child spends watching them. An hour a day really should be the limit. The powerful stimulus of the television screen will keep her attention for considerable lengths of time now, but do remember that the television doesn't answer questions, or explain the meaning of words, or even tell the little child what is fact and what fantasy.

The Book Shelf

This is a wonderful period for books, in which the little child can fully discover the delights of books as a means of obtaining information, as food for the imagination and as sheer, highly enjoyable entertainment.

As in play, children's individual preferences will begin to emerge more strongly, and it may be helpful to go to the library to discover what she really likes before buying her books. My daughter and my elder son loved anything and everything I read to them, and I was surprised when my younger son showed a very strong preference for particular stories, wanting them over and over again rather than different ones.

Interest in stories relating to the little child's everyday life is still strong, but she can also now enjoy imaginative stories. It's important to recognise that little children at this stage have much difficulty in separating fact from fiction, as their experience of the world and its wonders is still limited. They need adult help with this, particularly with stories that are potentially frightening. It's also important to recognise that although they are just beginning to recognise figures of speech, their understanding is in the main strictly literal, and they may therefore be confused by analogies which are not explained clearly to them. A sentence like 'a blanket of snow' may perplex her, being unable to see the connection between her cosy blanket and the cold outside.

Traditional stories like 'The House that Jack Built', 'The Three Little Pigs' and 'The Three Bears' are now hugely enjoyed. Little children love the repetitive words and sound patterns, and these stories all have elements that arouse surprise and humour over and over again.

CONTINUED

Little children love to hear them repeated many times, finding increasing pleasure in them, just as an adult does with repeated exposure to particular pieces of music. They love to predict what is coming next, and woe betide an adult who tries to change the wording even slightly.

You may find that your little child wants to take a turn telling you a story which has become very familiar.

She is likely to enjoy factual books about nature now, particularly those aspects she is familiar with. If she had seen some frogs, for example, she would love a book about how they develop from tadpoles.

Little children at this stage love to look at very detailed pictures and pick out particular parts of them.

She is also likely to be interested in books about concepts like colour, number, similarities and differences. Rhyme books are also likely to be much enjoyed.

You may well find that she is now interested in the print, as she will have realised that the words on the page actually correspond to the words we say. She may even recognise that a particular letter stands for a particular sound. If she spontaneously recognises words or letters, and tells you what they are, that's great, but once again, please *don't* set out to teach her. You are giving her in abundance all the important precursors to reading.

Do make sure that you continue to share a book every day. There is a wealth of lovely books for this age band. Those suggested below are a tiny sample, and as we said earlier, children already show strong individual tastes by this age. Follow the golden rule, and always give her the choice of book.

Stories relating to everyday life

★ *What Makes Me Happy?*, Laurence and Catherine Anholt (Walker Books)

★ *What's that Noise?*, Francesca Simon and David Melling (Hodder Children's)

CONTINUED

- ★ *Going to Playschool*, Sarah Garland (Puffin)
- ★ *One Snowy Night*, Nick Butterworth (Picture Lions)
- ★ The *Alfie* books, Shirley Hughes (Red Fox)

Stories with an element of imagination
- ★ *The Snowman*, Raymond Briggs (Puffin)
- ★ *Happy Days for Mouse and Mole*, Joyce Dunbar and James Mayhew (Picture Corgi)
- ★ *Alfie's Feet*, Shirley Hughes (Red Fox)
- ★ *The Tiger Who Came to Tea*, Judith Kerr (Picture Lions)
- ★ *Meg and Mog*, Helen Nicoll and Jan Pienkowski (Puffin)
- ★ *Can't you Sleep, Little Bear?*, Martin Wadell and Barbara Firth (Walker Books)
- ★ *The Bear*, Raymond Briggs (Red Fox)

Factual books
- ★ *Bugs and Slugs*, Judy Tatchell (Usborne)
- ★ *1001 Things to Spot on the Farm*, Gillian Doherty (Usborne)
- ★ *Farmyard Tales*, Stephen Cartwright (Usborne)

Books about concepts
- ★ *I Can Count*, Ray Gibson (Usborne)
- ★ *Fun with Numbers*, Ray Gibson (Usborne)
- ★ *Mouse Paint*, Ellen Stoll Walsh (Orchard)
- ★ *One Two Three with Ant and Bee*, Angela Banner (Mammoth)
- ★ *Starting to Count*, Jenny Tyler and Robyn Gee (Usborne)
- ★ *My Many Coloured Days*, Dr Seuss (Hutchinson)
- ★ *First Learning: Sizes*, J Tyler and R Gee (Usborne)
- ★ *Simpkin*, Quentin Blake (Red Fox)

Rhymes
- ★ *Each Peach Pear Plum*, Janet and Allan Ahlberg (Puffin)

Summary

To summarise, by the time she is four, your little child is likely to:

★ Be understood by people who are not familiar with her.
★ Give a connected account of recent events.
★ Give her address and age.
★ Ask endless questions.
★ Listen to and tell long stories.
★ Use language to bargain and negotiate.
★ Use social terms such as 'please' and 'thank you'.

Cause for concern

Below are circumstances in which it would be advisable to seek professional advice about your little child's development. (Please remember, though, that many children progress at slightly different rates.)

If you are in any doubt about your child, even if the reason for your concern is not mentioned here, do take her to see your Health Visitor or GP as soon as possible.

At four years it would be advisable to seek a professional opinion if:

★ She often looks puzzled, as if she doesn't understand what you have said, or doesn't do what you have asked her to.
★ She doesn't concentrate on anything for more than a few minutes.
★ She doesn't often use grammatical markers such as verb endings and plurals.
★ Her speech is very unclear.
★ She can't give you a clear account of something that happened when you were not present.

- ★ She doesn't ask lots of questions.
- ★ She doesn't want to play with other children.
- ★ She shows or tells you that she is aware of her non-fluency, or seems to be struggling to get the words out.

The Baby Talk Programme

HALF AN HOUR A DAY

Your little child, as we have heard, has moved into the stage where play with other children becomes increasingly important. She will gain enormous benefit now from spending some time in a playgroup or nursery setting, and from children coming to visit your home to play.

She still, however, will benefit hugely from her time alone with you, so please keep it up. This is still the best possible language learning situation, and it is still enormously helpful for her to be with an adult who understands her attention level. You can do so much, too, to introduce her to creative activities and to help her to extend her play. Your regular, reliable and unconditional attention, in which you have all the time in the world to listen to her, still serves to give her great emotional security, and the opportunities to discuss necessary prohibitions and requirements greatly reduces frustration for both you and your little child. It goes without saying that she will still relish the opportunity to have a captive adult to answer all her questions.

NON-FLUENCY

There is still another reason why this time is so important for this age group. Over half of all children between the ages of three and four go through a period of 'non-fluency', in which they repeat syllables or words, often many, many times. This happens because there is an enormous amount going on in their heads, and they don't yet have quite enough language to express it all. The repetitions occur when the little child is trying to figure out how to put what she wants to say. She is totally focused on this thought process, and totally unaware of the repetitions. This stage is a completely normal one, and will pass within a few weeks or months, as her language skills develop. I'm going to talk about this stage and how best to help your little child through it, as it can cause quite unnecessary alarm and despondency. Parents who have known someone with a stammer, particularly if this is one of the family, can leap to the entirely erroneous conclusion that their little child has started stammering, which can cause considerable panic. The danger is that what then commonly happens is that they start saying things to the little child which are meant to be helpful, such as 'Say it again, slower', 'Take a deep breath before you speak', and the little child, who was blissfully unaware of what was happening, is made aware, and begins to try to stop the repetitions. *This* can actually lead to struggle and a stammer.

Michael was an enchanting, curly-headed three year old, whose mother had asked me to see him as a matter of great urgency. She told me that she was panic stricken, as Michael had started stammering. She had two brothers who stammered, and she was very much aware what a disability this is. She had been trying to help Michael by constantly adjuring him to speak slowly, but felt that if anything, he was repeating words more and more frequently. Michael launched himself at the toy box, and began chatting away. He clearly had a great deal to say, and several times repeated a word up to fifteen times. It was evident that he was completely unaware of this, and was totally relaxed, unlike his mother.

Michael's mother was immensely relieved to hear that he was going through a totally normal stage. She phoned me a few weeks later, and told me that Michael's non-fluency had virtually stopped.

The golden rule, which we have discussed earlier, that we never, ever draw the little child's attention to how she is speaking is essential at this time.

Your playtimes are giving your little child exactly what she needs to come through this stage easily, by giving her experience of a situation in which there is no communicative stress. She is not competing to speak; you are giving her lots of time to speak; she is not being interrupted; and she is not being stressed by being asked to answer questions or say words. (As you will be aware, a very important part of the BabyTalk Programme is the avoidance at all times of communicative stress, which is why children who have gone through it emerge as such confident communicators.)

> **Never draw her attention to how she speaks**

The only additional thing that can be helpful at this stage is to slow your speech down a little if your child is a rapid speaker. This will automatically slow her down without her being at all aware of it.

THE SETTING FOR YOUR ONE-TO-ONE PLAYTIME

This can now vary considerably, as long as the two of you are alone together somewhere that is quiet. Your little child may, for example, love to spend time with you in activities such as gardening, setting up window boxes, putting out bird food or cooking. A walk or trip somewhere can be wonderful too.

If you are at home, it is now very helpful to make available to her materials for creative activities, like paint or clay, as well as some for investigative play and some for pretend.

HOW TO TALK

★ **Follow her focus of attention**
Although, as we have heard, your little child is likely to have developed the skill of shifting her attention focus, it is still important to follow her lead all the time in your playtimes. As

before, let her determine entirely the extent to which your conversation focus is about the 'here and now', and how much a discussion of past and future events.[5] When you are focused on the here and now, as before, avoid directions entirely, instead doing what I hope is natural to you now, and giving a 'running commentary' on what is happening, when you are not actually engaged in conversation. You might say, for example, something like 'Oh, it's going round and round. It goes round and round when you push it' as she twirls a toy roundabout.

As we discussed in the previous section, please do not be tempted to start to teach her. She will learn so much more when she is given information incidentally when it relates to what she is interested in at that moment. She will be able, for example, to show you when she is interested in concepts such as colour and number by her choice of books, or her conversation. Two studies, one dated and one more recent both showed that children whose parents played with them did better on later school-related tests than did those who had received early teaching.[6][7]

★ Help her to develop her play
You can still be of the very greatest help to your little child in terms of her investigative play by providing her with appropri-

Three-year-old Ben was brought to my clinic because he was only using two- to three-word sentences, and even those were not at all clear. Three weeks after I first met him, and after lots of discussion with his father, who had had great difficulty abandoning his desire to teach Ben, I watched the two of them having a wonderful play-session together. Ben had chosen a bag of large bricks of different shapes, and wanted to make a complicated roadway with them. As he placed the bricks, his father commented on what he was doing, mentioning the shapes of the bricks incidentally, saying, for example: 'That's a good idea. The square brick fits nicely beside the rectangular one', and 'The round one makes a very good traffic light'. Ben, who had been very confused about the names of shapes, was using their names correctly within a time space of less than an hour.

ate toys and play materials, and by showing her all the wonderful different ways in which she can use them. Interest in activities your little child has been doing for some time can very easily be much enhanced by providing new materials, such as felt-tipped pens for drawing, or sponges for painting. Adding paste to paint to change the texture, so that you can make patterns in it with twigs, comb or toothbrush, for example, can be great fun.

She would love to be given plasticene for modelling, perhaps with different cutters and shapes to press into it, and a new activity which may be found very interesting might be making rubbings of tree bark or other material, by putting paper on them and rubbing it with a crayon. You could show her how to make a scrap book by cutting out pictures from magazines, or a collage by crumpling pieces of tissue paper and gluing them on to coloured paper. (Wallpaper lining paper is a very cheap source of plentiful paper.)

This provision of materials is really important. Interestingly, an American study in the 1980s showed that the mere provision of appropriate play materials correlated with more advanced development in later childhood.[8]

Clearly, if in addition you show your child how these can be used, and help her to do so, she will gain immeasurable benefit. The two of you can have great fun experimenting with these and many other creative activities. She will love sharing them with you and, of course, they provide wonderful opportunities for rich language input. Think of the wonderful words which could be used in a tree-bark rubbing activity for example, including 'splintery', 'flaky', 'embossed', 'outstanding', and 'relief'.

As you did before, extend the skills she already has developed, showing her, for example, how you can make patterns on plasticene by pressing different materials onto it, once she has learned to manipulate it. You could also show her how to cut out shapes with scissors, once she can control her cutting well.

Admire her efforts

Praising and admiring what she produces does wonders for her confidence. She will love to see her pictures on the wall and her constructions on the window sill.

Your little child will love you to play simple board games and card games with her, and you can be of great help to her in explaining the rules before she plays the games with other children.

You can be of just as much help to her in terms of her pretend play. Once again, providing her with materials like an old skirt or shoes of yours, dressing-up clothes, and large boxes and tubes which can be made into garage, shop, fire station or house can be enormously helpful.

It's also still important to make sure that she has as many interesting experiences as possible, so that she can act them out later, and come to understand them and their place in her world more fully.

As she did in the last time period, your little child will love you to make lots of suggestions in order to extend her play, such as showing her, when she's playing at being a fireman, how firemen slide down a pole to get into the fire engine, and how they coil up the hoses. A shopping game could be extended by showing her how the stock is kept at the back of the shop, and the shelves re-filled from there.

Always resist the temptation to take over, however many wonderful ideas you might have. Never forget the golden rule of letting her lead. An American study clearly showed that parents who are too intrusive in their child's play actually hinder their development.[9]

> **Always let your child take the lead**

If you have a little group of children to play, you can also give them a lot of help. Try to ensure that they have adequate space in which to play, and at least half an hour in which to do so. Providing materials like a lot of boxes, cartons and blocks, so that they can create structures like boats or planes, will enable them to have a lot of fun.

You can also be very helpful in sorting out disagreements, as the children do not yet have very extensive skills in doing this.

★ Make sure that she continues to enjoy listening

It is still helpful to make sure that your little child continues to have lots of experiences in which listening is a lot of fun. She will now thoroughly enjoy singing, dancing to music and clapping to the rhythm. She will also adore repetitive rhymes like 'Old Macdonald Had a Farm' and 'There Was an Old Lady who Swallowed a Fly'.

Book time, too, gives wonderful experiences of delight in listening to voice, and when a group of children are around, games like 'Musical Bumps' and 'Pass the Parcel' which depend on listening, are much enjoyed.

It could also be fun to make funny noises to go with drawing and scribbling, like 'wheeeee' to a circular scribble, and 'di domp di domp' to a zig zag one. Your little child is still not too old to enjoy play sounds, associated for example with water play and play with vehicles. 'Shshshshsh' and 'gugugugug' as water comes from the tap and runs away are still found to be very amusing.

> **Make sure she still finds listening fun**

★ Sentence length

You no longer need to think about this. Just chat away. Your child will now be able to tell you if she doesn't know a word, and ask what it means, or let you know if she wants you to repeat what you have said.

There is no need to limit your use of words that might be new to her (although now that she is learning incidentally all the time, you will have to make a guess about this). They will be learned extremely easily in the context of her attention focus and already wide knowledge of the language. It is still helpful to put a word that you think probably is new into several sentences, like: 'It's an antelope. I think antelopes are a kind of deer. Antelopes seem even more graceful than some other kinds of deer.'

There is no need either, to continue to speak particularly slowly (unless your little child is going through the stage of non-fluency) or loudly or tunefully. She is well attuned to and interested in language now, and fully aware of how interesting it is to listen to.

She will still make some mistakes with grammar, and there are very likely to be some immaturities in the way she pronounces words. It is still helpful, when this happens, to say back clearly what she has said. Never, ever forget the rules, however, when you do this. Always make your response part of the natural conversation, and always start it with a 'yes'.

★ Continue to expand on what she has said

You will almost certainly find now that this is happening automatically lots of the time. As you did in the last age period, expand on what she tells you, adding some more information. She might say, for example, 'We went to the bouncy castle', and you could say 'Yes, we did, and teddy fell on his nose. Poor old teddy, he really did have a big bang on his nose.'

It is also helpful to add more information in response to her questions (watching carefully, of course, to make sure that she is still interested). If she asked you, for example, 'Why is that bird carrying a twig?' you could explain about nest-building to her. These conversations will now be driven much more by your child. She is likely to be asking endless questions, wanting explanations, and making it clear when the information she receives is not enough.

QUESTIONS

Carefully selected questions can at this stage really help the little child to think and to work things out. If she were having difficulty with a puzzle, for example, you could say something like 'What would happen if you turned that piece upside down?' or if she were building with bricks, 'What did putting the big one under all those little ones let us do?' Please do not ask many of these and, as before, be sure to answer them yourself if she doesn't.

The same rule still applies: never ask her questions in order to get her to answer. Little children, however poor or good their

When Nicholas came round for tea the other day, I commented on what he was doing as he played, and in no time we were enjoying a lengthy conversation, in which he revealed delightfully advanced language development. His mother was amazed at all this. She had defined Nicholas as a very shy child, as he usually took a very long time to start talking to adults he did not know. I let her into my very simple secret: that I had commented to Nicholas on what was happening, and had not asked him any questions. This led her to think of an elderly relative who had always initiated conversations with her by crossing her arms, fixing her eyes on her, and saying 'What's your news?' Nicholas' mother recalled exactly how she had felt, and understood very well why she preferred comments to questions.

language development, always know what you are up to, and very quickly become extremely inhibited.

SOME 'DON'TS' FOR THIS AGE PERIOD

★ **Several of the previous prohibitions still stand:**
Never correct your little child's speech. As before, this is extremely important. Remember, if her words or sentences are not clear, the helpful thing to do is to let her hear you say them clearly.

Never draw her attention to the way in which she is speaking. This is particularly important if she is going through the stage of non-fluency. Always respond to what she is communicating, and not how she does so.

OUTSIDE YOUR HALF HOUR

★ Give her time and space in which to play.
★ Let her do lots for herself when she wants to.
★ Be aware of her attention level.
★ Give her lots of opportunities to play with other children.
★ Give her lots of opportunities for active play outside, if possible.
★ Help her to discover the wonders of nature

Now that she is 4

THE USE OF LANGUAGE

As we have seen, the little child has basically mastered the language by the time she is four, having a wide vocabulary, and understanding and using all the basic sentence types in the language. She now continues to add to her vocabulary and to her knowledge of grammatical structures, and to use language in more mature ways.

She uses language increasingly often to think through and solve problems like how to reach a tree house, and to make play plans both for herself and in groups of children. Roles may be allocated, for example, and imaginative story lines developed. The little child becomes more and more skilled, not only in communicating her ideas, but also in bargaining and negotiating, making deals: for example, about the allocation of turns in having the lead role. She also becomes more adept at describing her experiences, and what she thought and felt about them.

She takes part in long, complicated conversations, and becomes increasingly able to adapt the way she speaks to the situation and the listener, being very clear, for example, that teachers are spoken to differently from little brothers. She becomes better at remembering the rules of politeness, and needs to be reminded to say 'please' and 'thank you' less often. She becomes very persistent in engaging an adult's attention when she wants to begin a conversation, and is better at picking the best moment to join other people's conversations, waiting for a pause rather than interrupting.

She enjoys language enormously in terms of riddles and jokes, and loves to listen to long and quite complicated stories.

Despite all this wonderful progress, however, she has still not long joined the party, and her immaturity shows in a number of ways. It is still absolutely normal in the fifth year to make grammatical errors such as 'goed' instead of 'went' at times; and most children still have immaturities in their speech sounds, most commonly using 'f' for 'th', 'th' for 's', and an 'r' sounding rather like a 'w'. The little child still doesn't always know the extent of other people's knowledge of her conversational topic, and may leave them a little baffled as to what she is talking about sometimes. She also fails at times to respond to her conversational partner's topic if her mind is elsewhere.

GENERAL DEVELOPMENT

The little child's skills in other areas also advance considerably in this year. She becomes very active and exuberant, and increasingly skilful at climbing and using large play equipment like a swing and a slide. By the time she is five, she is able to dance to music and to play ball games with great agility. A measure of her impressive control over her body is that by this age, she can walk downstairs carrying an object in her hands. She loves to draw, and her drawings become more recognisable. Some little children begin to write a few letters spontaneously at this age. She develops new skills including sewing, producing several large stitches. She becomes more and more interested in playing with other children, and more able to co-operate with them when she does so.

ATTENTION AND LISTENING

In terms of attention, by the time she reached the age of four, the little child was able to shift her own attention focus. In this succeeding year, she takes another big step forward. Her attention at last becomes two channelled, in that she is now able to continue what she is doing while listening to someone speak to her, without needing to stop and look at the speaker.[1] This happens in short spells at first, which gradually become longer. Arrival at this stage means that the little child is now ready for school, in that she will be able to listen to instructions about what she is doing, which is essential for learning in the classroom situation. (This ability, however, will not be fully established for another year.)

PLAY

The little child loves very active play now, and handles a bicycle and a ball very competently. She also loves to engage in the artistic and creative activities begun in the previous year, and makes more and more elaborate constructions with bricks and other building materials.

Playing with other children becomes very important indeed, and pretend play continues to be a highly social activity, with lots of joint planning and co-operation. Rules are made, and usually kept to. Imagination continues to flourish, and she often acts out stories she has encountered in books and television programmes.

HOW YOU CAN HELP

I hope that you find spending some time daily alone with your little child is so much fun that I don't really need to suggest that you continue to do so. As in the last year, this doesn't have to be in a special playtime, but can be spent involving her in activities of yours like cooking or gardening, or taking her swimming or to story time in the library. These times continue to give you wonderful opportunities for answering her questions and discussing with her the events in her life and how she feels about them. This is of particular importance if there has been a distressing event like the separation of her parents, the death of a family member or even of a beloved pet. Allowing her to express her feelings, helping her to understand what has happened, and in particular, reassuring her that the event was in no way her fault is extremely helpful to her.

Do continue to share a book with her every day. I hope that this is another habit that you are enjoying so much that it would be hard to break. Your little child will have very much developed her own individual taste in books now, and allowing her to choose library books is wonderful at this stage.

There are still things you can do to make sure that her language development continues to flourish. As was the case last year, you do not have to worry at all about restricting either the vocabulary you use, or the complexity of your sentences. Your little child will soon let you know if she is not clear about something you have said.

Continue to expand lots on what she has said. She might for example, say 'We're going to the park after lunch', and you might reply with something like: 'Yes, we are, and William and his dad are coming too, and then they are coming back to our house for tea.' This will probably be automatic with you by now.

If you notice a grammatical error, it's still helpful to model the correct version for her as part of the conversation, as you have done before. (A four-year-old girl was recently telling me how she 'choosed' her puppy, and I said: 'How lovely! You chose the tiny one. I think I'd have chosen him too.')

The same goes for mispronunciations, which are also likely still to occur. If your child said, for example, 'That bird has grey fevvers', you could say: 'Yes, he's got grey feathers on his head, and I think I can see red feathers on his tail.'

It's helpful, too, to be alert for the times when she overestimates what someone else knows. My little friend Charles was telling me recently all about how Joe fell in a puddle. His mother had to remind him that I didn't know whether Joe was a child or an animal.

Continue to help her play to develop by making sure that she has time and space in which to play, and increasingly, opportunities to play with other children.

Please still limit her television watching to a maximum of an hour a day. She can enjoy and learn much from children's programmes now, and they can stimulate her imagination and enable her to experience the wonders of nature that she cannot see in real life. She still, however, has an enormous need to play, to interact and converse with people, and to act out the events of her daily life so that she comes fully to understand them. She just hasn't got more than an hour to spare.

As before, she will benefit much more if you can watch with her and answer her questions, explain things that puzzle her, and discuss with her what she sees.

AND NOW TO SCHOOL...

The most important event of this year is likely to be starting school. If you have been able to do the BabyTalk Programme, your little child is likely to have developed the attention, listening and language skills that will enable her to enjoy school very much and happily participate in all the activities.

As I have mentioned, there is a huge controversy at present about the most appropriate timing for formal teaching of reading, writing and numbers. My experience leads me to think that later is better for many children, but most parents have no option about when and where their children start school. The important thing for you as a parent is to make sure that your little child has plenty of opportunities to play at home, and lots of enriching experiences like visits to the swimming pool, the park and the library. She may, of course, want to read, write and work with numbers at home at this time, and there is no problem with that. Just make sure that she always has the choice.

There is much you can do to help her with this great adventure of starting school. Some schools let you take your little child to have a look round before she starts, which is helpful. Talk to her a lot about what will happen at school, and make sure that you have time to answer all her questions. She will love to hear stories about when you started school. Above all, remember that your little child is extremely quick to pick up your attitudes to all the events of her life, and if you believe that starting school will be a positive and fun experience for her, so will she.

And finally . . .

I do hope that you have marvelled in and celebrated your little child's amazingly rapid progress from helpless infant to mature conversationalist.

I hope too that you have enjoyed knowing how best to talk and interact with her to enable her to reach her maximum potential, and that you have established a pattern of enjoying each other's company that will stand you in good stead for the rest of your life.

Above all, I hope that the BabyTalk Programme has been fun for you and your child.

If your answers to these hopes is in the affirmative, my purpose in writing this book will have been fulfilled.

Good luck for the future.

Labels

I'm going to talk briefly about some neurological impairments which cause long-term speech and language difficulties. These tend very strongly to run in families, and affected children need very long-term speech and language therapy, and many need special educational provision as well. I discuss them here, because in my opinion, based on extensive experience, although they are actually quite rare, their names are frequently used to 'label' children inappropriately.

Specific Language Impairment: Children with this disability experience severe and persistent language learning difficulties in the absence of other impairments such as hearing loss, autism or learning difficulties.

Dyspraxia: another neurologically based disability which causes children to experience delay in language development, with associated difficulties in co-ordinating the movements of tongue and lips to make the series of speech sounds needed to produce words. They also have difficulties in planning and organising their body movements: for example, to fit themselves into a small space, or to work out how to reach a toy by moving and climbing onto a chair. Affected children often appear generally clumsy and unco-ordinated, and their play can be very disorganised.

Attention Deficit Hyperactivitiy Disorder (ADHD): shows a particularly strong family history. It is a disability evidenced by very great difficulty in controlling attention, and in staying on task. The children are extremely distractable. Some are helped considerably by medication.

I have seen many children who have been given these labels, including some whose parents have been advised to teach them sign language, and to anticipate special educational needs. For a tiny number, this was absolutely appropriate, but for the great majority, the problems could have been prevented by help in early life with the development of their listening and attention skills, and with understanding words. This majority, when their parents followed our programme, rapidly reached normal limits, some ending up in the highly gifted range, both

---

At three, Sonia was a very attractive little girl, with huge blue eyes, the youngest of three children. She had had a number of assessments in different parts of the country, as her parents' anxiety about her slow speech development grew. She had been labelled 'Dyspraxic' as well as 'severely language delayed', and special educational provision was being discussed. Sonia was indeed clumsy, having no idea how to hold a pencil or scissors, and could not organise herself, for instance, to stand on a box to reach a toy. She understood and used only a few single words.

At first sight, Sonia did indeed seem like a child with serious difficulties. It emerged, however, that she had spent nearly all her life to date with a nanny, who although affectionate and caring, hardly ever spoke to her, and sat her in front of children's videos for most of the day. After just three weeks on the BabyTalk Programme, Sonia began to understand and use two- to three-word sentences. Her skills in drawing, building and cutting also developed very rapidly once she had opportunities to engage in these activities and was shown what to do. It is clear already that she will have no long-term educational problems. I was delighted to hear from her mother recently that at the age of five, she is now reading books normally read by six and a half year olds, and is very happy in school.

---

linguistically and in terms of general intelligence as measured by standardised tests – and all in a few short months.

> Another child who had been classified as affected by Specific Language Impairment turned out to have an amazingly original and creative mind. When I first met him at three years old, Ben had the understanding and use of language typical of a child of only sixteen months, and was being taught to use sign language. Almost unbelievably, six months into the BabyTalk Programme, he was taxing us all with questions like 'What is time?' and ' How do your bones get inside your skin?' By the time he was four, he had the language skills of a seven and a half year old.

Questions from Parents

Here are some questions commonly asked by parents who are doing, or thinking about doing, the BabyTalk Programme with their little children. I hope you find the answers helpful.

I have to go back to work when my baby is six months old. Will this be a problem?

I very much hope that by then you will have got into the habit of enjoying half an hour a day one to one with your baby, and that it won't be too difficult to keep it up when you are back at work. That half an hour a day can make the most enormous difference to your baby's development. If you can also share the BabyTalk principles with whoever is going to be your baby's main carer, so much the better, but even if this is not possible, rest assured that you will still be giving him all that is most important.

My wife is going back to work, and so I am going to be the main carer for our baby. Are there any worries about this?

None at all. I have worked with lots of fathers who are in charge, and all of them have done a wonderful job. The only difference I have noticed from working with mothers is that fathers find it much more difficult not to 'teach' their little children, and not to ask them questions. I hope that you will try very hard to follow the programme in these respects and resist the temptation. If you do, I'm sure that you will be successful, and above all that you will have lots of fun in the process.

I am a single parent with two older children. It will be very difficult to find time alone with the baby.
I do sympathise, and recognise how very difficult this can be. I do believe, however, that it is worth going to a lot of trouble to enlist the help of a friend, neighbour or relative to take care of the other children for a short time. It may also perhaps be possible to change your baby's routine so that she is awake at times when the other children are at school or playgroup. Even if this is not possible every day, your baby will still benefit a great deal from any time you can give her on her own. That precious half an hour a day can make such a difference.

We are going to have a nanny for our baby. What should we take into account?
If your nanny is to spend a substantial amount of time with your baby, it is important if possible to ensure that her first language is the same as yours. Best of all, share the BabyTalk Programme with her, so that she knows the principles – even if, as I hope, *you* will be doing the actual half an hour a day.

If it is not possible to have a nanny who shares your language, encourage her to talk and sing to your baby in her own mother tongue. Your baby will then have an opportunity to acquire more than one language, just as in the situation where family members speak more than one language. It is important to ensure that if you have to change to a different nanny that the subsequent one speaks the same language as the first. I have seen a number of children who were cared for by a succession of nannies who spoke different languages. Unfortunately, the children were making little progress in any of them.

I will have to put my baby into a day nursery while I work. Will it matter if they don't follow the BabyTalk Programme? I've heard the staff there asking the children lots of

questions, for example, and I have come to realise how much better it is not to do so.

When your little boy goes into the nursery, it is even more important that you do the programme consistently with him at home every day if you possibly can. Luckily, little children are very adaptable, and as long as you enable him to experience all the programme at home, he will still get very great benefit from it, which will not be undermined by the different approach taken in the nursery. He will benefit from all the play materials and toys in the nursery, and later on from the company of the other children. You might, in time, tactfully be able to share your views with the nursery staff.

I have a three year old, Michaela, who seems jealous of the fact that I have time alone with her little brother. She never gets any such time as the two of them go to bed at the same time, and the baby is always awake when Michaela is not at playgroup. What can I do?

Try putting the baby to bed a little earlier or letting Michaela stay up a little longer so that she does have some time alone with you. All children benefit so much from undivided attention from an adult, and I believe that this could help a great deal with her jealousy of your baby. You are likely to find that Michaela loves the part of the BabyTalk Programme for her age level.

My husband and I are getting divorced. Is there anything we can do to mimimise the effect on our three-year-old daughter?

You cannot, of course, prevent your little girl being upset by such a sad event. I believe, however, that by continuing to spend one-to-one time with her and giving her the time and the opportunity to talk about her feelings, and to answer her questions, you will be helping her a lot. You will be able to help her to understand, to however limited an extent, what is and is not going to happen. It is also important to recognise that children tend to assume that such events are their fault, and to reassure her repeatedly that this is not the case.

I am Italian, my wife is English, and we live in London. I should like my little boy to learn Italian, but I am worried that hearing two languages might confuse him. Am I right about this?

Babies and young children who have the chance of learning more than one language can do so extremely easily in the right circumstances, and are very fortunate in having the opportunity. They only become confused in two situations:

★ If the two languages are mixed together to a very great extent: that is, with several words of each language within the same sentence.

★ When a carer uses a language which he or she did not acquire in childhood. The reason for this is that, as we have seen, a very important part of the BabyTalk Programme is to modify the way we speak to babies and little children. It is well known that this is extremely difficult to do in a language other than mother tongue, or one acquired in early childhood. Adults would also be unlikely to know the traditional rhymes, songs and stories in a language not acquired in childhood, and these are a rich part of the heritage we share with our children.

My advice to you is to speak in Italian to your little boy whenever the two of you are alone together. For total perfection, you should do the BabyTalk Programme with him in Italian, and his mother should do it in English. He will learn the two languages extremely easily!

Further Reading

ON LANGUAGE

E. Lenneberg, *The Biological Foundations of Language* (New York, Wiley, 1967)

S. Pinker, *Language Development and Language Learnability* (Cambridge Mass., MIT Press, 1984)

N. Chomsky, *Aspects of the Development of Syntax* (Cambridge Mass., MIT Press, 1965)

G. Altmann, *The Ascent of Babel* (Oxford University Press, 1997)

D. Crystal (ed), *The Cambridge Encyclopaedia of Language* (Cambridge University Press, 1997)

S. Pinker, *The Language Instinct – the New Science of Language and Mind* (London, Penguin, 1994)

ON LANGUAGE DEVELOPMENT

C. Snow & C. Ferguson (eds), *Talking to Children* (Cambridge University Press, 1977)

J. Bloom, *Stability and Change in Human Characteristics* (New York, Wiley, 1964)

H. R. Shaffer (ed), *Studies in Mother–Child Interaction* (London, Academic Press, 1977)

C. Gallaway & B. Richards (eds), *Input and Interaction in Language Acquisition* (Cambridge University Press, 1994)

D. Messer, *The Development of Communication* (Chichester, Wiley, 1994)

E. Bates, I. Brotherton & L. Snyder, *From First Words to Grammar* (Cambridge University Press, 1988)

K. Nelson, *The Acquisition of a Shared Meaning System* (New York, Academic Press)

M. Bullowa (ed), *Before Speech* (Cambridge University Press, 1979)

J. Bruner, *Child's Talk* (New York, Norton, 1983)

K. Kaye, *The Mental and Social Life of Babies* (University of Chicago Press, 1982)

S. Bochner, P. Price & J. Jones, *Child Language Development* (London, Whurr, 1997)

ON INFANT PERCEPTION AND DEVELOPMENT

J. D. Osofsky (ed), *Handbook of Infant Development* (New York, Wiley, 1987)

C. Gramrud (ed), *Visual Perception and Cognition in Infancy* (1985)

J. Mehler & E. Dupoux, *What Infants Know: the New Cognitive Science of Infant Behaviour* (Cambridge Mass., Blackwell, 1994)

R. Feldman & B. Rune (eds), *Fundamentals of Human Behaviour* (New York, Cambridge University Press, 1985)

R. Griffiths, *The Abilities of Babies* (University of London Press, 1954)

C. Bremner, A. Slater & L. Butterworth, *Infant Development: Recent Advances* (Psychological Press, Taylor & Francis, 1997)

A. Gesell, *The First Five Years of Life* (London, Methuen, 1966)

P. Mussen (ed), *Carmichael's Manual of Child Psychology* (New York, Wiley, 1989)

ON PLAY

D. Singer & J. Singer, *The House of Make-Believe* (Harvard University Press, 1990)

E. Matterson, *Play with a Purpose for the Under Sevens* (third edition) (London, Penguin, 1989)

K. Macdonald (ed), *Parent-Child Play* (State University of New York Press, 1993)

R. McConkey, D. Jeffree & S. Hewson, *Let Me Play* (London, Souvenir Press, 1964)

References

INTRODUCTION

1 T. Walpaw, J. Nation & D. Aram, 'Developmental Language Disability – a Follow-up Study' in M. Burns & J. Andrew (eds), *Selected Papers in Language and Phonology,* No. 1

2 T. Fundudis, J. Kolvin & R.Garside, *Speech in Retarded and Deaf Children* (London, Academic Press, 1979)

3 P. Silva, 'The Prevalence and Stability of Language Delay From Three to Seven Years' in *Folio Phoniatrica* 35 no 3-4 (1983)

4 N. Richman, J. Stevenson & P. Graham, *Pre-school to School – a Behavioural Study* (London, Academic Press, 1982)

5 C. Drillien & M. Drummond, 'Developmental Screening and the Child with Special Needs' in *Clinics in Developmental Medicine*, vol. 86 (Heinemann Medical Books, 1983)

6 S. Ward, 'An Investigation Into the Effectiveness of an Early Intervention Method for Language Delayed Children' in *International Journal of Disorders of Language and Communication,* 34 vol. 3, pp. 243-264 (1999)

7 D. Wechsler, *Wechsler Intelligence Scale for Children* (Third UK Edition) (Sidcup, Kent, The Psychological Corporation, 1992)

8 J. Rust, *Wechsler Objective Language Dimensions* (The Psychological Corporation, Harcourt Brace & Co, 1996)

9 J. Rust, S. Golombok & G. Trickey, *Wechsler Objective Reading Dimensions* (Sidcup, Kent, The Psychological Corporation, 1992)

10 L. M. Dunn, L. M. Dunn & C. Whetton with D. Pintilie, *British Picture Vocabulary Test* (NFER Nelson, 1982)

11   B. Skinner, *Verbal Behaviour* (New York, Appleton Century Crofts, 1957)

12   N. Chomsky, 'A Review of "Verbal Behaviour" by B. Skinner' in *Language*, 35, pp. 26-58 (1959)

13   N. Chomsky, *Aspects of the Theory of Syntax* (Cambridge Mass., MIT Press, 1965)

14   N. Chomsky, *Knowledge of Language: Its Nature, Uses and Origin* (New York, Praeger, 1986)

15   S. Pinker, *The Language Instinct* (London, Penguin, 1994)

16   K. Kaye, 'Towards the Origins of Dialogue' in H. R. Shaffer (ed), *Studies in Mother–Child Interaction* (New York, Academic Press, 1977)

17   C. Trevarthen, 'A Descriptive Analysis of Infant Communicative Behaviour' in H. R. Shaffer (ed), *Studies in Mother–Child Interaction* (New York, Academic Press, 1977)

18   L. Vygotsky, *Thought and Language* (Cambridge Mass., MIT Press, 1962)

19   E. Hoff Ginsberg, 'Methodological and Social Concerns in the Study of Children's Language Learning Environments' in *First Language*, 12, pp. 251-255 (1992)

20   J. Huttenlocher, W. Haight, A. Bryk, M. Selzer & T. Lyons, 'Early Vocabulary Growth' in *Developmental Psychology*, 27, pp. 236-248 (1991)

21   G. Wells & W. Robinson, 'The Role of Adult Speech in Language Development' in C. Fraser & K. Scherer (eds) *The Social Psychology of Language* (Cambridge University Press, 1982)

22   M. Tomasello & J. Todd, 'Joint Attention and Lexical Acquisition Style' in *First Language*, 4, pp. 197-212 (1983)

23   A. Fernald & P. Khul, 'Acoustic Determinants of Infants' Preference for Motherese' in *Infant Behaviour and Development*, 10, pp. 279-293 (1987)

24   K. Nelson, 'Towards a Rare Event Comparison Theory of Syntax Acquisition' in P. Dale & D. Ingram (eds), *Child Language – an Interactional Perspective* (Baltimore MD, University Park Press, 1981)

25   E. Lenneberg, *The Biological Foundations of Language* (New York, Wiley, 1967)

26   B. Thorpe, *Birdsong – The Biology of Vocal Communication and Expression in Birds* (Cambridge University Press, 1961)

27   J. Law, *The Early Identification of Language Disabled Children* (London, Chapman and Hall, 1989)

28   M. Sheridan, 'Children of Seven Years With Marked Speech Defects' in *British Journal of Disorders of Communication*, 8, pp. 1-8 (1973)

29   M. Bax, H. Hart & S. Jenkins, 'The Assessment of Speech and Language Development in Young Children' *Paediatrics*, 3, pp. 19-26 (1980)

30   P. Macintyre & R. Umansky, 'Speech and Language Screenings as Predictors of Communicative Problems in Young Children' in *Folio Phoniatrica* 35, no 3-4 (1983)

31   L. Bliss & D. Allen, 'Screening Kit of Language Development' in *Journal of Communication Disorders*, 17, pp. 133-141 (1984)

32   M. Nash in *Time Magazine* (24 February 1997) reporting on the work of: Researchers at the Baylor College of Medicine Houston, Harry Chugain – Wayne State University Belmont, Corey Goodman & Carla Shatz – University of California Berkeley, Stanley Greenspan – George Washington University, Eric Kandel – Columbia University

33   J. Cooper, M. Moodley & J. Reynell, *Helping Language Development* (London, Edward Arnold, 1978)

0–3 MONTHS

1   B. Stern, B. Beebe, J. Jaffe & S. Bennet, 'The Infant's Stimulus World During Social Interaction' in H. R. Shaffer (ed), *Studies in Mother–Child Interaction* (London, Academic Press, 1977)

2   A. Slater, D. Rose & V. Morison, 'Newborn Infants' Perception of Similarities and Differences Between Two and Three Dimensional Stimuli' in *British Journal of Developmental Psychology*, 2, pp. 287-94 (1984)

3   R. Fantz, 'Pattern Discrimination and Selective Attention as Determinants of Perceptual Development From Birth' in A. Kidd & J. Rivoire (eds), *Perceptual Development in Children* (New York, International Universities Press 1966)

4   E. Melhuish, 'Visual Attention to Mothers' and Strangers' Faces and Facial Contrast in One-month Olds' in *Developmental Psychology*, 18, pp. 299-331

5   I. Bushnell, F. Sai & J. Mullin, 'Neonatal Recognition of Mother's Face' in *British Journal of Developmental Psychology*, 7, pp. 3-15 (1989)

6   B. Berthenthal, D. Profitt, N. Spetner & M. Thomas, 'The
    Development of Infant Sensitivity to Biomechancial Motions' in
    Child Development, 56, pp. 531-543 (1985)

7   A. Melfzoff & K. Moore, 'Newborn Infants Imitate Adult Facial
    Gestures' in *Child Development*, 54, pp. 702-709 (1983)

8   A. Melfzoff & A. Goprick, 'The Role of Imitation in
    Understanding Persons and Developing a Theory of Mind' in
    S. Baron-Cohen, H. Tager-Flushberg & D. Cohen (eds),
    Understanding Other Minds – Perspectives From Autism (Oxford
    University Press, 1993)

9   L. Camras, C. Malatesta & C. Izard, 'The Development of Facial
    Expression in Infancy' in R. Feldman & B. Rime (eds),
    Fundamentals of Nonverbal Behaviour (New York, Cambridge
    University Press, 1991)

10 T. M. Field, R. Woodson & C. Cohen, 'Discrimination and
    Imitation of Facial Expressions by Neonates' in *Science*, 218,
    pp. 179-181 (1982)

11 G. Bremner, 'Object Tracking and Search in Infancy' in
    Developmental Review, 5, pp. 371-396 (1985)

12 A. Slater, V. Morrison, C. Town & D. Rose, 'Movement Identity
    and Identity: Constancy in the Newborn Baby' in *British Journal
    of Developmental Psychology*, 3, pp. 211-220 (1985)

13 A. DeCasper & W. Fifer, 'On Human Bonding' in *Science*, 208,
    pp. 1174-76 (1980)

14 A. DeCasper & W. Fifer, 'On Human Bonding' in *Science*, 208,
    pp. 1174-76 (1980)

15 R. Aslin, 'Visual and Auditory Development in Infancy' in J. D.
    Osofsky (ed), *Handbook of Infant Development* (New York,
    Wiley, 1987)

16 W. Fifer & C. Moon, 'Psychobiology of Human Newborn
    Preferences' in *Seminars in Perinatology*, 13, pp. 430-433 (1989)

17 D. Messer, *The Development of Communication* (Chichester,
    Wiley, 1994)

18 R. Cooper & R. Aslin, 'Preference for Child Directed Speech in
    the First Month After Birth' in *Child Development* 61, pp. 1584-
    1595 (1990)

19 P. Hepper, 'An Examination of Fetal Learning Before and After
    Birth' in *Irish Journal of Psychology*, 12, pp. 95-107 (1991)

20 C. Trevarthen, 'A Descriptive Analysis of Infant Communicative
    Behaviour' in H. R. Shaffer (ed) *Studies in Mother–Infant
    Interaction*, pp. 227-70 (London, Academic Press, 1977)

21   P. Eimas, E. Sequeland, P. Jusczyk & J. Vigorito, 'Speech Perception in Infants' in *Science*, 171, pp. 303-306 (1971)

22   L. Camras, C. Malatesta & C. Izard, 'The Development of Facial Expression in Infancy' in R. Feldman & B. Rime (eds), *Fundamentals of Nonverbal Behaviour* (New York, Cambridge University Press, 1991)

23   P. Slater, 'Visual Perceptual Abilities at Birth' in B. de Boysson-Bardies, S. de Sconen, P. Jusczyk, P. McNeilage & J. Morton (eds), *Developmental Neurecognition – Speech and Face Processing in the First Year of Life* (Dordrecht Boston, 1993)

24   G. Bremner, 'Object Tracking and Search in Infancy' in *Developmental Review*, 5, pp. 371-396 (1985)

25   P. Eimas & P. Quinn, 'Studies on the Formation of Perceptually Based Basic Level Categories in Young Children' in *Child Development*, 65, pp. 903-18 (1994)

26   E. Hoff-Ginsberg, 'Methodological and Social Concerns in the Study of Children's Language Learning Environments' in *First Language*, 12, pp. 251-5 (1992)

27   J. Huttenlocher, W. Haight, A. Bryk, M. Selzer & T. Lyons, 'Early Vocabulary Growth: Relationship to Language Input and Gender' in *Developmental Psychology*, 27, pp. 236-248 (1991)

28   E. Bates, I. Brotherton & L. Snyder, *From First Words to Grammar* (Cambridge University Press, 1988)

29   D. Messer, *The Development of Communication* (Chichester, Wiley, 1994)

3–6 MONTHS

1   G. Bremner, 'Object Tracking and Search in Infancy' in *Developmental Review*, 5, pp. 371-396 (1985)

2   M. Ruddy & M. Bornstein, 'Cognitive Correlates of Infant Attention and Maternal Stimuli Over the First Year of Life' in *Child Development*, 82, pp. 53-183

3   M. Ruddy & M. Bornstein, 'Cognitive Correlates of Infant Attention and Maternal Stimuli Over the First Year of Life' in *Child Development*, 82, pp. 53-183

4   K. Bzoch & R. League, *Receptive-Expressive Emergent Language Scales* (Pro-Ed Inc, 1991)

5   K. Hirsch-Pasek, E. Kemler, D. Nelson, P. Jusczyk, K. Cassidy, D. Benjamin, L. Kennedy, 'Clauses are Perceptual Units for Children' in *Cognition*, 26, pp. 269-286 (1987)

6   D. Hay, A. Nash & J. Pederson, 'Interactions Between Six-month Old Peers' in *Child Development*, 54, pp. 557-562 (1983)
7   M. Ruddy & M. Bornstein, 'Cognitive Correlates of Infant Attention and Maternal Stimuli Over the First Year of Life' in *Child Development*, 82, pp. 53-183
8   A. Fernald & P. Khul, 'Acoustic Determinants of Infants' Preference for Motherese' in *Infant Behaviour and Development*, 10, pp. 279-293 (1987)
9   J. Werker & P. Mcleod, 'Infant Preference for Both Male and Female Infant Directed Talk' in *Canadian J Psychology*, 43, pp. 230-246 (1989)
10   A. Fernald, 'Four-month-olds Prefer to Listen to Motherese' in *Infant Behaviour and Development*, 8, pp. 181-95
11   M. Papousiek, M. Bornstein & I. Nuzzo, 'Infant Responses to Prototypical Melodic Contours in Parental Speech' in *Infant Behaviour and Development*, 13, pp. 539-545
12   J. Ryther-Duncan, D. Scheumeman, J. Bradley, M. Jensen, D. Hansen & P. Kaplan, 'Infant Versus Adult Directed Speech as Signals for Faces,' Poster at Biennial Meeting of SRCD New Orleans (1993)

6–9 MONTHS

1   K. Bzoch & R. League, *Receptive-Expressive Emergent Language Scales* (Pro-Ed Inc, 1991)
2   S. Bochner, 'The Development of Vocalisation of Handicapped Children in a Hospital Setting' in *Australian and New Zealand Journal of Developmental Disabilities*, 12, pp. 55-63 (1986)
3   K. Bzoch & R. League, *Receptive-Expressive Emergent Language Scales* (Pro-Ed Inc, 1991)
4   J. Bruner, *Child's Talk: Learning to Use Language* (New York, Norton, 1983)
5   C. Trevarthen, 'Communication and Co-operation in Early Infancy' in M. Bullowa (ed), *Before Speech* (Cambridge University Press, 1979)
6   D. Messer, *The Development of Communication* (Chichester, Wiley, 1994)
7   M. Turvey, R. Shaw, W. Mace, 'Issues in the Theory of Action' in J. Requin (ed), *Attention and Performance*, 7, pp. 557-595 (Hillsdale, New Jersey Lawrence Erlbaum Associates Inc., 1978)

8   R. Baillergeon, 'The Object-Concept Revisited' in C. Gramrud (ed), *Visual Perception and Cognition in Infancy* (Hillsdale, New Jersey, Lawrence Erlbaum Associates Inc., 1993)

9   E. Lenneberg, *The Biological Foundations of Language* (New York, Wiley, 1967)

10   C. Murphy & D. Messer, 'Mothers, Infants and Pointing' in H. R. Shaffer (ed), *Studies in Mother-Infant Interaction* (London, Academic Press, 1977)

11   J. Mandler, P. Bauer, L. McDonagh, 'Separating the Sheep From the Goats' *Cognitive Psychology*, 23, pp. 263-298 (1991)

12   R. Griffiths, *The Abilities of Babies* (University of London Press, 1954)

13   G. Collis, 'Visual Co-orientation and Maternal Speech' in H. R. Shaffer (ed), *Studies in Mother-Infant Interaction* (London, Academic Press, 1977)

14   K. Bzoch & R. League, *Receptive-Expressive Emergent Language Scales* (Pro-Ed Inc, 1991)

15   C. Trevarthen, 'The Development of Intersubjective Motor Control in Infants' in M. G. Wade (ed), *Motor Development in Children* (Dordrecht Martinus Nyhof, 1986)

16   C. Trevarthen, 'Communication and Co-operation in Early Infancy' in M. Bullowa (ed), *Before Speech* (Cambridge University Press, 1979)

17   A. Nelson, 'Constraints on Word Learning?' in *Cognitive Development*, 3, pp. 221-246 (1988)

18   K. Clarke-Stewart, 'Interaction Between Mothers and Young Children' in *Monographs of the Society for Research in Child Development*, no 153, vol. 38, pp. 96-97 (1973)

9 – 12 MONTHS

1   M. Carpenter, K. Nagell & M. Tomasello, 'Social Cognition, Joint Attention and Communicative Competence from Nine to Fifteen Months' in *Monographs of the Society for Research in Child Development*, 4, No. 255 (1998)

2   K. Nelson, 'Structure and Strategy in Learning to Talk' in *Monographs of the Society for Research in Child Development*, 38, 1-2, No. 149 (1973)

3   S. Ward, 'The Predictive Accuracy and Validity of a Screening Test for Language Delay and Auditory Perceptual Disorder' in *European Journal of Disorders of Communication*, 27, pp. 55-72 (1992)

4   C. Trevarthen, 'Signs Before Speech' in T. A. Sebeok & J. Umiker-Sebeok (eds), *The Semiotic Web* (Berlin, Amsterdam, Mouton de Gruyter, 1990)

5   K. Bzoch & R. League, *Receptive-Expressive Emergent Language Scales* (Pro-Ed Inc, 1991)

6   J. Cooper, M. Moodley & J. Reynell, *Helping Language Development* (London, Edward Arnold, 1978)

7   M. Adamson & T. Bakeman, 'Affect and Attention: Infants Observed With Mothers and Peers' in *Child Development*, 56, pp. 582-593 (1985)

8   D. Hay & H. Posse, 'The Social Nature of Early Conflict' in *Child Development*, 53, pp. 105-113 (1982)

9   S. Pinker, *The Language Instinct: The New Science of Language and Mind* (London, Penguin, 1994)

10 J. Bruner, 'Early Social Interactions and Language Acquisition' in H. R. Shaffer (ed), *Studies in Mother–Child Interaction* (London, Academic Press, 1977)

11 K. Kaye, *The Mental and Social Life of Babies* (University of Chicago Press, 1982)

12 E. Hoff Ginsberg, 'Methodological and Social Concerns in the Study of Children's Language Learning Environments' in *First Language*, 12, pp. 251-255 (1992)

13 K. Nelson, *Making Sense: The Acquisition of the Child's Shared Meaning System* (New York, Academic Press, 1985)

14 C. Snow, R. Perlman & P. Nathan, 'Why Routines are Different' in K. Nelson & A. Kleek (eds), *Children's Language*, 6, Hillsdale, New Jersey Lawrence Erlbaum Associates Inc., 1987)

15 G. Wells & W. Robinson, 'The Role of Adult Speech in Child Development' in C. Fraser & K. Scherer (eds), *The Social Psychology of Language* (Cambridge University Press, 1982)

16 M. Tomasello & Farrer, 'Joint Attention and Early Language' in *Child Development*, 57, pp. 1454-1463 (1986)

17 L. Baumwell, C. Tamis-Lemanda, R. Kahana-Kalman & J. McClune, 'Maternal Responsiveness and Infant Language Comprehension', SRCD Conference New Orleans (1993)

18   M. Tomasello & J. Todd, 'Joint Attention and Lexical Acquisition Style' in *First Language*, 7, pp. 197-212

19   M. Carpenter, K. Nagell & M. Tomasello, 'Social Cognition, Joint Attention and Communicative Competence from Nine to Fifteen Months', *Monographs of the Society for Research in Child Development*, 4, No. 255.

20   M. Tomasello & J. Todd, 'Joint Attention and Lexical Acquisition Style', *First Language*, 7, pp. 197-212

21   V. Reddy, D. Hay, I. Murray & C. Trevarthen, 'Communication in Infancy' in G. Bremner, A. Slater & G. Butterworth (eds), *Infant Development – Recent Advances* (Psychological Press, Taylor & Francis, 1997)

12–16 MONTHS

1   J. Huttenlocher, 'Origins of Language Comprehension' in R. Solso (ed) *Theories in Cognitive Psychology*, 5th edition (Loyola Symposium Potomac MD Erlbaum, 1974)

2   K. Nelson, *Making Sense: the Acquisition of Shared Meaning* (New York, Academic Press, 1985)

3   D. Furrow, K. Nelson & H. Benedict, 'Mother's Speech to Children and Syntactic Development: Some Simple Relationships', *Journal of Child Language*, 6, pp. 423-42 (1979)

4   J. Cooper, M. Moodley & J. Reynell, *Helping Language Development* (London, Edward Arnold, 1978)

5   M. Beeghley, 'Parent Infant Play' in K. Macdonald (ed) *Parent Child Play* (State University of New York Press, 1993)

6   K. Bzoch & R. League, *Receptive-Expressive Emergent Language Scales* (Pro-Ed Inc, 1991)

7   J. Mandler, 'The Development of Categorisation: Perceptual and Conceptual Categories' in G. Bremner, A. Slater & G. Butterworth (eds), *Infant Development: Recent Advances* (Psychological Press, Taylor & Francis, 1997)

8   M. Beeghley, 'Parent Infant Play' in K. Macdonald (ed) *Parent Child Play* (State University of New York Press, 1993)

9   C. Snow, A. Arlmann-Rupp, Y. Hassin, J. Jobse, J. Jooten & J. Vorster, 'Mothers' Speech in Three Social Classes' in *Journal of Psycholinguistic Research*, 5, pp. 1-20 (1976)

10 J. Sachs & M. Johnson, 'Language Development in a Hearing Child of Deaf Parents', paper given at the International Symposium on First Language Acquisition, Florence, Italy (1972)

11 M. Tomasello & J. Todd, 'Joint Attention and Lexical Acquisition Style' in *First Language*, 4, pp. 197-212 (1983)

12 M. Della Court & B. P. Keene, 'The Relationship Between Pragmatic Dimensions of Mothers' Speech to the Referential-Expressive Distinction' in *Journal of Child Language*, 10, pp. 35-44 (1983)

13 D. Furrow, K. Nelson & H. Benedict, 'Mothers' Speech to Children and Syntactic Development' in *Journal of Child Language*, 6, pp. 423-442 (1979)

14 M. Beeghley, 'Parent Infant Play' in K. Macdonald (ed) *Parent Child Play* (State University of New York Press, 1993)

16–20 MONTHS

1 J. Huttenlocher, W. Haight, A. Bryk, M. Selzer & T. Lyons, 'Early Vocabulary Growth: Relationship to Language Input and Gender' in *Developmental Psychology*, 27, pp. 236-248 (1991)

2 J. Cooper, M. Moodley & J. Reynell, *Helping Language Development* (London, Edward Arnold, 1978)

3 R. Baldwin, 'Infants' Contribution to the Achievement of Joint Reference' in *Child Development*, 62, pp. 875-890.

4 M. Tomasello & J. Todd, 'Joint Attention and Lexical Acquisition Style' in *First Language*, 4, pp. 197-212 (1983)

5 P. Dunham, F. Dunham & A. Curwin, 'Joint Attention and Lexical Acquisition at Eighteen Months' in *Developmental Psychology*, 29, pp. 827-831.

20–24 MONTHS

1 K. Bzoch & R. League, *Receptive-Expressive Emergent Language Scales* (Pro-Ed Inc, 1991)

2 R. Griffiths, *The Abilities of Babies* (University of London Press, 1954)

3 A. Gesell, *The First Five Years of Life* (London, Methuen, 1954)

4 M. Tomasello & J. Farrer, 'Joint Attention and Early Language' in *Child Development*, 57, pp. 1454-1463 (1986)

5 N. Cohen & A. Barwick, Department of Research, Hinks Bellcrest Institute, University of Toronto

6 L. Gleitman, E. Newport & H. Gleitman, 'The Current Status of the Motherese Hypothesis' in *Journal of Child Language*, 11, pp. 43-79 (1984)

7   C. Wells, 'Adjustments in Adult Child Conversation: Some Effects of Interaction' in H. Giles, W. Robinson & P. Smith (eds), *Language; Social and Psychological Perspectives* (Oxford, Pergammon, 1980)

8   M. J. Farrer, 'Discourse and the Acquisition of Grammatical Morphemes' in *Journal of Child Language*, 17, pp. 607-23

9   R. Brown & U. Bellugi, 'Three Processes Involved in Language Acquisition of Syntax' in *Harvard Educational Review*, 34, pp. 133-51 (1964)

2 – 2¹/₂ YEARS

1   A. Gesell, *The First Five Years of Life* (London, Methuen, 1954)

2   J. Cooper, M. Moodley & J. Reynell, *Helping Language Development* (London, Edward Arnold, 1977)

3   S. Edwards, P. Fletcher, M. Garman, A. Hughes, C. Letts & I. Sinka, *Reynell Developmental Language Scales* (NFER Nelson, 1997)

4   R. Brown, *A First Language – the Early Stages* (Cambridge, Mass., Harvard University Press, 1973)

5   R. McConkey, D. Jeffree, S. Hewson, *Let Me Play* (London, Souvenir Press, 1964)

6   R. Battin, 'Psychological and Educational Assessment of Children with Language Learning Problems' in R. Roes & M. Downs (eds), *Auditory Disorders in School Children* (New York, Theime Stratton, 1987)

7   D. Johnson, *Learning Disabilities* (New York, Grune and Stratton Inc, 1976)

8   D. Cantwell and I. Baker, 'Psychiatric Disorder in Children with Speech and Language Retardation' in *Archives of General Psychiatry*, 34, pp. 583-591 (1977)

9   M. Hadley & P. Rice, *Journal of Speech and Hearing Research*, 34, pp. 1308-1317 (1991)

10 S. Baron-Cohen and H. Ring, 'A Model of the Mind Reading System' in C. Lewis & P. Mitchell (eds), *Children's Early Understanding of the Mind* (Hove Erlbaum, 1994)

11 N. Cohen & A. Barwick, Hincks Bellcrest Institute, University of Toronto

12 R. Brown & V. Bellugi, 'Three Processes in Children's Acquisition of Syntax' in *Harvard Educational Review*, 34, pp. 133-151 (1964)

13 M. Farrer, 'Discourse and the Acquisition of Grammatical Morphemes' in *Journal of Child Language*, 17, pp. 607-624 (1990)

14 C. Wells, 'Adjustments in Adult Child Conversation' in H. Giles, W. Robinson & P. Smith (eds), *Language: Social and Psychological Perspectives* (Oxford, Pergammon, 1980)

2$^1/_2$–3 YEARS

1 J. Cooper, M. Moodley & J. Reynell, *Helping Language Development* (London, Edward Arnold, 1978)

2 S. Edwards, P. Fletcher, M. Garman, A. Hughes, C. Letts & I. Sinka, *Reynell Developmental Language Scales* (NFER Nelson, 1997)

3 K. Bzoch & R. League, *Receptive-Expressive Emergent Language Scales* (Pro-Ed Inc, 1991)

4 R. Griffiths, *The Abilities of Babies* (University of London Press, 1954)

5 P. Levenstein & J. O'Hara, 'The Necessary Lightness of Mother Child Play' in K. Macdonald (ed), *Parent Child Play: Descriptions and Implications* (State University of New York Press, 1993)

6 M. Barton & M. Tomasello, 'Joint Attention and Conversation in Mother-Infant Sibling Triads' in *Child Development*, 62, pp. 517-529 (1991)

3–4 YEARS

1 J. Cooper, M. Moodley & J. Reynell, *Helping Language Development* (London, Edward Arnold, 1978)

2 L. M. Dunn & C. Whetton with D. Pintilie, *British Picture Vocabulary Test* (NFER Nelson, 1982)

3 R. McConkey, D. Jeffree & S. Hewson, *Let Me Play* (London, Souvenir Press, 1964)

4 J. Singer and D. Singer, 'Combinatorial Play, Conceptual Development and Early Multi-Word Speech' in *American Psychologist*, 2, pp. 184-90 (1990)

5 M. Tomasello, *Joint Attention as Social Cognition: Origins and Role in Development* (Hillsdale NJ Erlbaum, 1995)

6 P. Levenstein, 'Cognitive Growth in Pre-school Children Through Verbal Interaction with Mothers' in *Journal of Orthopsychiatry*, 40, pp. 426-32 (1970)

7   M. Bornstein, 'Maternal Responsiveness; Characteristics and Consequences', *New Directions for Child Development*, 43 (1989)

8   H. Gottfried & I. Caldwell (eds), *Play Interaction* (Lexington Mass., Lexington Books)

9   D. Singer & J. Singer, *The House of Make-Believe* (Harvard University Press, 1990)

NOW THAT SHE IS FOUR

1   J. Cooper, M. Moodley & J. Reynell, *Helping Language Development* (London, Edward Arnold, 1978)

TRAVELLING ABROAD
WITH CHILDREN

Samantha Gore-Lyons

The essential book for all parents who want to take a holiday abroad with their children

From deciding when to take your child away for the first time and choosing somewhere you will all be happy, to selecting accommodation and your means of travel, this book will provide you with all the answers.

It includes an indispensable guide to what to pack and what to leave at home, details about getting visas and inoculations, ways of making your journey easier, reminders about high-risk food and drinks, and much, much more. The invaluable health and first-aid section gives advice on coping with bites and stings and dealing with more serious accidents and emergencies.

Travelling Abroad With Children will ensure a safer, healthier and happier holiday for the whole family.

Arrow Books
£7.99
ISBN 0 09 944525 5

THE BEST START IN LIFE

*How a woman's diet can protect her child
from disease in later life*

Professor David Barker

Current medical thinking states that heart disease is caused by rich food and a sedentary lifestyle. However, recent research by Professor David Barker and his colleagues at the University of Southampton has shown that it starts with poor nutrition in the womb – that the food a mother eats before and during pregnancy, and how she feeds her child in the first three crucial years after birth, can protect the child against a heart attack, a stroke or diabetes later in life.

This pioneering medical research is supported by the British Heart Foundation. In a clear, easy-to-follow style, *The Best Start in Life* will guide women through the foods they should eat during pregnancy and the food they should give to their children, explaining how a baby grows and develops, and how this is determined by the food it receives.

This book is a must-have for all parents and parents-to-be. It could ensure a healthier future for your child.

Century
£9.99
ISBN 1 8441 3152 1

Buy Arrow

Order further Random House titles from
your local bookshop, or have them delivered
direct to your door by Bookpost

☐	Travelling Abroad with Children	0099445255	£7.99
☐	The Best Start in Life	1844131521	£9.99

FREE POST AND PACKING
Overseas customers allow £2 per paperback

PHONE: 01624 677237

POST: Random House Books
c/o Bookpost, PO Box 29, Douglas
Isle of Man, IM99 1BQ

FAX: 01624 670923

EMAIL: bookshop@enterprise.net

Cheques (payable to Bookpost) and credit cards accepted

Prices and availability subject to change without notice
Allow 28 days for delivery
When placing your order, please state if you do not wish
to receive any additional information.

www.randomhouse.co.uk